South Africa

D0228007

South Africa:

Human Rights and the Rule of Law

International Commission of Jurists

Edited by Geoffrey Bindman

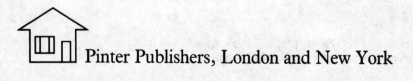 Pinter Publishers, London and New York

© International Commission of Jurists, 1988

First published in Great Britain in 1988 by
Pinter Publishers Limited
25 Floral Street, London WC2E 9DS

All rights reserved. No part of this publication may be
reproduced, stored in a retrieval system, or transmitted by any
other means without the prior written permission of the copyright
holder. Please direct all enquiries to the publishers.

Reprinted in paperback with a new chapter in 1989.

British Library Cataloguing in Publication Data

A CIP catalogue record for this book is available
from the British Library

ISBN 0 86187 979 1
    0 86187 779 9 (PBK)

Library of Congress Cataloging-in-Publication Data

CIP available from the Library of Congress

ISBN 0 86187-979-1

Typeset by Florencetype Ltd, Kewstoke, Avon
Printed in Great Britain by Biddles, Guildford

Contents

SOUTH AFRICA AND NEIGHBOURING STATES

ZIMBABWE

MOZAMBIQUE

BOTSWANA

NAMIBIA

VENDA

GAZANKULU

TRANSVAAL

LEBOWA
Pietersburg

NDEBELE
Mamelodi
PRETORIA
SWAZI

Johannesburg
Soweto
Sebokeng

BOPUTHATSWANA

SWAZILAND

ORANGE
FREE STATE

NATAL

KWA ZULU

Kimberley

BASOTHO-QWAQWA

MASERU

LESOTHO

Durban

CAPE PROVINCE

Western Cape

TRANSKEI
Umtata
Queenstown

Eastern Cape

CISKEI

King Williams Town
Mdantsane   East London

ATLANTIC OCEAN

CAPE TOWN
Langa
Crossroads

Port Elizabeth

INDIAN OCEAN

KEY

- - - · - International Boundary

· · · · · · Provincial Boundary

◉ Capital Cities

● Major Cities

● Towns

SWAZI Bantustans

0   400 kilometres

Michael Green

Reproduced from South Africa in the 1980's State of Emergency, *published by the Catholic Institute for International Relations, 22 Coleman Fields, London N1 7A7.*

1 Preface

With increasing reports of the tensions and repression of blacks in South Africa, the International Commission of Jurists decided to send a mission to South Africa.

Their terms of reference were to examine the degree of compliance in South Africa with international human rights law as embodied in the Universal Declaration of Human Rights and other relevant instruments. The particular subjects they considered were trade union rights, the repeal of the pass laws and other discriminatory legislation, the independence of judges and lawyers, the security system, the treatment of children under the legal system, the state of education, freedom of speech and political activity, legal services in rural areas, and human rights in the homelands.

In accordance with its normal practice, the International Commission of Jurists informed the South African government at the beginning of July of its intention to send a mission in September, and of the subjects to be studied and the places to be visited. The Commission asked if the mission could have meetings with government ministers and senior officials at the end of its visit. Shortly before this a state of emergency had been declared in South Africa, covering the whole country. The South African ambassador to the United Nations in Geneva thought it likely that the government would ask that the mission be postponed in view of the state of emergency, and this proved to be the case.

Accordingly, it was decided to postpone the mission until the beginning of 1987. By that time it became clear that the emergency was likely to be prolonged, so a decision was taken to send the mission to South Africa and to wait until the later stages of its visit before seeking appointments with ministers and other representatives of the South African government.

The mission was composed of four lawyers, each having expertise on the apartheid system. They were Geoffrey Bindman, a solicitor practising in London; Jean-Marie Crettaz, a member of the Council of the Geneva Bar; Henry Downing, an Irish barrister; and Guenter Witzsch, Professor of Public Law in the University of Munster, in the Federal Republic of Germany.

The mission went to South Africa for a period of three weeks in February 1987. A programme of meetings and visits was arranged. The team began with a series of meetings in Johannesburg and then divided into two pairs. One travelled to Bophuthatswana and then to Port Elizabeth and Ciskei. The other to Durban and Cape Town, where they were later joined by the other pair. The whole team then went to Bloemfontein and spent a final few days in Pretoria and Johannesburg. They met a wide range of practising and academic lawyers, judges, community workers, political and trade union leaders, human rights activists and ordinary residents of townships. At the end of their stay they met government officials and the Deputy Minister of Law and Order.

The team had secretarial assistance throughout which enabled them to record and transcribe virtually all their interviews. They obtained copies of many affidavits, court documents, reports and publications relevant to their enquiry.

A preliminary report of this mission, written by Geoffrey Bindman, was published in the *International Commision of Jurists' Review*, No. 38, in June 1987. The participants in the mission felt, however, that they could only do justice to the vast information and documentation they received by making a comprehensive review of the present state of apartheid, including the historical background to the legislation and practice where this is needed, to enable the reader to understand more fully the present critical stage in the evolution of the apartheid system.

The International Commission of Jurists joins with the members of the mission in expressing their deep gratitude to all those who devoted so much time and effort to help the mission in its task. The International Commission of Jurists is also deeply grateful to the members of the mission, in particular to Geoffrey Bindman for editing this report as well as being its principal author, and to the Swedish International Development Authority and the Ford Foundation for their grants which made the mission possible.

The concluding chapter in this edition, which updates this report, is also by Geoffrey Bindman.

Geneva, December 1987 and March 1989   Niall MacDermot
Secretary-General
International Commission of Jurists

Editorial note

The members of the mission were able to travel freely in Southern Africa but many of those who talked to us clearly did so at some personal risk. For this reason the identity of many informants cannot be disclosed. Since our visit in February 1987 we have been able to maintain contact with some of them and have continued to receive much information from published and other sources. The report therefore takes into account developments up to the end of February 1988.

Geoffrey Bindman   London, March 1988
Jean-Marie Crettaz
Henry Downing
Guenter Witzsch

Chapter 19 covers further developments up to the end of March 1989.

Geoffrey Bindman

2 General Introduction[1]

The country and its people

The Republic of South Africa covers an area of over five times the size of the United Kingdom. The country is divided into four provinces, the Transvaal, the Orange Free State, Natal and the Cape Province. In addition, the South African government has established 'self-governing' African 'homelands' and has granted 'independence' to four so called 'homelands': Transkei, Bophuthatswana, Venda and Ciskei. This independent status has not been recognized by the international community,[2] and indeed has been condemned by resolutions of the United Nations.[3]

The estimated population of South Africa in 1985 was over 29,000,000. This figure is made up of 21,197,253 classified as Africans, 4,590,639 whites, 2,853,964 coloured and 801,758 Asians. Precisely 5,954,425 people live in the four so-called independent homelands. The black African people make up 72 per cent of the total population of South Africa, whereas the white population represent 15.6 per cent of the total.[4] Different birth rates for the whites and Africans will lead to a steadily increasing black majority.

Every South African is classified at birth as belonging to a particular racial group. By virtue of the Population Registration Act 1950,[5] a register of the entire population is kept in which each person is classified as belonging to a particular racial group: white, coloured, Indian (Asian) or African. The term 'coloured' refers to people regarded as of mixed racial descent. A person's social, political, civil and economic rights are determined by the race or ethnic group to which he is deemed to belong, and, therefore, this Act provides the basis for separate and unfavourable treatment under other legislation and is at the root of the apartheid system.

English and Afrikaans are the two official languages of South Africa. In addition, there are a large number of African languages. Most South Africans are members of the Christian faith, but there are also a small number of Jews, Moslems and Hindus. The majority of whites belong to the Dutch Reformed Church.

Historical background

In 1652 the Cape was occupied by the Dutch East India Company for the purpose of establishing a resting point for its ships. In 1795 the British occupied the Cape to protect its sea route to India, but in 1803 it was returned to the Netherlands. In 1806 the Cape was recolonized by Britain and the Cape became a British Colony. In 1843 Natal was taken over by Britain. The Dutch settlers moved into the interior and established the Orange Free State and—in the territory which is now the Transvaal—the South African Republic. The British fought the Dutch settlers in the Anglo-Boer War of 1899–1902. In 1910 the four colonies joined together to form the Union of South Africa, which then became a self-governing dominion. The Union of South Africa of 1910 attempted to consolidate white power by bringing together the Boer republics and the British colonies. Unity of the white settlers was essential for the economic exploitation of the mineral wealth of the country. In 1931 South Africa became an independent state within the British Commonwealth of nations, and in 1961 the South African Parliament converted the state into a Republic.[6]

In 1948, the National Party came to power on the platform of apartheid and has retained power ever since. Initially, the legislation enacted by the National Party government was directed towards the achievement of racial segregation in the social, economic, educational and political life of the country. However, as opposition to this policy mounted, the government enacted a number of security laws designed to suppress political opposition. More recently again, in response to both national and international pressure, the National Party government has repealed some of the discriminatory laws and has promised to repeal others. However, at the same time, the government has intensified its security programme in order to suppress all internal opposition to its policies.

In 1960 the South African government declared a state of emergency for 156 days. However, this resulted in a loss of confidence in the economy of South Africa, and thereafter the government seemed reluctant to repeat such action. Instead, the government enacted a number of security laws that were part of the ordinary law of South Africa. However, in 1985 these measures were thought to be insufficient and a new six months' emergency was declared covering a number of specified areas. In June 1986 a national state of emergency was declared, and this state of emergency has been renewed in 1987. It looks destined to continue indefinitely.

The apartheid system is based on the notion of 'apartness' or racial segregation. The South African government today prefers to use the term 'separate development' in substitution for apartheid, and it claims that it desires 'separate but equal' development for the people of South Africa. The government justifies 'separate development' as 'constructive', enabling each racial group to develop and live according to its own cultural and social norms. The theory is that each ethnic group has the right to self-determination in its own territory. As will be seen, the government has now acknowledged that this theory cannot be implemented in practice.[7]

Apartheid laws fall into two categories: first, the laws which set out the personal, social, economic, cultural and educational status of the individual in society, and second, the laws that set up the institutions of separate development and determine the political status of the individual. The cornerstone of both types of legislation is the Population Registration Act 1950, by virtue of which every individual is classified as belonging to a particular racial group. All subsequent legislation is designed to accord to the citizens of South African different rights and privileges according to this racial classification. The second type of legislation has manifested itself in the separate homeland policy. The notion behind this policy is that the Bantu peoples of South Africa do not constitute a homogeneous race but form separate national units on the basis of language and culture. The government intended that these separate cultures would form self-governing national units. The so-called 'independent homelands' have separate parliaments, governments and courts, with judges often seconded from the Supreme Court of South Africa.

The government's purpose was to justify the claim that it discriminated between individuals on the grounds of nationality rather than on the grounds of race. The 'separate but equal' policy of the National Party culminated in the 1983 Constitution.

In 1978 P.W. Botha became the Leader of the National Party. This is seen by many in South Africa as being the beginning of a reform era. The legislation that has been passed from that date shows a pattern of reforming social discrimination while at the same time entrenching white power. These reforms have effected no fundamental change, but they are aimed at getting rid of what is called 'petty apartheid'. The pass laws[8] and the influx control laws[9] have been abolished. There has been a considerable development in labour relations legislation, and blacks are now entitled to own businesses in central districts. The parks have been opened up, and the cinemas have been desegregated. In 1985 the legislation prohibiting inter-racial marriages[10] and inter-racial sexual relations[11] was repealed.

Government and Parliament

The pre-1983 system of government was based on one parliamentary chamber, were members were elected by whites only in single-member constituencies. As a result of the Republic of South Africa Constitution Act 1983,[12] Parliament was drastically altered. Parliament now consists of three chambers. The House of Assembly is for whites, the House of Representatives is for coloured people, and the House of Delegates is for Indians.

The State President is both head of state and head of government. He is elected by a 'college', the majority of which are white, and he is aided by the President's Council, which is heavily weighted in favour of the ruling National Party. The State President in theory acts on the advice of the ministerial council for the relevant population group in respect of 'own affairs', that is affairs that only affect that particular group. But, in respect of 'general affairs' (i.e. matters that have an effect on all racial groups) the President is supposed to act on the advice of the Cabinet over which he presides.

Parliamentary Supremacy

Parliamentary supremacy is the fundamental principle of South African law. Under this doctrine laws enacted by Parliament cannot be invalidated by the courts. Judicial review of legislation is thus excluded, except in relation to the 'entrenched clauses' which protect the equality of English and Afrikaans as the two official languages. The courts can enquire as to whether or not the procedural requirement[13] of legislation affecting the status of the two languages has been met. The 1983 Constitution expressly provides that 'no Court of law shall be competent to enquire into or pronounce upon the validity of an Act of Parliament'.[14] There are thus no legal restraints on Parliament's will. One academic has commented that 'civil liberty and the rule of law were sacrificed on the altar of parliamentary supremacy to the idol of apartheid'.[15]

The South African legal system

South African common law is essentially a mixture of Roman–Dutch and English law. The common law together with legislation make up the law of South Africa. Roman–Dutch law consists of Germanic custom supplemented by Roman law and was brought to the Cape in 1652 by the Dutch East India Company. After the annexation of the Cape by Britain in 1806, local common law was gradually influenced by English legal doctrine.[16] The court system was adopted from England, and English criminal procedure is followed.

In some instances, particularly in relation to certain aspects of African family relations, African customary law is still used.

The courts and the legal profession

There are two types of judicial officers in South Africa: judges, who sit in the Supreme Court, and magistrates, who handle a much larger proportion of the civil and criminal work load, and who sit in the Magistrates Courts. The Supreme Court of South Africa consists of an Appellate Division, which is the highest Court of Appeal, and a General Division, which is made up of provincial and local divisions and which is both an Appeal Court from the decisions of the Magistrates Courts and a court of first instance.[17] The Supreme Court has both civil and criminal jurisdiction. Supreme Court judges are appointed from the ranks of senior advocates (barristers) by the State President in council. The Appellate Division consists of a chief justice and ten judges of appeal. There are about 130 Supreme Court judges in South Africa. Each provincial division is presided over by a Judge President, who is responsible for the administration of that division. Supreme Court judges have tenure until the age of 70, and can only be removed before that date on the grounds of incapacity or misconduct.[18]

The lower courts consist of District Magistrates Courts, which have both civil and criminal jurisdiction, and Regional Magistrates Courts, which have criminal jurisdiction only. In criminal matters, the District Magistrate is limited to imposing a maximum sentence of one year's imprisonment, a fine of R.1,000 or a whipping, whereas the Regional Magistrate can impose a maximum prison sentence of ten years' imprisonment, a fine of R.10,000 or a whipping. The magistrates are full-time civil servants. Whipping is a common form of punishment.

A system of judicial precedent exists whereby lower courts are bound by the decisions of the higher courts within the same province and by the decisions of the Appellate Division. South Africa has an adversarial system of criminal justice on the Anglo-American model and the prosecution of criminal offences is vested in the Attorney General—a civil servant—for each division.

The legal profession consists of advocates (barristers) and attorneys (solicitors). The advocates make up the Bar, which is divided into Senior and Junior Counsel, the former of which represents the most senior and experienced lawyers in South Africa, and makes up the pool from which judges are appointed. Advocates have exclusive rights of audience before the Supreme Court. The advocate is instructed or 'briefed' by the attorney, who is a member of the Side-Bar and who deals with the client directly. The advocate only deals with the client through the attorney. In the case of capital offences, however, an advocate may be instructed by the state to appear *pro bono* for an indigent accused without the instructions of a briefing attorney. The vast majority of advocates and attorneys in South Africa are white. There are approximately 900 advocates and 6,000 attorneys in practice in South Africa.[19]

The security forces

The South African Police (SAP) is a national police force charged with the preservation of internal security, the maintenance of law and order, the investigation of offences and the prevention of crime. In 1984 the force was made up of 23,206 whites and 21,490 non-whites.[20] There are 1.4 policemen for every 1,000 people, a smaller proportion than in most other countries. In addition, there are two reserve police forces and railway police. The security branch of the SAP is responsible for the investigation of matters of state security and is the most controversial branch of the force. This branch has far-reaching *de jure* and *de facto* powers.

The South African government spent R.95,000,000 on intelligence services during the financial year 1985/6.[22] In addition to the security branch of the SAP, the intelligence services are made up of Military Intelligence, the Intelligence Evaluation Section of the Department of Foreign Affairs, and the National Intelligence Service.[23] The Cabinet has a sub-committee, the State Security Council, to deal with matters of state security, and there is a huge security structure which reaches from the State Security Council down to each local community. This structure is co-ordinated through joint management centres, who operate in secret and of which little is known.[24]

Welfare and Education

There is an acute housing shortage in South Africa for non-white groups, but particularly for Africans. Social welfare services are run by different government departments for each racial group. The average school career of a white child in South Africa is twelve years. The final matriculation examination is taken at the end of the twelfth year, and the result of this examination determines entry to universities and third-level education. Different government departments control the educational systems for the four racial groups. There is a separate system of education for black children. The per capita state expenditure on African children is less than one-sixth of that spent on each white child.[25] Corporal punishment is permitted in all schools, and whipping is the most common sentence given to males convicted in the Juvenile Courts.[26]

Notes

1. For a detailed introduction to the South African legal system see J. Dugard, *Human Rights and the South African Legal Order*, Princeton, NJ, 1978, p. 1 et seq.
2. For example, Boputhatswana is recognized only by Taiwan and Israel.
3. See those listed in A.O. Ozgur, *Apartheid: The United Nations and Peaceful Change in South Africa*, Transnational Publishers, 1982.
4. Race Relations Survey, 1985, South African Institute of Race Relations, 1986, pp. 1 & 2.
5. See Dugard.
6. Hugh Corder, *Judges at Work*, Johannesburg, 1984.
7. The South African Constitution Act 1961, Act no. 32 of 1961.
7. See p. 130.
8. Blacks (Abolition of Passes and Co-ordination of Documents) Act 1952, Act no. 67 of 1952.
9. Black (Urban Areas) Consolidation Act 1945, Act no. 25 of 1945.
10. Prohibition of Mixed Marriages Act 1949, Act no. 55 of 1949.
11. Immorality Amendment Act 1950, Act no. 21 of 1950.
12. Act no. 110 of 1983.
13. Sections 137, 152, South African Act 1909, and the South African Amendment Act 1956, Act no. 9 of 1956.
14. Section 30 of the Republic of South Africa Constitution Act, no. 110 of 1983.
15. Dugard, p. 28 and Ch. 2.
16. Hugh Corder, Judges at Work, Johannesburg, 1984, pp. 15 & 16.
17. The Supreme Court Act 1959, Act no. 59 of 1959.
18. Ibid., Section 10(7).
19. Interview with Henri Viljoen, Chairman of the Bar Council, February 1987.
20. Race Relations Survey, 1985, p. 480.

21. Dugard, p. 12.
22. Race Relations Survey 1985, p. 464.
23. Interview Capetown, February 1987.
24. See Chapter 13 below, 'The Security System'.
25. South African Institute of Race Relations, Social and Economic Update, 8 November 1987. The per capita expenditure on African children (outside the homelands) for 1986 is stated to be R.395. For white children the figure is R.2746 for the same period.
26. McLachlan, 'Children in Prison in South Africa', Institute of Criminology, University of Capetown, 1984.

3   Legal Structures of Apartheid

Is apartheid 'dead', as Pik Botha, the Foreign Minister, claimed in 1985? Is a black president in South Africa acceptable to the National Party, even 'inevitable', as Pik Botha, considered a 'liberal' within the National Party said in January 1986—rather prematurely as it appears since he was immediately rebuffed, in strong terms, by the State President. Is apartheid 'outdated', as P.W. Botha stated in Parliament in January 1986? Is it to be dismantled and eventually abolished altogether, or is it only to be 'reformed', leaving its basic structures unchanged? Inconsistent public utterances by prominent National Party officials suggest that the government may be confused about its intentions. This became particularly apparent when in August 1985, in the wave of mounting international threats of sanctions, Pik Botha travelled through some Western countries and hinted that President Botha, in a speech in Durban on 15 August 1985, would announce dramatic reforms. International expectations ran high but were bitterly disappointed by a speech that defied international criticism and practically called for a retreat into the 'laager'.

Although we found no evidence of any intention of relinquishing white minority control, we acknowledge that there has been some relaxation in the legal structure of apartheid in recent years. The following is a brief overview.

The new 1983 Constitution, which provides for the first time parliamentary representation for non-whites, that is so-called coloureds and Indians roughly in proportion to population group, was claimed by the government to be a major breakthrough. A breakthrough it is, in the sense that the white electorate now accepts that it is not the only group to be represented in Parliament.

No genuine shift in political or economic power has taken place, however, and the Constitution excludes from parliamentary representation the huge disenfranchised African majority. It reinforces the apartheid structure by allowing the three racial groups to express their political wishes and views only in three separate houses, with the white House of Assembly effectively having a veto power. There is thus no prospect of bringing about meaningful changes against the majority of the white house even in the unlikely case of the members of the two other houses and a minority of the House of Assembly mustering more votes than the majority of the latter house. Also, in the event of disagreement between the houses of Parliament about any piece of legislation, the President's Council, which is heavily weighted in favour of the ruling National Party, decides which view prevails.

There is also an array of apartheid legislation which has recently been repealed or amended. This especially relates to 'petty apartheid'. The Reservation of Separate Amenities Act 1953 legalized the provision of separate buildings, services and conveniences for different racial groups. It did not compel segregation but permitted it to be enforced by local or state ordinance.[1] Since 1979 there has been a policy of granting blanket exemptions to legalize multi-racial use of facilities. The government has in recent years discouraged what former Prime Minister Vorster described as 'unnecessary and purely irritating race discriminatory measures not essential to separate development'. As a consequence, those most blatant signs of apartheid, such as racially segregated public toilet facilities in airports or 'whites only' benches in public parks have all but disappeared. But during our visit, four young girls were prosecuted in Durban accused of unlawfully bathing from a beach reserved for whites and—a well-publicized case—a black schoolboy was refused participation in a national sporting event by the governors of the white host school.

The Immorality Act 1957 and the Mixed Marriages Act 1949, which made inter-racial sexual relations illegal,[2] have been repealed, but the Group Areas Act, which assigns residential areas to each population group to the exclusion of other groups, still prevents couples living together across the colour line without government permission. The reluctance of the government to waive the requirements of that Act is illustrated by its refusal to allow even its own ambassador to the European Communities, Professor Ranchod, classified as Indian, to reside in a neighbourhood designated for whites only. The Act though has not been uniformly enforced; economic or political exegiences occasionally make exceptions politically desirable. Thus black diplomats may reside in white areas. To avoid embarrassment of the Japanese business community—a category of people very much courted in sanction-threatened South Africa—the government had declared all Japanese 'honorary whites' already many years ago. The Group Areas Act also clashes with a new law which allows blacks to own freehold land in urban areas when until recently they could acquire only a 99-year leasehold on real property (in November 1987 two blacks in Johannesburg were the first to make use of the new laws). It is therefore possible for a black family to own a house in which they are not allowed to live.

The abolition of the pass laws which affected black people only has been hailed by the government as signalling the demise of apartheid. These laws, indeed, were the cause of particular bitterness among black people, especially the infamous Section 10 (1) of the Black (Urban Areas) Consolidation Act 1945, which made it illegal for most blacks to remain in white areas for more than seventy-two hours. To enforce the pass laws more easily, each black person was required to always carry and show on demand a so-called passbook which gave information on the holder's place of work, employer's name and signature and showed whether or not the holder was allowed to stay in a particular white area. During 1983 alone, 262,905 blacks were arrested for pass law offences,[3] and since 1916 altogether 18 million.[4] This, at least, has changed. Black South Africans no longer find themselves liable to arrest at any moment for being in the wrong place. There is now a uniform identity document for all South Africans which, in theory, is deracialized and colour-blind. No longer does it contain a number which reflects the racial group. But contrary to government claims, we are satisfied that from the identity number one still may trace the racial classification recorded in the central records office in Pretoria.

As much as the black community welcomed the abolition of the pass law system and the scrapping of thirty-four discriminatory influx control laws,[5] it is a marginal advance. Influx control is still imposed by the enforcement of other laws. The Prevention of Illegal Squatting Act criminalizes residence in an unauthorized area and empowers the authorities to remove a person to any other land which the appropriate Minister may designate. The enforced deprivation of South African citizenship for those consigned to the 'independent' homelands makes their presence outside those homelands illegal, unless they can establish permanent residence to the satisfaction of a hostile bureaucracy. Those who still have South African citizenship cannot move without both home and job to go to—virtually impossible in present circumstances. Experienced observers to whom we spoke saw the abolition of the pass laws as part of a new government strategy to bypass the courts: instead of prosecuting offenders publicly in the courts, an administrative discretion is substituted which the judges cannot easily supervise.

The Restoration of Citizenship Act 1986 has also been hailed as a progressive change, and undoubtedly it marks a turning-point from the policy which sought to exclude every black person from South African citizenship and eventually to make all blacks aliens in their country of birth. Discrimination would then no longer have been based on race but nationality —a form of discrimination accepted by all other states. The government has evidently recognized that this policy cannot be fully implemented—the people in the non-independent homelands are refusing independence because they can see that conditions in those homelands that have opted for independence are even worse than in South Africa itself. But citizens of the independent homelands who now see the possibility of reclaiming South African citizenship are likely to be disappointed. Only those already permanently resident with home and job outside the homeland will qualify, and they are at the mercy of bureaucratic discretion.

The structure of apartheid remains untouched by the cosmetic changes which the government has so far made. No changes are proposed in the segregated public school system. Possibly even the Group Areas Act could be repealed without threatening white domination. Perhaps even the Population Registration Act, the corner-stone of South Africa's 'pigmentocracy' according to which each individual South African is to be racially classified and on which the segregated franchise depends,[7] could be sacrificed in the last resort, but as long as it remains, the government's claim that it is dismantling apartheid will be a hollow one.

Notes

1. See Dugard, p. 63.
2. See pages 9 and 10.
3. Graham Leach, *South Africa*, London 1986, p. 81.
4. Ibid., p. 94. See also Amnesty International, USA, *South Africa: Imprisonment under the Pass Laws*, New York, 1986.
5. Leach, p. 94.
6. See also the Aliens Act and the Admission of Persons to the republic Regulations Act.
7. For more details, see Dugard, pp. 60ff.

4   Freedom of Movement and Forced Removals

Freedom of movement and the restrictions placed on it nowadays in South
Africa must be examined in the light of two separate components: on one
side, the individual's right to move freely and to choose his dwelling inside
the national borders of his country and, on the other side, the right to leave
his country and to return to it.[1]

Group areas

The Group Areas Act, together with the Mixed Marriage and Population
Registration Acts constitute 'one of the foundation deeds of the Apartheid
Revolution'.[2] When, during the campaign previous to the constitutional
referendum of 1983, P.W. Botha announced that apartheid was about to be
extinguished, the Group Areas Act was abundantly criticized by many who
saw it as a keystone of the system.

The Mixed Marriage Act was abolished in 1985, but significantly the
Group Areas Act was not, and the intention of the governing party is
evidently to keep it on the statute book:

When, on a number of occasions, the Government was challenged to abolish the
Group Areas Act—once by a maverick section of the National Party in Port Elizabeth,
more frequently by Opposition spokesmen—the State President generally responded
with some vigour that the Act was there to stay. Along with the Population
Registration Act, it remained the central guarantee of residential and ultimately
cultural differentiation on which the distinction between 'own' and 'general' affairs in
the 1983 Constitution was based.[3]

However, this legislation remains in force, with the consequence that even
if mixed marriages are nowadays legally authorized, they are frequently
prevented as long as mixed couples are not allowed to live in the same place.

The Group Areas Act was adopted in 1950 on the proposal of Minister
Donges (who was the governmental protagonist in the constitutional fight of
the 1950s about the Separate Representation of Voters Act). Many times
amended, it was consolidated in 1957, and again in 1966.

The Act does not establish new principles. By 1923, under the Union,
separate residences in the cities were already set up for Africans. Likewise,
residential segregation among whites, coloureds and Indians already existed,
either in an informal way or as a result of local legislation (e.g. the prohibition

on Indian people living in the Orange Free State and in certain parts of North Natal).

The innovative aspect of the Group Areas Act was that it 'was to turn this fairly limited and unsystematic form of segregation into a rigid system that applied throughout the country'.[4]

The Act compels people to live in specific zones which have been proclaimed for people of their racial group only and whose classification is determined by the government.

The creation of 'group areas' in towns and cities for white, African and coloured is prescribed by this Act, the last group having been subdivided, as a result of a Presidential Proclamation, into Indian, Chinese, Malayan and 'other coloured' people.

Residential intermingling had advanced so far in many cities that it was impossible to implement the final goal of the Act—separate 'race areas' for residential and business purposes—with immediate effect. Consequently the Act provides for different stages of implementation. Some areas are thus proclaimed 'controlled areas' within which existing ownership and occupation patterns are pegged. The ultimate aim, however, is the establishment of separate 'group areas' set aside for the exclusive ownership or occupation of the different racial groups. Disqualified persons—that is, those belonging to a racial group other than that for which the area has been proclaimed— are prohibited from acquiring property for ownership in such an area, if the group area has been proclaimed for ownership; or are obliged to vacate premises by a specified date under threat of criminal sanction if the group area has been proclaimed for occupation. The Act distinguishes between group areas for occupation and for ownership and in practice emphasizes occupation. The emphasis is explained by a sometime law adviser to the Group Areas Board, Mr. F.P. Rousseau, as follows: 'The clashes and difficulties between persons of different races which other countries have experienced have had their origins almost entirely in undesired occupation. If your neighbour by reason of his race has a way of living different from yours, so that his proximity offends you, you are not likely to worry about the racial group of his landlord.'[5]

Since the beginning of 1985, under economic and external pressures, the government has freed the central business districts of big cities from the group areas legislation. They are now opened to people of all races. However, it is only for professional purposes that non-white people can occupy premises in the centres of the cities. At night they must go back to the zones reserved for their housing, which means that they must often travel long distances.

The Act established a Land Tenure Advisory Board (then named the Group Areas Board and, later, the Community Development Board) consisting of white state employees reporting to the Ministry of Interior. Their function is to recommend exclusive ownership or occupation (or both) of certain areas by particular racial groups. The object of the legislation is nothing less than 'a complete unscrambling of the residential patterns in South-African towns'.[6]

Once a group area has been decreed, all residents who are not qualified to live there because they do not belong to the right racial group must leave their homes and may be forced to go to places allocated to them.

As a result of this process, many massive removals were ordered in the middle of the 1950s.

We are in no doubt that the Group Areas Act has been applied in a grossly discriminatory way to the advantage of the white population: in 1982, 80,053 coloured families and 38,472 Indian families were shifted as compared with 2,262 white families.[7]

To those official figures, which only take into account the non-African population (because Africans are controlled by other means), we must add the number of Africans who have been evicted from their urban housing by the application of the Group Areas Act; as an example, 80,000 Africans were evicted from the centre of the city of Durban in 1961 when it was declared a 'white zone'.[8]

Similarly, 60,000 Africans were evicted from Sophiatown, a lively and dynamic suburb of Johannesburg founded in 1905 and suddenly proclaimed a 'white zone'.[9] It is sometimes thought that the Group Areas Act, which the government has no intention of repealing, is no longer enforced. This is largely true. It is because the objective has been reached: 'The whole Republic had been covered by the racial zoning plans of the Board and its regional subdivisions by the mid-1970s, and in almost all respects these zoning plans had been finalized.'[10] However, its effects remain and the government uses it as last resource when it deems it appropriate.[11] The example of Professor Ranchod illustrates this (see p. 12).

In February 1987, during our visit, the government expressly used the group areas regulations against the 3,000 to 5,000 black people living in the township of Lawaaikamp in George, Western Cape. The land on which the tin shanty houses were built belongs to the municipality of George, but has been proclaimed a coloured group area. Consequently, according to the terms of the Group Areas Act, the occupation by black people is illegal.[12] Having issued a notice requiring all black residents to leave Lawaaikamp by a deadline expiring on 30 December 1986, the government realized that it had acted illegally, and in February 1987 it was announced that the government was basing its demand of removal on the Group Areas Act, in addition to the alleged public health grounds, which were also mentioned.[13]

Implementation of this unique legislation leads to the following assessment. First of all, in most cases the removal of a population implies the destruction of an integrated and lively community. The case of District Six is a striking example. District Six is an area in the heart of Cape Town which had been occupied by coloured people since 1834. Its estimated population was 61,000 coloured and 800 whites. This quarter was extremely lively and every year the whole city used to go there for the carnival.

Very suddenly, on 11 February 1966, District Six was proclaimed a white zone and its coloured inhabitants were moved to new settlements situated from 20 to 40 kilometres away in the Cape Flats. District Six was demolished. Even today, it is nothing but a huge waste ground of the city, all buildings having been demolished except churches and mosques.

By forcing hundreds of thousands of black people to live in segregated ghettos, the Group Areas Act generates splits and suspicions among the

urban working-class but also strengthens the relationships between white
people who are separated from black people and yet who among themselves
are not divided into group areas, for British, Afrikaners, Greeks or Portu-
guese.

The Act incites non-white people to consider themselves as 'coloured',
'Indian' or 'African' rather than to unite to find a solution to their common
problems. New ghettos are created in order to be easily controlled. They are
crossed by large perpendicular streets, convenient for police patrols and
military vehicles. They are situated far away from the centre of the cities and
often they have only two entrances which can be easily blocked by the police.

When visiting a shanty town at Crossroads, the mission members and their
courier were quickly located by a small aeroplane flying over the township
which identified their location with a sign of its wing. Within minutes, an
Army Casspir arrived on the scene. An armed officer rushed towards the
group and very thoroughly interrogated the courier about the object of our
visit before ordering us to leave the area immediately.

The Group Areas Act is also used as a means of economic control. New
townships are often created next to industrial areas in order to supply the
necessary labour force. The Group Areas Act penalizes Indian traders by
excluding them from working in town and city centres. Many white
shopkeepers profit from this situation at the expense of their ousted
competitors.

Finally, white people have made huge profits out of property deals as a
result of the Act. White speculators have made fortunes from forced sales of
buildings belonging to coloured or Indian people who suddenly found they
were not qualified to live there anymore:

Often, the speculators have had close connections with the inner circles of the
National Party. They have known in advance where and when the next proclamation
is to fall. Having bought these black houses for very little, they then renovate them
and sell them to white buyers as charming cottages at enormously inflated prices.[14]

Influx control

As seen above, the Group Areas Act essentially affects Indians and coloured
people. The control of the constantly increasing African population in urban
areas was a much more serious and urgent problem for the government.

'Influx control' is the name given to 'the network of legislation and
regulations which controls African access to the urban-industrial centres
situated in what is claimed to be white South Africa'.[15]

The Group Areas Act and its enforcement have caused the residence of
hundreds of thousands of African people in the urban areas to be deemed
illegal. Since the early 1950s, the government has sought to engage in 'an
ongoing and increasingly vicious battle to root out the people living "illegally" in town', trying to reduce the number of Africans allowed to stay
permanently in the urban areas and to control strictly those who remain. The

opening shot of this battle was the Prevention of Illegal Squatting Act 1951, which empowered the authorities to remove squatters from public or private land and send them elsewhere at their discretion, and gave every local authority the right (or the duty, on ministerial command) to 'establish' . . . an emergency camp for homeless persons'.[16] The same Act empowers the authorities to demolish the buildings of the ousted people.

The next step was the passing in 1952 of two central Acts, the Natives (Abolition of Passes and Coordination of Documents) Act which requires all Africans including those exempted under the pass laws (and including women for the first time) to carry 'reference books' containing their photographs, and information about their places of origin, their employment records, their tax payments and their encounters with the police. Thus the government was able to exercise the control of African Influx into the towns.

The second Act, the Native Laws Amendment Act, which amended the Black (Urban Areas) Act, is the central measure of influx control. This Act prohibited Africans from remaining in 'prescribed' areas for more than seventy-two hours unless they could produce either formal exemption from the prohibition, or permission to be there. Affecting initially only urban areas, the Act was amended in 1964 'in order to plug gaps in the system of controls', to extend influx control to peri-urban districts so that the urban area and the peri-urban districts became known collectively as 'prescribed areas'.[17]

An *exemption* could be obtained by a sustained period of lawful residence or employment in the area. The exemptions were colloquially known as 'Section 10 rights'. Section 10 of this Act specifies four conditions for urban residence. People who meet these conditions did not qualify for residence in *any* urban area. Their qualification was for a specific area only and no other.

The four categories of legal urban residence created in this way were:

(a) People who had been born in the urban area and lived there continuously ever since;
(b) People who had worked continuously for ten years for one employer in the same urban area, or who had lived lawfully and continuously in the urban area for at least 15 years;
(c) The wives and married daughters and the son under 18 years of age of anybody who qualified in terms of (a) or (b);
(d) Those who had been given special permission to be in the urban area by the authorities, generally because they were migrant workers on contract to work there.

Those people qualified under either (a) or (b) would be able to live permanently in the urban area, unless they were found to be 'idle and undesirable', in which case they would be expelled. Those who were qualified as per (c) could stay only as long as their status did not change.

If, for instance, a wife became widowed or a daughter got married or a son became of age, then they would have to leave the area *unless* they already qualified in their own right, under provisions (a) or (b).

Those who qualified under (d) would be able to stay only as long as their permission remained valid. As soon as the time stipulated on their pass ended, then they would no longer qualify to be there and would have to leave. Those people not so exempted could apply for *permission* to remain in the area. This was generally granted only for purposes of employment, and then only for a period of up to a year at a time. Many were unable to obtain such permission despite having offers of employment.

Simultaneously, the influx control policy was refined by a sophisticated migrant labour system. A network of labour bureaux was established in order to control the number of people allowed to enter an urban area for job purposes and to direct labour to those areas and sectors most in need of it, especially in the mining and construction industries.

Labour bureau officials acquired arbitrary powers over the work-seekers:

With one stamp they could determine where one could work, for how long one could work there, even what kind of work one could do. Once a rural person got 'farm worker only' stamped in his pass, it was virtually impossible for him ever to break from that category legally.[18]

In 1964 the powers of the labour bureaux were extended to cover the employment of all African workers in the urban areas, whether permanent residents or migrants. From 1968 their control became even more far-reaching and labour bureaux were set up in the Bantustans. Control over which residents of rural areas were to be allowed to work in town was to be exercised prior to their removal to the rural areas; they were already subject to control while still in the area of departure. At the same time, to prevent acquisition of 'Section 10 rights' it became compulsory for migrant workers who had jobs to return to their 'place of origin' once a year. Large numbers of Africans would come to the city for a year, to take up employment. They were not permitted to bring their families with them. Most were required to spend the year in single-sex hostels, generally under grim conditions. Members of the mission were able to observe these conditions. At the end of each year, they had to return to their rural place of origin. The government interpretation of the statute was that ten successive one-year periods of employment under migrant labour contracts did not amount to ten years continuous employment in the urban area, so that the qualification for Section 10 (b) rights was never achieved.

This interpretation survived unchallenged until September 1981 when it was finally rejected by the ruling of the Rand Supreme Court in the celebrated *Rikhoto* case. Although Rikhoto was a contract worker, and therefore required to return to his homeland annually to break the continuity of his residence in town, the court held these annual holidays did not destroy his Section 10 rights.

Another successful application to the court was made by Mrs Nonceba Komani who, in August 1980, won the right to live with her husband in an urban area despite the fact that she had not been entered by officials on her husband's lodging permit. 'It was estimated that 143,000 out of 800,000 migrant workers would benefit immediately'.[19]

As customary when it is defeated by a court, the government reacted by issuing blocking legislation. In this case, new laws were introduced in August 1983 to remove the effects of the *Komani* and *Rikhoto* decisions.

As to the *Komani* decision, the new legislation obliges the wives and children of urban African to prove they had already been living with qualified men of their choice before 26 August 1983; those whose residence began after that date are excluded. To contain the effects of the *Rikhoto* decision, the new legislation says that contract workers seeking Section 10 rights must now show that they either own, rent or occupy houses in their own names; the occupation of a room in another house is not regarded as adequate.

In passing this new law, the government and Parliament must have been aware that these new requirements cannot be met by most of those affected.

In fact, during the past thirty years, housing policy has been designed and used by the government to give effect to the policy of influx control, to limit the number of Africans who can find a permanent place of urban residence. The enforcement of the Group Areas Act means that urban housing provision for Africans has been deliberately restricted. Pursuing the policy of favouring the white minority, the government has chosen to limit the funds made available for African family housing in urban areas, urban funds being channelled to single-sex hostel development and the construction of new family housing curtailed in favour of family housing in the homelands.

But the government's well-known and widely proclaimed intention of rooting the black population out of the cities could not be achieved. Facts are stubborn and the object of influx control proved unattainable. As a result of the very poor economic situation in the homelands, which the white minority has perpetuated, large numbers of Africans continued to leave the rural areas, where land is poor and unemployment very high, to live illegally in the cities in order to find a way of providing for their families.

To do this they were prepared to risk imprisonment. By working for three months in Cape Town, then spending nine months in jail, a person from Ciskei can earn three times more than by working for one year in Ciskei— even if he could find a job there. As a result of the government policy, the African urban housing shortage has rocketed. By March 1985 it had reached 538,000 houses for Africans outside the Bantustans, 52,000 for coloured and 44,000 for Indians.

In economic terms alone, this policy is a nonsense, since at the same time there was actually a surplus of housing units available for people classified by the government as white. This was not, of course, available for other groups, because of the Group Areas Act.

Refusing to face the facts it had itself created, the government tried to find new legal means to get rid of the black population in urban areas. The result was the Black Community Development Act 1983. Section 37 of this Act empowered the Minister of Co-operation and Development (as the Minister for 'Bantu Affairs' was now called, after a brief spell as 'Plural Relations') to 'disestablish' a place on the sole condition that *he* is *satisfied* that it is desirable, for either health reasons or town planning reasons. Disestablishment meant that the inhabitants were physically forced off the land. This device of creating illegal squatters enabled the government to keep alive influx control while claiming credit for repealing the main influx control legislation. The discretionary power of decision of government officials is the crucial point: one sole official is empowered to destroy a community at will. Because it is discretionary, a decision of one sole person may be difficult if not impossible to challenge in court. Objections against the opinion of the official are limited to showing an improper motive or failing to consider relevant questions. Furthermore, lawyers hesitate to launch judicial challenges because they know from hard experience that a successful outcome will soon be nullified by amending legislation.

Attempting to change the Minister's mind seems futile. The members of the mission noted the response of the Minister to several applications: he made it clear that he had made up his mind that he was simply not prepared to reconsider or enter into any further discussions. The victims have little choice but to wait for the axe to fall. When the eviction takes place, the authorities use whatever violence they consider necessary. Nor do those who are evicted even receive any compensation for their lost homes: it is paid only to those whom the government regards as legal residents. Squatters do not qualify.

In his speech at the opening of Parliament on 31 January 1986, President Botha announced that he intended to abolish influx control measures and on 24 June 1986, Parliament passed the Abolition of Influx Control Act which became law on 1 July 1986. This Act repeals all the legislation comprising the core of the pass laws and particularly the entirety of the Black (Urban Areas) Consolidation Act. The Group Areas Act remains in force, as well as the Prevention of Illegal Squatting Act (with amendments), and the Black Community Development Act.

This historical review of the influx control legislation is necessary to explain the consequences and the real impact of the Abolition of Influx Control Act, which is very far from restoring freedom of movement to non-white people in South Africa. This will become even more apparent when we examine the other side of influx control, namely the 'homelands' policy; and when we describe the practical consequences of the enforcement of the influx control, especially the forced removal of hundreds of thousands of people in South Africa. It will be seen that the Abolition of Influx Control Act does not mean the end of apartheid. Influx control of black people is continuing apace, and the right to freedom of movement for the majority of South Africans is constantly violated.

The 'homelands' policy

The creation of Bantustans (previously named 'reserves', then 'homelands', also later on 'national states') constitutes the second part of the influx control policy. Like the Group Areas Act, the creation of the homelands by the post-1948 government was not new. The only novelty was the systematic elaboration of the policy. Since the mid-nineteenth century, the British had experimented in Natal with a system of 'Natives' reserves', which are the forebears of the Bantustans and of the homelands of apartheid.

Under the South African Union, the Native Land Act was adopted by the Parliament of South Africa in 1913. It confined the black majority of the population to land representing 7.3 per cent of the country's surface. This law is the starting point of a policy of separation which was to be developed later. This same law was responsible for the first forced removals of the black rural population to areas reserved for it ('scheduled land').

In 1936 the Native Trust and Land Act established once and for all the proportion of the land designated to become native reserves, the area of which represents approximately 13 per cent of the whole country.[20] The land reserved for the black population by the 1936 law is distributed among the four provinces on a quota basis.

The 'quota land' thus represents the maximum area which may be occupied or owned by Africans in each province. In order to enable the smaller scheduled areas of 1913 to reach the new 1936 quota, an official institution was created by the government, the South African Native Trust (which later became the South African Bantu Trust, then the South African Development Trust) to manage the acquisition and the administration of the land to be added to the scheduled areas (released land).

When the Nationalists came to power in 1948, the Trust was far from having completed its mission and many 'Black Spots' were still in existence all over the country. 'Black Spot' is an official expression usually designating African freehold land which was located outside of the scheduled or released areas. When proceeding with the establishment of the homelands, the government's particular intention was to obtain the elimination of 'Black Spots'. It was also the government's intention to transfer the 'surplus' black population from the urban white areas into those reserves as well as the blacks established in white rural areas who were not owners of their land. The latter became undesirable as a result of the mechanization of agriculture and constituted a second category of 'surplus people' (redundant workers, ex-labour tenants and their families).

Finally, in order to appease international public opinion deeply troubled by the situation in South Africa, the government conceived the homelands as a way of giving blacks political rights within the boundaries of their former reserves, thereby providing a kind of justification for the deprivation of political rights on the national level.

The first Bantustans were thus born in the ruins of the old native reserves, which were economic deserts. The first step in creating the Bantustans was the Bantu Authorities Act 1951, which established tribal, regional and territorial authorities with limited powers within the reserves.

The pick of the tribal leaders soon became salaried officials—local controlling agents on behalf of the central government. Several of those who had been in the forefront of resistance to colonialism became protagonists of the white apartheid government.

The decisive step forward was the introduction in 1959 of the Promotion of Bantu Self-Government Act, which inaugurated the separate development policy and changed the reserves into Bantustans. The preamble of this Act expressed the theory which the government tried to impose: 'The Bantu people of the Union of South Africa do not constitute a homogenous people but form separate national units on the basis of language and culture.'

The law extends the system of tribal and territorial authority established in 1951, devolves considerable executive powers to territorial authorities and offers to each national unit the prospect of eventually becoming self-governing and even independent.

At the beginning, the government was only able to identify eight national units: North Sotho, South Sotho, Tswana, Zulu, Swazi, Xhosa, Tsonga and Venda. The system was subsequently extended: Xhosa were divided into two units, the Transkeians and the Ciskeians. Then, by the mid-1970s the national unit of Ndebele was discovered and added to the list. The ten homelands which became national states and which today appear on the map of South Africa are the following: Bophuthatswana (Tswana), Ciskei (Xhosa), Gazankulu (Shangaans and Tsongas), KwaNgwane (Swazis), KwaNdebele (Ndebeles), KwaZulu (Zulus), Lebowa (North-Sotho), QuaQua (South-Sotho), Transkei (Xhosa) and Venda (Vendas).

The new law refines the manipulation of the ethnic principle. While under the Group Areas Act the African population is largely defined as one single group, it is now identified as a series of separate tribal groups.

The geographical distribution of the land allocated to the ten homelands is hopelessly irrational and consists of a large number of separate tracts scattered over the map like confetti (see map). Kwazulu, for example, contains no less than twenty-nine main areas and forty-one secondary areas spread all over the province of Natal.

Bophuthatswana comprises seven sections located in three different provinces. Lebowa contains four separate parcels. As one journalist wrote, South Africa is not only a patchwork but a cartographer's nightmare.

What the Group Areas Act accomplished on a local level, the Promotion of Bantu Self-Government Act achieved on a national scale.

The creation of national units led to the same consequences as the Group Areas Act. It institutionalized and encouraged arbitrary group rivalries and tensions. (Why, for example, has a policy which claims to be based on 'tribal' unity divided Xhosas into Transkeians and Ciskeians?) It is difficult not to believe that the real purpose in creating the homelands was to counter the political message of African nationalism and democracy.[21]

The suppression of the 'Black Spots', or in the words of a 1965 circular of the Bantu Administration and Development Department, 'the suspension of property rights vested in Bantu in land situated in white areas'[22] has allowed white people to make huge profits out of forced sales of land. For example, in six districts of the Province of Natal, the occupants of thirty-eight African farms were evicted in 1973: twenty-two of them had important coal resources in their soil, and in 1982 sixteen of these properties had been transformed into mines after having been sold to whites.

It was the creation of the homelands which allowed the South African Development Trust, during the 1960s to acquire African land on a large scale in accordance with the quota provisions of the Land Act 1936. The 'surplus people' ousted from the cities and rural zones have been installed in relocation camps or simply removed from their farms without any concern for their resettlement.

Over the years, the homeland's function as a huge relocation camp became more and more important. In 1970 the most radical legislation on influx control was adopted with the Bantu Homelands Citizenship Act. This Act ascribes to all South Africans of African descent the citizenship of one or other 'homeland' on the basis of linguistic, cultural, familial or geographical ties.

Transfer of citizenship for all Africans was the automatic result of the 1970 Act passed by the white South African Parliament. It applied to all Africans, with or without their consent and even if they had never lived outside a 'white area'.

In the following year the Bantu Homelands Constitution Act was adopted, giving power to the State President to give to each homeland self-government by proclamation. This had already been given to Transkei in 1963 in order to demonstrate to the International Court of Justice (before which South Africa was arraigned in connection with Namibia) the sincerity of South Africa's intentions under its separate development programme.

The status of 'independence' was attributed to four homelands (Transkei, Venda, Bophuthatswana and Ciskei) by South Africa in obvious violation of the international law principle of self-determination. The constitution of these 'states' were adopted in Pretoria. A very large number of persons living in the homelands were settled there against their will and about half of the population of the homelands lives outside the national territory allocated to them.

The government's objective in creating 'independent' homelands was clearly defined in 1978 by the Minister for Bantu Affairs: 'If our policy is taken to its logical conclusion as far as the black people are concerned, there will not be one black person with South African citizenship'.

According to the constitution of the 'independent' states, the situation of their citizens would change drastically as soon as their so-called 'homeland' became constitutionally 'independent'. By a stroke of the pen, they automatically lost their South African nationality and became foreigners in South Africa, where many of them were born and had been living since their birth. This 'denationalization' affected about 8,250,000 Africans. It can be compared only to the Nazi statutory order denationalizing the German Jews. Foreigners in their own country, the new citizens of 'independent' homelands were, from the day of 'independence', considered in white zones as 'guest workers' even if they were born and had always remained there.

Once a person becomes a foreigner, he is subjected to influx control rules contained in the Aliens Act. He cannot enter the South African Republic without permission and cannot apply for a job without permission. He is subjected to summary arrest and to deportation procedures. People who provide employment or accommodation to such 'foreigners' without the necessary official permission commit a criminal offence and are subject to very heavy penalties.

As soon as 'independence' was granted, the governments of Transkei and South Africa concluded an agreement whose first article declares:

No citizen of Transkei engaged in Transkei for employment in the Republic of South Africa shall enter the Republic of South Africa for the purpose of taking up employment unless he complies with the laws and regulations relating to the admission to, residence in, and departure from the Republic of South Africa.

Another agreement was concluded in 1976 between the same two governments 'relating to the movement of citizens of Transkei and of the Republic of South Africa across the common borders'. Its first article provides: 'the movement to and the sojourn in the Republic of South Africa of the citizen of Transkei . . . shall be governed by the laws and regulations governing the admission to, residence in, and departure from the country'.

Similar agreements were concluded with the governments of Bophuthatswana, Venda and Ciskei at the time of independence.[23]

The constitutions of the 'independent' states expressly prescribe the preservation of 'Section 10 rights' of their citizens but, by applying its usual policy of 'one step forward, two steps back', the South African government soon robbed this concession of any value for black people. By a 1978 amendment to the Black (Urban Areas) Consolidation Act 1945, children born after 'independence' to 'new foreigners' became automatically foreigners, *wherever they were born.*

This amendment also drastically weakened the effect of another 1978 government concession: blacks qualified to remain in urban areas according to Section 10 (a) or (b) were granted from that year the right to obtain 99-year leasehold rights to property. What might otherwise have been a substantial advance in reality benefited very few people.

Deprived of their South African citizenship, the 'new foreigners' are nevertheless subject to most of the discriminatory laws of South Africa which are applied to blacks regardless of their citizenship. For example, the Population Registration Act is applied not only to black South African citizens, but to all persons of 'native' descent. The same is true of the rights of residence of blacks in the urban areas. The rules governing education in separate schools for blacks are applicable to them, as well as the Black (Prohibition of Interdicts) Act 1956, which deprives blacks of the rights to obtain judicial interdicts against unfavourable determinations of their residence rights.

Another result of 'independence' is that homeland citizens, considered as 'new foreigners' in South Africa, become subject to South African laws on deportation of foreigners. These laws grant extended powers to the South African government to deport political opponents. Section 45 of the Admission of Persons to the Republic Regulation Act empowers the Minister of Interior, 'if he considers it to be in the public interest', to order the removal from the Republic of 'any person who is not a South African citizen'. This law grants the Minister of Interior absolute powers, because he is the only judge of 'public interest'. His decision 'shall not be subject to appeal or to review by any Court of Law and no person shall be furnished with any reasons for such decision'.[24]

Section 14 of the Internal Security Act permits the deportation of a non-South African citizen who is convicted of certain offences under this Act or who is deemed by the State President to be an undesirable inhabitant 'because he is communist' (see p. 66).

Following international pressure, including the earliest economic sanctions by the United States, the State President announced in September 1985 that South African nationality would be reinstated for all those who had been deprived of it as a result of the independence of certain homelands. The State President admitted that there were 5 million 'new foreigners' in the 'independent states' and 4 million in South Africa, outside those states.

The legislation restoring South African citizenship was published in June 1986 and its real meaning will be examined later (see p. 33).

The consequences of the enforcement of influx control

In execution of the influx control policy, approximately 3,500,000 blacks were moved between 1960 to 1982, and at that date 2 million persons still remained under the threat of removal in the near future. Those figures are derived from the study published in 1983 by the Surplus People Project which described the redrawing of the South African map. We have set out at length at the end of this chapter Professor Davenport's description of the scale of removals throughout South Africa (see Appendix I, p. 37).

Another writer has said:

'Four million is clearly the minimum number of forced removals since 1948 and the true figure may be almsot double this. In qualitative terms the social upheaval of so many millions of people moved in so short a time is analogous to that of the industrial revolution in Europe in the late eighteenth and early nineteenth centuries, or the mass migrations of people made refugees in World War II, and subsequent conflicts in Europe, Asia and the Middle East. It is unclear if the totals include children.[24A]

These impressive figures have never been seriously challenged by a government which juggles statistics at will; thus in an official statement of 1983 Minister Kornhoof publicized statistics which compared the number of white *individuals* moved with the number of black *families* moved during the same period of time in order to convey the impression that almost as many white people had been moved as Blacks.[25] Furthermore, the government in 1982 procured the passing of a law to ensure 'the preservation of secrecy in connection with matters dealt with by the Commission of Co-operation and Development'.[26] This was intended to apply to the consolidation of the homelands (Laws on Co-operation and Development Act 1982).

Removals are usually carried out rudely and often with violence. Administration trucks which are identifiable by their 'GG' licence plages arrive early in the morning or even in the middle of the night to pick up the evicted families who will be lucky to be able to take with them more than a few personal belongings collected in haste. The families are then taken to a homeland, a resettlement zone or a shanty town. Usually, they are given three months to build new housing and their shanty houses are then available for new arrivals.

The most important group of removed persons is the Africans living on white territories with their families through informal sharecropping or farm-leasing agreements with white farmers. In return for permission to settle on the land, they agree to perform seasonal work for the white farmers, but the government has brought pressure on white farmers to employ farm workers and to mechanize their farming businesses, thereby forcing the eviction of 1 million Africans and putting an end to many amicable relationships. The second group of resettled people is made up of the inhabitants of the 'Black Spots', who formerly owned land in the middle of white agricultural areas. They were dispossessed of their land and moved to areas which, very often, were subsequently united with a homeland.

A third category comprises the victims of the homelands consolidation policy, one of the essential elements of apartheid. The case of Moutse, a rural district of Transvaal province with 120,000 inhabitants, is a striking example. Officially, the homelands policy purports to enable each ethnic group to keep its identity. But in Moutse, the Pedi population which is linked to the Sotho ethnic group was suddenly and by a stroke of the pen of the State President, excised from Lebowa and united with the KwaNdebele homeland, which belongs to the ethnic group of Ndebele.[27] This decision by the State President resulted from bargaining between the government of the white minority and the local authorities of KwaNdebele to whom the Moutse district was offered as an inducement to seek 'independence'. Serious protests by the Moutse population followed, but the change of border decided by Pretoria was carried out with extreme brutality in 1986:

On the morning of January 1st, militia of the autonomous Government of Kwa-Ndebele proceeded to Moutse where the inhabitants were barricaded; they kidnapped 260 persons who were taken to the capital Syabuswa. There, Simon Skosana, 'Prime Minister' of the territory ordered them to accept his authority or be flogged. 22 deaths resulted from the confrontation between the militia and the inhabits of the village of Moutse.[28]

The Pretoria government dismissed these events as 'tribal confrontations and black on black violence'. Today the resistance of the Moutse inhabitants still continues and legal proceedings are currently pending before the Supreme Court. This type of population displacement is obviously not included in the official statistics because there is no removal of people, merely the alteration of borders. The last category of removed people is the inhabitants of the cities who are evicted as a result of pass law legislation.

The paradox of the influx control policy is that it has failed, despite its systematic character based on sophisticated legislation which gives huge powers to the government. Its failure is demonstrated by the fact that more Africans than whites are living in the 'white areas'. In addition, the financial cost of the influx control policy has been extremely high for South Africa.

The cost of maintaining numerous government employees in several ministries to deal with these questions is itself enormous. Then there is the acquisition and maintenance of the 'GG' truck fleet permanently installed in the rural regions where the removals are to take place. Then again, there is the exorbitant transportation cost of the workers whom the government compels to settle away from their place of work. Putco, a private bus company established by Italian immigrants has the monopoly for the transport of black workers who commute long distances daily between their homes and the industrial areas. Over one-third of the revenue of Putco is derived from grants by the government to subsidise costs which black workers could not otherwise afford. The distances in KwaNdebele being the longest, they get the highest subsidies. The government is spending tens of millions of rands each year for these subsidies—a sad contrast to the inadequate budget allocated to black education (see p. 43).

The 'reforms' of 1 July 1986

On 1 July 1986 the Abolition of Influx Control Act and the Restoration of Citizenship Act came into effect. It can be conceded that these made important changes, but restrictions on the freedom of movement continue to be a heavy burden for the non-white population of South Africa.

The abolition of influx control

On 31 January 1986, addressing the white Parliament, the State President, P.W. Botha, announced the abolition of passes and their replacement by one single identification document for all South Africans. The two statutes purporting to implement this promise repealed all pass law legislation and, in particular, the entire Black (Urban Areas) Consolidation Act 1945, as well as the Black (Prohibition of Interdicts) Act of 1956.

A new identity document (ID) is required for persons of all racial groups and is in similar form for all. Any person residing *permanently and lawfully* in South Africa may obtain one. This includes all South African citizens as well as foreigners residing permanently with a permit in South Africa. The ID has become a non-racial identity document in the sense that the racial code of each individual which appeared on the previous document (00 for whites, 01 for mixed races of Cape Town, 05 for Indians, 08 for blacks) has disappeared.

By reading the ID, it is no longer possible to identify the racial group of the bearer. However, the identity number allocated to each person enables officials to detect the birth entry number registered with the central administration in Pretoria and which, in turn, enables the racial group to be determined. Lastly, the issue of IDs is separately administered for whites and blacks.[29] For example, white people apply to the office of the Department of Home Affairs located in Johannesburg at Harrison Street while black people must apply to the office of the Department of Co-operation and Development, also in Johannesburg, but at 15 Market Street.

The positive effects of this reform are essentially the following: Africans no longer need an exemption or a permit to reside or work in white urban areas, and employers are now authorized to hire whomever they wish without applying to the 'pass office'. Africans are also authorized to take their families to their place of work or residence.

Another statutory improvement in the situation of the blacks is related to the right they now have to buy a piece of land or a house with freehold title within a black township. Rights under Section 10 (a) or (b) are no longer obtainable since this section has disappeared from the statute book with the repeal of the entire Black (Urban Areas) Consolidation Act 1945.

This, however, only applies to black townships. Under the provisions of the Land Act, which is still in force, blacks are still denied the right to purchase agricultural land in the rural zones outside the homelands.

The right to buy land in the townships is, however, illusory. Virtually all land in the townships is already the property of local authorities (through the medium of the State Administration Boards or the Town Council or the Provincial Administration). Furthermore, the Abolition of Influx Control Act does not in fact abolish influx control and forced removals are being regularly implemented by other means. For example, the provisions of the Group Areas Act remain in force and which are being applied.[30] In February 1987, in the Cape Town area, about 100 Lansdowne residents of all races launched a campaign to prevent the government from evicting coloured home-owners and tenants to comply with Group Areas Act.[31]

The Black Community Development Act 1983 also remains in force, and the government continues to rely on Section 37 to disestablish a township whenever it deems it desirable to do so.

Brits is a good example to illustrate this procedure. It was adopted by Minister Heunis on 17 October 1986 through publication in the government gazette of an announcement whereby, with immediate effect, the township of Brits was no longer a township and was consequently no longer a place reserved for occupation by blacks. Brits is a small industrial town located north of Pretoria whose black township has existed for over fifty years. It has been appallingly neglected: there are no proper social services; no proper maintenance services, no adequate water supply, no decent water sewerage and the roads are blocked up. Originally, the township was separated from the city, but as the white residential zone grew, it became closer and closer. White people wanted to take possession of the township to develop their own residential zone yet further. In addition, they disliked living close to blacks. These are the reasons for the decision of the Minister to disestablish the township.

Brits' black population of 10,000 people was allocated a new piece of land in a township 25 kilometres away. Since 17 October 1986 the inhabitants of the township have been awaiting their forced eviction, and a war of attrition is still going on between the government, which has cut off services and is trying to run the place down until people are forced to move to the new place reserved for them. The latter is equipped with all services, and the contrast increases as the existing township deteriorates.[32]

The inhabitants of the township of Langa at Uitenhage in the Eastern Cape province did not enjoy the respite of a war of attrition. They were threatened with removal by force under the new policy of orderly urbanization based on the Prevention of Illegal Squatting Act, the implementation of which was substantially facilitated by the emergency. The objective of this policy is to depopulate any area which the government deems overcrowded. The inhabitants of Langa township like those of Red Location in Port Elizabeth were only given a verbal warning by the SADF, who circled round the township and announced through loudspeakers that 'this place is dirty, there are too many people, you must move to Motherwell or you must move to KwaNobuhle'. People started shouting, screaming and throwing stones. The soldiers invaded the township using tear gas and sjamboks. This became a situation of 'unrest', which brought the emergency regulations into play: no one was allowed to enter the township, and the press were not allowed to report the event. At Langa the removals were implemented in the middle of the night.[33]

In many cases, as an alternative to threats shouted by the security forces, the inhabitants of townships are being notified of their evictions by notices sent by their town council. These require them to demolish their houses within ten days, failing which they are subject to criminal sanctions including demolition of their houses by the authorities with confiscation of their property. Some town councils use private lawyers for this task (see Appendix II, p. 40). The policy of 'orderly urbanization' based on the Prevention of Illegal Squatting Act has been applied systematically at Old Crossroads in Cape Town, at Duncan Village in East London and the townships of Port Elizabeth.

Illegality is no hindrance for the government employees of the town council: we received evidence that in November 1986, the township of Ibahyi issued an eviction notice entitled 'removal of unauthorized structures' with the threat to the recipient of the notice of sanctions as specified under Section 44 of Blacks (Urban Areas) Consolidation Act 1945. The authorities had overlooked (or did not care) that this Act had been repealed in its entirety on 1 July 1986 (see Appendix II, p. 40). Persons receiving eviction notices are invited to sign a form as follows: 'I am moving voluntarily and I accept this as voluntary and I am signing this document freely and any action which might be taken now or in the future would be ungrounded'. We were supplied with copies of these forms, which are in Afrikaans.

Of course, as it was put to us, 'when a man is standing over you with a rifle, you sign it'. At Brits, we were informed that soldiers appeared with blank pieces of paper requiring people to sign them. We conclude that this is the reality of the removals which the government presents as 'voluntary'.

Another notably hypocritical method used by the government for the control of the black population is the Slums Act, amended in 1987. Until 1987 the Slums Act only applied to whites, coloured and Indians. The recent amendment makes it applicable to everybody and, in particular, to Africans. This enabled the State President to declare that from now on the Slums Act has become a non-discriminatory law. But, of course, townships and housing built for Africans frequently falls far short of complying with the standards required by the Slums Act. Thus by making its provisions applicable to everybody, the police can walk into any township and require any family to move where, for example, more people live in one room than the Slums Act permits. The inhabitants of the black townships subjected to eviction threats since 1 July 1986 under this new influx control system are practically defenceless.

The enforcement of the Slums Act is made even easier by the emergency situation, as can be observed by the active role played by the police forces and the Army in removals. The lawyers whom the inhabitants employ in desperation are molested and harassed. Several have been arrested. One of them, David Naidoo of Port Elizabeth, one morning found his office totally empty. His tape recorders, typewriters and all his files had vanished.

The Director of the Legal Resources Centre in Johannesburg has described the situation of many Africans who today live in the urban areas as follows:

Despite the housing shortage, the urban African population has continued to grow. In the absence of formal housing provision, people have built their own 'informal' structures, not authorised by the housing authorities. The mid-1970s saw the growth of large 'Squatter' communities, particularly in the Western Cape where the influx control policy was most rigidly enforced. The best known of these communities was Crossroads. The authorities first attempted to demolish Crossroads by prosecuting 'Squatters' under existing legislation. However, the process of prosecuting individuals was slow and cumbersome, and an important test case resulted in a failure of the prosecution. The result was a series of legislative amendments which placed 'squatters' in an increasingly vulnerable position. Now, government officials and landowners may summarily demolish their homes, without first obtaining a court order or even giving them prior notice. The jurisdiction of the courts to prevent demolitions is effectively ousted by procedural requirements. And the legislation makes it possible for a magistrate, acting in an administrative capacity, to order the removal of 'squatters' and their 'transfer' to such place as he may deem appropriate.

Very many African people today living in the urban areas are officially regarded as 'squatters', and potentially subject to this sort of action.[34]

Despite administrative decentralization which allocates powers to local authorities, the central government in Pretoria keeps control of the entire policy of influx control. In the case of Lawaaikamp it clearly appeared to the lawyer who represented the residents in negotiating with the local town council that the latter was seeking instructions from higher up, that is from the Members of Parliament and the central administration. There was no doubt in his mind that the strings were being pulled by the Joint Management Committee (JMC). The fate of Lawaaikamp was still at the time of writing in the hands of the JMC which had this item on its agenda for its session in February 1987.[35]

Finally, the government continues to apply its policy of consolidation of the homelands which, and as far as the black rural population is concerned, constitutes another kind of removal. It does not involve shifting people, it involves shifting boundaries. Territories located outside of the boundaries of the homelands are being incorporated into the homelands. So, a population living one day in South Africa may by a stroke of the pen find itself living in the independent Republic of Venda. Note also that the State President is the author of such decisions, which tells us something about the real character of the so-called independent states within South Africa.

The case of the Moutse community has already been mentioned. On 18 February 1987 it was announced that the community of Botsabelo (Onverwacht) would be incorporated in the homeland of Qwa-Qwa, which is the next homeland scheduled to acquire 'independent' status.[36]

The restoration of citizenship

The commitment made by President Botha in September 1985 to restore South African citizenship to those individuals who had been deprived of it by virtue of the 'independence' of certain homelands was, at first sight, implemented by the Restoration of Citizenship Act 1986, which took effect on 1 July 1986. However, on closer examination it seems improbable that this new legislation will bring about the result promised by the State President.

The law foresees the restoration of citizenship by birth, by descent, by registration or by naturalization. Sheena Duncan has summarized its provisions as follows:

Citizenship by descent

Section 3. The minor child, who has never been married, of a person who has become South African in terms of 2(a) above and who was born in the homeland after the Status Act and entered S.A. before the 1st July 1986 and was lawfully and permanently resident in S.A. immediately before 1st July 1986.

Citizenship by registration

Section 4(1). A person who is a citizen of an independent homeland because of a Status Act and who was a citizen of S.A. before that Status Act can apply for registration as an S.A. citizen and be entitled to registration IF HE *CONVINCES* THE DIREC-TOR GENERAL THAT he entered S.A. after the Status Act but before 1st July 1986 and that he is lawfully and permanently resident in S.A. and has been lawfully and permanently resident for a continuous period of one year immediately before making the application and has in addition been lawfully and permanently resident in S.A. for a further period of at least 4 years during the 8 years immediately preceding his application. He must not be under the age of 16 years at the time of making the application.

Section 4(3). A minor who is a citizen of a TVBC state in terms of a Status Act, who has never been married and whose father or mother has become a S.A. citizen in terms of Section 2 or 4(1) and who is lawfully and permanently resident in S.A. may be registered by the Director General as an S.A. citizen.

Citizenship by naturalization

Section 5. A person who is a citizen of an independent homeland by virtue of the provisions of a Status Act and who was born in that homeland before or after the Status Act or whose father or mother was born in the homeland before or after independence and who enters South Africa lawfully (i.e. with permission) after the 1st July 1986 may apply for naturalization in terms of Section 10 of the South African Citizenship Act.

Section 10 of the Citizenship Act requires that the applicant

- is not a minor
- has been lawfully admitted to S.A. for *PERMANENT RESIDENCE* i.e. has been granted a permanent residence permit as outlined below
- has been ordinarily resident for a full year immediately preceding the application and for a further 4 years during the 8 years immediately preceding the application (he cannot count any period of imprisonment or detention as a period of residence)
- is of good character
- intends to continue to reside in South Africa
- is able to read and write one of the official languages to the satisfaction of the Minister
- has an adequate knowledge of the responsibilities and privileges of South African citizenship
- has, if he is over 14 years of age, within 6 months of notification of the granting of a certificate of naturalization taken an oath of allegiance
- etc. etc.

The grant of a certificate of naturalization shall . . . be in the absolute discretion of the Minister and he may, without assigning any reason, grant or refuse a certificate as he thinks most conducive to the public good, and no appeal shall lie from his decision.[37]

This summary makes it immediately clear that only a small percentage of those who were deprived of their citizenship will be able to regain it. More specifically, the 5 million or more persons living within the boundaries of the 'independent' homelands will not qualify. They will remain foreigners because they do not meet the basic requirement of permanent residence in non-homeland South Africa. Nor is it likely that any significant number of them could obtain a permanent residence permit in South Africa.

The numerous migrant workers who arrived in South Africa after 'independence' of their homelands met severe obstacles in acquiring permanent residence rights. The Admission of Persons to the Republic Act stipulates that periods spent in South Africa in terms of Labour Agreements are not taken into consideration in determining whether a person has acquired residence rights in the Republic.

The truth is that the Restoration of Citizenship Act will only restore citizenship for those who were already in possession of Section 10 rights under the Black (Urban Areas) Consolidation Act before its abolition, to those who owned land in the 'Black Spots' with freehold title and those who were lawful residents on white-owned farms for many years. Furthermore, administrative harassment must also be taken into consideration as the following example illustrates. A young black contacted the 'white' Office of

Home Affairs to obtain an identity document which is the right of any person who is lawfully and permanently resident in South Africa. He was received with relative courtesy but was then sent to the Bantu Commissioners for the collection of his fingerprints under the pretext that the equipment to do this was not yet available at the 'white' office (in the past fingerprints were only collected from black persons, but today people of all races must provide all ten fingerprints). He went to the 'black' office where he produced a baptism certificate as required by the Department's circular concerning identity documents. He was shouted at for having dared contact the 'white' office. His request was turned down until he delivered a birth certificate.[38]

The basic qualification required to obtain restoration of citizenship is an extended permanent period of residence in the Republic of South Africa. Thus only a limited number of new foreigners living outside the homelands will be able to apply for the restoration of citizenship. The Minister of Home Affairs informed Parliament that the number of such persons was 1,750,400 according to a government estimate.

It is generally accepted by observers that the government's interpretation of the notion of 'permanent residence' remains linked to Section 10 rights of the abrogated legislation. In other words, at the very moment where the old pass laws disappeared as a means of influx control, influx control comes back as means to determine citizenship, which, in turn, constitutes the key to freedom of movement. Thus over 7 million people will remain foreigners and will be denied freedom of movement within South Africa.

There remains the possibility that 'aliens' may obtain a work permit in South Africa. If they get a permit, they are part of the notorious system of migrant labour, living in single-sex hostels. The position of these migrant workers may well be worse under the new law. The penalties for infringement of the Aliens Act are much more severe than those under the Black (Urban Areas) Consolidation Act. The Aliens Act allows deportation of foreigners even if they possess a work permit. In this way too they can be denied the opportunity of acquiring permanent residence rights. The *Rikhoto* principle (see page 20) is no longer applicable in today's situation.

Soon after the 1986 law was adopted, the Minister of Home Affairs made the following statement to the press:

Prior to 1st July 1986 the position in terms of the exemptions and agreements was that citizens of the TBVC states who wished to work in the RSA, had to have prior consent.. . . The Restoration of South African Citizenship Act, 1986, and the repeal of Influx control measures with effect from 1st July 1986 have in no way altered the situation.

Theoretically, the new foreigners are still given the possibility to obtain South African naturalization. A large majority of those foreigners would have to prove that they have permanently and lawfully resided in South Africa for a full year immediately preceding the application *and* for a further four years while the application is pending (Section 10 of the South African Citizenship Act). It is important to note that periods of imprisonment or detention are not considered as periods of residence. This will inevitably affect many black people because of the emergency situation.

Last but not least, the Aliens Act provides that a permanent residence permit may not be issued to any person unles he or she does not and is not likely to pursue an occupation, in which, in the opinion of the 'Immigrant Selection Board', a sufficient number of persons is already engaged in the Republic to meet the requirements of the inhabitants of the Republic.

In view of the endemic unemployment prevailing in South Africa, this amounts to *de facto* adoption of a new kind of 'labour preference policy' for the benefit of white people.

There is yet more: to understand the real limitations upon freedom of movement under the Restoration of Citizenship Act, we must take into account another statute passed by Parliament during the last days of its 1986 session — the Borders of Particular States Extension Amendment Act 1986. This Act authorized the State President to declare the transfer of land from the Republic to certain 'sovereign and independent' states so that the land, thus transferred, ceases to be part of the Republic and becomes part of the state to which it has been transferred. The Act provides for the incorporation of land into the 'independent' homelands of Transkei, Bophuthatswana, Ciskei and Venda at the direction of the State President. (As for the 'sovereign and independent' character of the homelands, it is worth noting that the governments of Transkei, Bophuthatswana, Venda and Ciskei were merely *informed* of the South African decision.)

Thus the government can incorporate tens of thousands of people into 'independent' homelands. For the time being, these persons are permanent and lawful residents of the Republic of South Africa. They are at present entitled to have their South African citizenship restored to them, and to be issued with a new identity document. But after incorporation they will be entitled to nothing. They will become aliens, dependent on a temporary permit to work in South Africa and they will be condemned to permanent alienation from their own country, now and in the future. Their children and grandchildren will remain foreign.

This Act is closely linked to forced removals. Under the new law, the territory of the black community of Bloedfontein in central Transvaal was added to the independent homeland of Bophuthatswana. Bloedfontein is a community of 15,000 persons who are living on lands purchased by their ancestors in the 1920s. However, the majority of them are not Tswana speaking, and Bophuthatswana refused to accept them. A strange deal was then concluded between the South African government, the 'independent' government of Bophuthatswana and the self-governing KwaNdebele.

The deal totally ignores and rides roughshod over the 15,000 persons concerned. The deal is to remove them forcibly to a piece of land which will be offered to KwaNdebele; they will be dispossessed of their homes by force.[39]

The fate of other black communities in Transvaal will be sealed under the new law. Those communities had hitherto successfully fought against the threat of forced removals. Braklaagte in the district Marico of Western

Transvaal has resisted attempted removals since 1937. Today, after a half-century's resistance, the population of Braklaagte sees the end of its fight in a change of borderlines: it will be incorporated into Bophuthatswana and it inhabitants, many of whom had already initiated the formalities for obtaining the restoration of their South African citizenship, will remain foreigners.[40] The same applies to the community of Machakaneng near Brits, which has fought for many years unsuccessfully against government attempts to remove it from its land. Eventually, in 1983 the tenants were evicted without prior warning by security forces with rifles and helicopters. The remaining families of the landowners were subsequently told to move, but they continued to refuse.[41]

Nevertheless, the government can achieve its objective simply by the incorporation of this territory into Bophuthatswana. Once more, by a stroke of the pen of the State President, a black community loses both its South African nationality and its land.

The Right to Travel Abroad

Banning orders or conditions put on release on bail are commonly used to preclude South African citizens critical to the Government policies from travelling abroad. The Government disposes of another means to silence the opponents' voice. It is empowered to arbitrary, "at his pleasure", withdraw or cancel a passport. The Supreme Court has endorsed that arbitrary power. Suffice to quote the following preamble of Mr Justice Friedman in Bishop Tutu's case: 'Passports now contain the condition which . . . provides that applicant's passport shall remain the property of the Government of the Republic of South Africa and may be amended, withdrawn or cancelled at any time at the pleasure of the Minister of the Interior on behalf of the Government.'[43]

Appendix I to Chapter 4: T.R.H. Davenport on forced removals

But there was another side to the story. An unofficial five-volume report by a group of researchers calling themselves the Surplus People Project, published thirteen years after Cosmas Desmond's *Discarded People*, came out in 1983 under the title *Forced Removals in South Africa*. It quoted official figures to show that in the interest of Homeland consolidation and for other reasons approximately 3,500,000 people had been moved, many of them under some measure of duress, between 1960 and 1982. At the time their Report was completed, the participants in the Surplus People Project estimated that a further two million people were 'threatened with removal in the near future'. In May 1984 the Department of Cooperation and Development, making use of a different set of figures, rebutted these allegations with a statement that only 1,971,908 people had been removed, and that it was not possible to state how many were still under threat of removal.

The Western Cape removals have to be related to the policy under which Coloured people were as a general rule to be granted employment in preference to Africans west of a line from the Fish and Kat rivers to Aliwal North, from which Port Elizabeth and Uitenhage were exempted only in 1978. The Government began to establish large settlements for Coloured people at Atlantis north of Cape Town, and at Mitchell's Plain on the False Bay coast, and announced its intention during 1984 of making the existing

African residential areas on the Cape Flats (Langa, Nyanga and Guguletu) available in the longer term for Coloured settlement. Meanwhile the historic predominantly Coloured suburb of District Six was flattened under powers acquired by Community Development in terms of the Group Areas Act, leaving a great scar on the slopes of Devil's Peak where a vibrant, poor, colourful, gang-ridden community had lived since about the time of slave emancipation in 1838.

Behind the Western Cape removals lay the Government's desire to reduce the number of Africans with residential rights and replace them with contract workers. Hence the destruction of the squatter settlements on the Cape Flats in 1977–8, and above all the much publicised saga of Crossroads, a squatter settlement which had grown up close to the southern end of Cape Town's main airport. At the last of these, an energetic women's committee, with some backing from sympathetic whites and considerable international press publicity, encouraged the people to stand their ground despite forceful attempts by the authorities to disperse the settlement. Eventually, in 1981, Dr Koornhof agreed that those with residential rights in the Cape Peninsula should be allowed to stay. This was an inducement for many more to try for rights, and on 20 August the police deported over 1,000 Transkeians back to Umtata as prohibited immigrants (Transkei being technically a foreign state), but allowed the Ciskeians (whose leaders had not yet opted for independence) to stay. But Crossroads remained, and the number of squatters grew, spreading into the surrounding bush and thereby creating further problems for officialdom. Crossroads residents and the 'Bush People' were among the most successful of all squatters to resist removal. But in January 1983 there were added to their number another group who occupied an empty site close to the nearby K.T.C. Bazaar. In a continuing fight with Board officials, their shacks were repeatedly demolished and as rapidly rebuilt. Violence broke out on 16 May when youths threw stones at police, who were using dogs and sneeze machines in another attempt to demolish shelters, after the winter rains had set in. In one of the system's weirdest compromises, 'legals' were then allowed to keep their beds provided no shelters were erected over them, and the 'Bed people' joined the 'Bush people' in the continuing saga of popular resistance. But by 1985 the Crossroads community was badly divided, and it had also become clear that the Government intended in due course to move them, along with the residents of all the settled black townships on the Cape Flats, to a new controlled settlement at Khayelitsha, on the False Bay coast.

In the Eastern Cape, where a good deal of publicity had already attended the establishment of Dimbaza, near King William's Town, removals escalated with the migration of about 56,000 people from Herschel and Glen Grey into the Hewu district of the Ciskei to escape Transkeian rule, after the Transkei had taken transfer of the former districts on becoming independent in 1976. The settlers were moved on to very well-developed agricultural land in such large numbers that within a year or two the land had been reduced to near desert conditions, and the people became dependent on rations. The Government also began to clear politically inconvenient black settlements like that of the Mfengu community who had lived and farmed near Humansdorp, west of Port Elizabeth, since the 1830s. Their appeals to be allowed to remain rather than move to the Keiskamma valley in the Ciskei were rejected by Parliament. They went. Resistance to removals was also particularly strong at Mgwali, a Presbyterian settlement in the 'white corridor' between East London and Queenstown, which occupied land originally given to the Xhosa hymnologist Tiyo Soga by Sandile, the Xhosa paramount, and kept by the residents as a reward for their loyalty during the cattle-killing of 1857. The African population of Ciskei grew from 357,801 to 630,353 in 1970–80, net immigration as a result of removals amounting to 142,350. The drought of 1982–4, and the very undeveloped infrastructure of Ciskei added to the problems of resettlement there, despite efforts of the Ciskeian authorities to create more employment opportunities.

In the Orange Free State, the policy led to the building of an enormous location at Onverwacht, south of Bloemfontein, and to the packing of large numbers of people into the

Rolong and Sotho Homelands of Thaba'Nchu and Qwaqwa. Onverwacht became, in the words of the Surplus People Project, a 'sprawling slum' of something between 100,000 and 200,000 people, a disease trap lacking most basic amenities and with very little grazing land on which the residents, most of whom had been brought from farms in the Free State, could run their few remaining stock. Thaba'Nchu was equally crowded. Qwaqwa, the official name for the Mopedi location at Witzieshoek, was considerably worse, with a population which had risen very fast from 24,000 in 1970 to something between 200,000 and 300,000 in 1980, its density increasing over the same period from 54 to 622 per square kilometre—a settlement described by Benbo, a government agency, as 'overpopulated in relation to available employment opportunities . . . poorly situated with regard to industrial areas and markets . . . [possessing] no notable mineral or agricultural riches', yet with 'a limited tourism potential' close to the beautiful Golden Gate nature reserve.

In the Transvaal, where the largest amount of land for black settlement had to be found in terms of the Beaumont Report (1916) and the 1936 Land Act, most moves resulted from the policy of relocating Africans into territorial Bantustans. 1,153,000 had been moved by 1982, and another 585,000 were under threat of relocation. Of those removed, 400,000 had been taken from farms, 350,000 as a result of urban relocation, 280,000 in terms of 'black spot' removal, and 120,000 in the name of territorial consolidation. The Surplus People Project listed 58 black spots, and 29 towns whose black residential areas had been moved. Little detailed work has been done on most resettlement areas in the Transvaal, but some evidence of resistance to removal has emerged from places such as Rooigrond, near Mafeking, an area whose turbulent history goes back to the days of the Republic of Goshen; and Mogopa, whose people were moved with a considerable show of force to Pachsdraai at the end of 1983 and in early 1984. Both these places were in the Western Transvaal. Parts of the farms Driefontein, Daggaskraal and KwaNgema in the Wakkerstroom district of the South-eastern Transvaal (a community comprising some 5,000 Swazi-, Zulu- and Sotho-speaking adults, 1,500 of whom were landowners in 1982) had been bought by P. ka I. Seme on behalf of the Native Farmers' Association of Africa in 1912, shortly before the Land Act made black purchases in this area unlawful. According to the Surplus People Project, the total population grew to between 30,000 and 50,000. The Government decided to remove this black spot, and to relocate the people to their respective Homelands according to their home languages, and also to build a dam covering part of their land. The first indications that removal was intended were given in 1965, but pressure was only brought to bear in 1981. At this point the residents elected a board of directors, with Saul Mkhize, a well-respected community leader, as its chairman. The authorities chose not to recognise the board. Relations between the community and the authorities deteriorated during 1982 and 1983, as a series of petty incidents showed. Eventually, on 2 April 1983 Mkhize called a meeting at the Cabanangi school, supposedly to discuss the move. Two policemen arrived beforehand to ban the meeting. There were altercations and the judge who later heard the case, accepted police evidence that stones had been thrown. Mkhize was shot and killed by a policeman, who was subsequently charged with murder and acquitted. The residents were eventually granted permission to remain on their land in 1985.

The number of people relocated in Natal between 1948 and 1982 was calculated by the Surplus People Project at 745,000, nearly half of whom were farm residents, 105,000 lived in 'black spots', and 295,000 had been moved under the Group Areas Act. A further 606,000 were said to be under threat of removal, mainly from black spots and urban areas.

Reports by the Association for Rural Advancement in Natal during the early 1980s reveal a gradual switch of emphasis from the removal of labour tenants on white farms to the clearing of black spots, especially in Northern Natal, where the squatters on white-owned land had attracted the attention of the Du Toit Commission in 1959–60 (Davenport and Hunt). By 1983 black freehold in northern Natal had largely been cleared, and the authorities were beginning to turn their attention to Ladysmith and the Natal Midlands. The Limehill example had alerted the authorities to the need for more careful preparation in the provision of infrastructures before relocating people, but the scale of operations made this extremely difficult to implement, as was the case in the Eastern Cape, where the early publicity given to Dimbaza had been comparable. Consequently Natal removals were far from lacking in distress stories, as is shown by the detailed research which lies behind the Natal volume of *Forced Removals*, with references to places like Mzimhlophe, where no water supply had been laid on during the eight years since the removal in 1975, where unemployment was high, diet insufficient, and the provision of schools, clinics and shops generally inadequate.[42]

Appendix II to Chapter 4

REMOVAL OF UNAUTHORISED STRUCTURES
VERWYDERING VAN ONGEMAGTIGDE STRUKTUUR

To: N.I.
Aan: _____   *P.N.* _____
Take notice that being the registered occupier of
Neem kennis dat u as geregistreerde bewoner van _____

and being the owner of an unsightly structure/unauthorised structure/prefabricated
en synde die eianaar van en ongoglike struktuur/ongemagtigde struktuur/voorafvervaardigde
building/moveable structure/to wit
gebou/vers kuifbare struktuur te wete _____
are hereby ordered in terms of Regulation 13(16) of Chapter II of Government Notice
hiermee gelas word, kragtens Regulasie 13(16) van Hoofstuk II van Goewermentskennis-
No. R1036 dated 14th June, 1968, read with Proclamation No. R1267 dated the 26th
gewing Nr. R1036, gedateer 14 Junie 1968, saamgelees met Proklamasie Nr. R1267,
July, 1968, to remove above-mentioned structure/building within 10 days of service of
gedateer 26 Julie 1968, om bogenoemde struktuur/gebou binne 10 dae na ontvangs van
this Notice from the Bantu Residential Area.
hierdie Kennisgewing uit die Bantoewoongebied te verwyder.

Failure to do so, without reasonable cause will render you liable to Prosecution in
Indien u sonder 'n grondige rede in gebreke bly om aan hierdie Kennisgewing te voldoen, stel
terms of Regulation 47(1)(h) of Chapter II of Government Notice R1036 dated 14th
u u bloot aan vervolging kragtens Regulasie 47(1)(h) van Hoofstuk II van Goewerments-
June, 1968, and the penalties prescribed under Section 44 of Act 25 of 1945 as
kennisgewing Nr. R1036, gedateer 14 Junie 1968, en die strafbepaling voorgeskryf in
amended.
Artikel 44 van Wet 25 van 1945, soos gewysig.

Date: _____
Datum: *SUPERINTENDENT*

MODE OF SERVICE/WYSE VAN BEDIENING

I , being an official in the employ of the Bantu
Ek , *as 'n beampte in diens van die Bantoesake-*
Affairs Administration Board, and authorised to serve documents and processes
Administrasieraad, en gemagtig om dokumente en prosesstukke kragtens wet te bedien,
according to law do hereby certify that at (place)
sertifiseer dat ek persoonlik op (plek) _____

on (date) at (time) I served a true copy of this
op (datum) _____ *om (tyd)* _____ , *'n ware afskrif van hierdie*
document on (name) N.I./V.F.
dokument op (naam) _____ *P.N./V.* _____
personally and explained to him/her the nature of the contents.
gedien het en aan hom/haar die aard van die inhoud verduidelik het.

Date: _____
Datum: SIGNATURE/*HANDTEKENING*

Notes

1. See Universal Declaration of Human Rights, Art. 13; International Covenant on Civil and Political Rights, Art. 12.
2. T.R.H. Davenport, *South Africa: A Modern History*, 3rd edn, Johannesburg, 1987.
3. Ibid., p. 563.
4. L. Platzky and C. Walker, *'The Surplus People': Forced Removals in South Africa*, Johannesburg, 1985, p. 99.
5. J. Dugard, *Human Rights and the South African Legal Order*, Princeton, NJ, 1978, pp. 80–1.
6. Davenport, p. 362.
7. Ibid., p. 562; Dugard, p. 82.
8. Platzky and Walker, p. 100.
9. Ibid.; P. Haski, *L'Afrique blanche*, Paris, 1987, p. 69.
10. Davenport, p. 563.
11. *Weekly Mail*, 12/18 June 1987.
12. E. Unterhalter, *Forced Removal*, London, 1987, pp. 84 and 123; *Weekly Mail*, 20/6 March 1987, p. 7.
13. Interview with South African lawyer acting in the case, February 1987.
14. Platzky and Walker, pp. 101 and 102.
15. Ibid., p. ix.
16. Davenport, p. 407.
17. Ibid., p. 545.
18. Platzky and Walker, p. 108.
19. Unterhalter, p. 37.
20. Ibid., p. 8.
21. Platzky and Walker, p. 113.

22. Ibid., p. 115.
23. J. Dugard, 'South Africa's "Independent" Homelands: An Exercise in De-nationalization', *Denver Journal of International Law and Policy*, 1980, pp. 31–2.
24. Platzky and Walker, p. 395.
24A.Untrhalter, p. 3.
25. Ibid., p. 14.
26. Ibid., p. 15.
27. Unterhalter, p. 107.
28. Interview with a social worker, February 1987.
29. Interview with lawyers, February 1987.
30. See statement by Minister Heunis, p. 30 above.
31. *Cape Times*, 20 February 1987, p. 3.
32. Unterhalter, p. 84.
33. The people were forced at gunpoint to transfer their possessions to tents erected for them (Unterhalter, p. 84).
34. G. Budlender, 'Influx Control in the Western Cape: From Pass Laws to Passports', Johannesburg, 21 August 1986, p. 6.
35. Interview with lawyer, February 1987. As to JMC's, see p. 122.
36. *Weekly Mail*, 20/6 March 1987, p. 7.
37. Sheena Duncan, Black Sash, Johannesburg, 17 July 1987.
38. Black Sash, 'Working Notes for Advice Offices', Johannesburg, July 1986.
39. Unterhalter, pp. 108 and 119.
40. Ibid., p. 112.
41. *South African Journal of Human Rights*, pp. 387–8, (November 1986).
42. Davenport, pp. 445–449.
43. Tutu vs. Minister of Internal Affairs 1982(4) SA 571T.

5 Education and Access to the Professions

Another major area of policy in which there is no sign of the abandonment of apartheid is education. Segregation in schools is a corner-stone of the doctrine of white domination, and the policy of the National Party has been to ensure a separate and inferior education system for black people. Dr Verwoerd was responsible for introducing 'Bantu education' in 1953. It was designed to equip black children for the menial role which the apartheid system assigned to them.[1]

The schools provided for black children are starved of resources (notwithstanding increases in government funding in recent years) and the curriculum has excluded subjects in most schools necessary to prepare them for higher education and admission to skilled and professional occupations. There is gross discrimination in the funds provided by the state for black and white children. Per capita expenditure is six times greater for white children than for black.[2] Those black children who have gained admission to universities either belong to the very small minority who have been accepted in church or private schools or they have succeeded by exceptional ability and hard work to overcome the huge disadvantages of the public education system. Black students have in recent years protested vigorously against the discrimination inflicted on them and have been in the forefront of anti-apartheid activity. Boycotts of schools have taken place across the whole country. In consequence children have been the target of violent repression by the state. Police and soldiers have carried out arrests on school premises and have, by their frequent presence, provoked resistance which is then held to justify arrests, detentions and violent assaults including many killings of children by the security forces. We consider the powers and conduct of the security forces in more detail later.[3]

In an attempt to persuade the government to change their education policy and to involve the parents and the community in decision-making, a National Education Crisis Committee was established in early 1986. Its consultative conference in Durban in April 1986 was attacked by busloads of Inkatha vigilantes, but the conference nevertheless concluded its business and it decided that the national schools boycott should be ended and the children should return to school notwithstanding the failure of the government to meet its demands for reforms in the system. On their return to school it was intended that the students should implement 'people's education', rejecting the inferior structure provided by the authorities.

The Soweto uprising of 1976 was a protest against education policies. These included the compulsory teaching of the Afrikaans language, which many regarded as the language of oppression. The teaching of history also aroused considerable resentment because of the distortion of the relative achievements and values of black and white people. Because the curriculum reflected the notion of black inferiority, it was an inadequate basis for entry to higher education to which more and more young black people aspired. Ironically, that aspiration was encouraged by industrial development which created a demand for skilled workers which the white minority could not satisfy. Thus the doctrines of apartheid were shown to conflict with the interests of business and the seeds sown of dissension within the white community.

It was the planned commemoration of the anniversary of Soweto on 16 June 1986 which led the government to declare a state of emergency on 12 June in that year. The NECC was a major target of the government, and it has been severely hampered since then by the detention of many of its leaders. Those who were not arrested have had to go into hiding to avoid arrest. Many school children were detained. Though a substantial number are said to have been released before the new emergency was declared on 12 June 1987, many are still in detention. We were told that children who have been released from detention have great difficulty in being readmitted to school. They are excluded on the instructions of the security police. The powers given to the security police and the government by the emergency regulations to control the educational system are described elsewhere.[4]

Even the independent universities are now being put under severe pressure by the government to control or prevent criticism of the government. We understand that 80 per cent of their funding comes from sources which are controlled by the government, which has announced in September 1987 that it is prepared to withdraw those funds unless its wishes are carried out. This attempt to curtail academic freedom appears to us to be a gross abuse of a basic human right by the government. The universities themselves, which are jealous of their liberal tradition, have made it clear that they will not passively accept such interference. It remains to be seen whether they will be able to resist it successfully.

We had the advantage of interviewing one of the leading members of the NECC—one of the very few not imprisoned. He gave us a graphic account of the alienation felt by many children within the segregated public school system. The intrusive and domineering behaviour of the security forces towards the principals and teachers undermined, he told us, the respect of the pupils for the authority of the teaching staff. It was common for elderly black teachers to be threatened and intimidated by young soldiers and policemen who knew they could humiliate them with impunity.

The schools are a focal point in the conflict between the government and the opponents of apartheid. The government recognize this but their attempt to impose discipline in the classroom by the use of military force has inevitably led to an escalation of violence and bitterness. The Deputy Minister of Law and Order expressed the opinion to us that youngsters were indoctrinated and incited by terrorists to carry out their violent objectives, and that this gave the government no choice but to use force against them in response, however young they might be. We find this an improbable scenario. We accept that pupils feel involved in the wider anti-apartheid struggle, and it is also no doubt true that some believe that pupils that by violent acts, such as burning of classrooms, they can contribute to the end of apartheid. The slogan 'liberation now, education later!' demonstrates the exasperation of many students with the current educational system. But no such reaction justifies the brutality of the government's response. In any event no degree of violence or misbehaviour by a child can justify treating them as adults. We were told of many cases in which violent assaults and torture were inflicted on school-children and many examples of detention under the emergency regulations of children of 13 and younger are well authenticated. The case of Makhajane to which we refer later[6] is a striking but, we conclude, far from isolated example of wholly exaggerated and disproportionate action taken against a child for what could at most have been a breach of school discipline. When we drew the attention of the Deputy Minister to the prevalence of brutality and torture of school-children, he said that such cases were fully investigated and disciplinary action taken wherever a complaint was substantiated. However, he also acknowledged that there was no machinery for investigation except by the police themselves. To complain to the police about police misconduct is futile, as has been demonstrated in other countries, and in South Africa it is plain that the complainant would be vulnerable to victimization. The fact that action against members of the security forces is so rare, even in the most glaring cases, demonstrates the absence of any serious attempt to control abuses.

We paid special attention to the problems of black people in gaining access to the legal profession. The number of black lawyers remains small and disproportionately very low in comparison with the number of white lawyers, though the proportion is increasing. An article in the first issue of the *African Law Review* gives some useful statistics. In 1986 there were 686 black attorneys (from all non-white groups). In 1982 there were only 286. However, the total number of attorneys in South Africa is over 6,000, of whom blacks are still therefore only about 10 per cent. The rate of increase is likely to grow in the immediate future because there are 626 black articled clerks out of a total of 2,369. But the number of black law graduates went down from 284 in 1984 to 250 in 1985. Because of disruption of classes in the so-called black universities in 1986, the number of graduates in that year was thought to have declined again, though no final figures were available when the article was written. Unrest also reduced the number of black students sitting matriculation examinations, so that the number qualifying to enter university to study law will be less.

The number and proportion of black attorneys may be small, but the paucity of black advocates is even more striking. We were told that there were only two black advocates practising in Johannesburg and not more than a dozen or so in Cape Town and Durban. There are only two black senior counsel in the whole country and no black judges.[8] The chairman of the Bar told us that there were about 900 advocates altogether. The ratio of black advocates is thus even lower than that of black attorneys. The difficulties for black youngsters who wish to become lawyers are formidable. Those who come from government schools (obviously all but a handful) have the unenviable task of passing examinations in Latin, a subject which is not normally taught in black schools. We were told that at the University of Cape Town, for example, black students may have to extend their studies by up to two years to achieve the minimum Latin qualification, which the government has recently made more stringent.

Those black students who succeed in passing the professional examinations still have to surmount the hurdle of gaining acceptance by a firm of attorneys as an articled clerk or as a pupil in advocate's chambers. We heard strong criticisms of the failure of the professional organizations to make adequate provision for the admission of black lawyers and the Chairman of the Bar acknowledged that his branch of the legal profession had failed to come to grips with the problem. We were assured that the Bar was now fully aware of its responsibilities and was now urgently seeking ways of fulfilling them. In particular, the financial difficulties facing many advocates starting practice were more likely to affect young black advocates because they were less likely to have sources of funding. For this reason more scholarships were being given. The inadequate representation of black people in the legal profession seems inevitable while apartheid persists.

Notes

1. R. Omond, *The Apartheid Handbook* (Harmondsworth, 1985), p. 80.
2. Ibid., p. 77.
3. See chapters 10, 11 and 14.
4. See report in *Weekly Mail*, 20/6 November 1987, p. 5; see also p. 99.
5. As this book goes to press, it is reported that a Supreme Court judge has upheld a challenge to restrictions imposed on universities under the emergency regulations, but full details are lacking.
6. See p. 106.
7. Published by the Black Lawyers' Association, Johannesburg, January 1987.
8. The absence of black judges is partly explained by the strong opposition of democratic lawyers' organisations to the acceptance of judicial appointments. When Hassan Mall S.C., accepted a temporary appointment in early 1987, he was heavily criticised by professional colleagues. See also p. 113.

6 Freedom of Speech and Expression

As we will see in Chapter 10, the state of emergency, which has covered the whole country since 12 June 1986, has drastically curtailed freedom of expression. The purpose of this chapter is to study the ordinary and permanent law relating to this topic outside the emergency regulations. Our conclusion is that the permanent security legislation authorizes blatant violations of the rule of law. We have placed considerable reliance in reaching this conclusion on Professor Anthony Mathews' magisterial book published in 1986,[1] which reviews the position thoroughly, as well as upon interviews with South African writers, journalists and lawyers, and our experience of South Africa broadcasting and the Press.

Speech and information

Any newspaper to be printed or published in South Africa has to be registered. Up to 1982 the freedom to establish newspapers was guaranteed by the Newspaper and Imprint Registration Act 1971. The Minister of Internal Affairs had an obligation to register if the application fulfilled formal requirements. The Internal Security Act 1982 curtailed this freedom by making registration of a newspaper conditional on a deposit not exceeding R.40,000, which the Minister of Law and Order may require from the proprietor within twenty-one days of submission of the application. The Minister may require such a deposit 'whenever he is not satisfied' that a ban on the newspaper 'will not at any time become necessary'.[2]

The banning provisions of the Act empower the Minister of Law and Order, without notice to any person concerned, by notice in the *Government Gazette*, to prohibit the printing, publication or dissemination of any publication, if he is satisfied that the publication in question endangers state security or the maintenance of law and order, promotes communism or any of its objects.[3]

The Minister's powers are quite arbitrary and his opinion cannot be challenged in court except in proved cases of dishonesty or impropriety. 'Court intervention is clearly a theoretical possibility not an actual one'.[4] The requirements of procedural justice are denied to the publisher since the Minister 'is not required to disclose his reasons or to afford a hearing'.[5]

In practice, the opinion of the Minister is formed by members of the South African Police, to whom the matter is referred by the Department of Home Affairs, during the twenty-one day period, in order to enable them to advise the Minister of Law and Order on the possibilities of a future ban on the newspaper.[6] Newspapers already in existence are not subjected to this 'Damoclean form of press control',[7] unless their registration lapses; that is, if the printing and publishing is not commenced within one month after registration, or if the newspaper is at any time not printed and published during a period exceeding one month, or if the newspaper changes hands.[8]

The deposit provision has a drastic effect on freedom of the press. Many proprietors are unable or unwilling to pay the deposit, and it is believed that up to 1986 more than ten had to abandon their plans to publish.[9] If they manage to raise the money required and pay the deposit, they will remain vulnerable to the risk of banning with the additional consequence of losing the money deposited. Members of the mission met the editor of a new newspaper who had hesitated for a long time before applying for registration, because he feared the economic results of a banning order. He was not prepared to compromise his professional duty by falling into line with the government's political requirements.

The provisions of the Internal Security Act are applicable to any newspaper or publication in South Africa. Many other prohibitions are found in the Act, for example in Section 56, which makes it an offence for any person, without the consent of the Minister of Law and Order, to print, publish or disseminate any speech, utterance, writing or statement or any extract from or recording or reproduction thereof made at any time by prohibited persons. In December 1985, Tony Heard, the editor of the *Cape Times*, published an interview with the President of the ANC, Mr Oliver Tambo. Heard believed it was important for whites in South Africa to have access to the thinking and personalities of the ANC because the ANC is necessarily a part of the solution to South Africa's problems. Heard was charged in terms of Section 56 (1) of the Internal Security Act for quoting a banned person.[10] Such a charge makes him liable to a penalty of imprisonment up to three years. The provisions of the Internal Security Act are used in parallel with the emergency regulations which at the time of Tony Heard's interview, were amended to prevent television coverage of situations of an arrest in the townships without police approval so that television and photographic coverage were effectively blocked. At the same period there were reports of increased police harassment of journalists in the black townships.[11]

The Publications Act 1974

In 1962 the Newspaper Press Union, composed of the prominent daily and weekly newspapers in South Africa constituted the S.A. Media Council, with a Conference of Editors, 'in an endeavour to ensure the achievement and maintenance of highest standards of conduct in the newspaper industry'.[12] This was a response to 'various degrees of government pressure'.[13] The Council has a code of conduct and it asserts over its members a quasi-judicial disciplinary control. The Supreme Court has a limited power of review of its decisions.

In passing the Publications Act Parliament accepted that any newspaper which is published by a member of the Newspaper Press Union is excluded from the definition in the Act of 'publication or object' and is therefore exempted from the operation of the Publication Act. All other newspapers are subject to the provisions of the Act which is 'the chief engine of censorship' in South Africa.[14]

The Publications Act applies not only to newspapers but to books, periodicals, pamphlets, posters or other printed matter, writing or typed scripts, which are published or duplicated in any way, drawings, pictures or illustrations, paintings, prints, photographs or engravings, carvings, statues and models, and records or other forms of sound reproduction.[15] The definition is so broad that even a writing or a drawing on underpants has been held to be covered by the Act.[16] The Act has created a committee under the control of the government which controls the censorship of publications. Banning under the Publications Act takes the form of a declaration that the publication or object in question is *undesirable*. Outside the field of indecency, obscenity or blasphemy the grounds of 'undesirability' are very broadly and imprecisely described as follows: 'harmful to the relations between any sections of the inhabitants of the Republic' and 'prejudicial to the safety of the State, the general welfare the peace and good order.'[17]

According to a Supreme Court decision, publications expressing criticism of police action in the townships can be declared unlawful.[18] The declaration of unlawfulness need not precede publication and a person may be convicted even if the committee makes its declaration after the event.[19] The insidious nature of political censorship is illustrated by the judgment of the Supreme Court in *S. v. Simoko*,[20] where the Court found the accused publishers to be negligent because their publication dealt with certain political issues *which they should have anticipated could be declared undesirable*.[21] It is a criminal offence under this Act to distribute a publication declared undesirable, and the mere possession of a banned publication may also constitute a crime. The finding of a committee of censorship may be appealed to the Publications Appeal Board (PAB), whose members are appointed by the government. There may be an appeal even against a decision by the committee *in favour* of publication. The only remedy against a decision of the PAB is a limited right of review in the Supreme Court. Procedurally, there are serious objections to the system of prior censorship since 'both the work and the composition of publication committees is blanketed in secrecy'.[22]

This conditional process of registration is particularly harmful for poor black publishers and opponents of the system of government in South Africa. Establishing a newspaper opposed to the National Party has become a virtually impossible task.

The Prisons Act 1959

It is a crime to publish any false information concerning the experience in prison of any prisoner or ex-prisoner or relating to the administration of any prison. In the leading case,[23] it was held that generalized accounts of prison experiences are covered by the prohibition and, moreover, that revelations about the behaviour of a particular prison warder will be regarded as a reflection of the administration of the prison and therefore within the scope of the prohibition. In that case, the *Rand Daily Mail* had published a series of articles about conditions and experiences in a number of South African prisons. The newspaper had first-hand accounts by former prisoners and prison warders. The prosecution persuaded the court that all was well with the prison system, a proposition which subsequent revelations have stripped of credibility.[24] One of the authors of the newspaper articles was jailed and the editor was fined. The newspaper itself was also fined.[25]

Since 1974, the Minister of Justice has introduced a new procedure by which information regarding prisons or prisoners must prior to publication be communicated in full to the Media Liaison Section of the S.A. Prison Service in Pretoria. The Prison Service checks the information and makes comments to the newspaper, which is then obliged to publish those comments with the same degree of prominence as the report itself.[26] Mathews describes this arrangement:

A sophisticated form of press co-optation which has ensured, and will ensure in the future, that newspapers will not go overboard on prison conditions.. . . An editor who publishes a dramatic exposé in breach of the arrangements is likely to be prosecuted; and one who submits to the scheme for verification is unlikely to make shocking revelations.[26]

The Prisons Act and its procedures are a severe curb on freedom of expression.

The Police Act 1958

Introduced by an amendment in 1979, Section 27 (b) of this Act is similar to the provision of the Prisons Act first discussed. It makes it a crime to publish any untrue matter about the police force, or any part of it, or about any member of the force in relation to the performance of his functions as such a member, without having reasonable grounds for believing it to be true. If it is proved that the publisher cannot satisfy the burden of reasonable grounds, he is liable to a fine of R.10,000 or imprisonment up to five years, or both. 'Force' includes all ranks and even temporary members of the police reserve (Section 1 of the Act) and members of the Railway Police since they were incorporated into the regular police force in 1986.

Section 27 (b) discourages journalists from reporting information of vital concern to the public. The police hold people *incommunicado* in police cells in terms of the Internal Security Act and allegations of ill-treatment of detainees are numerous. When they operate in black townships they 'often seal off areas in which "sensitive" actions are occurring, thereby preventing the more objective evidence of journalists and photographers being available'.[28] Moreover, quite frequently journalists who operate in the black townships are detained or banned. Journalists told us of many occasions when they have been harassed by police. During police actions the man with the camera is a particular target. He is likely to be in front. Police have been known to aim a teargas canister at the lens, or even to shoot at cameras. Expensive cameras are sometimes destroyed by the police and one journalist told us that he was detained for sixty-seven days during 1985 without charge.

We endorse the conclusion of Professor Mathews:

The high degree of official protectiveness towards the police in South Africa and of white ignorance of how they act and are viewed in the black townships, makes a gloves-off account of police conduct an urgent necessity. Though such an attack on police behaviour will be seen by many whites as unpatriotic, the opposite is in fact true. Police lawlessness is not just bad; it is a deadly poison that is spreading through the body politic thereby creating an incurable hostility between its constituent parts and the certainty of prolonged instability.[29]

Even more stringent control of the Press was imposed at the end of August 1987. The Minister of Home Affairs, Stoffel Botha, announced in Parliament new measures paving the way for the appointment of Press censors and setting up a quicker procedure for the banning of newspapers: 'For the first time, the Government has given itself the power to approve—or censor—the content of a newspaper *before* publication'.[30]

Notes

1. A. Mathews, *Freedom, State Security and the Rule of Law*, Cape Town and Johannesburg, 1986. Anthony Mathews is Professor of Law at the University of Natal, Pietermaritzburg.
2. Internal Security Act 1982, s. 15.
3. For the definition of 'communism' in South Africa, see p. 66.
4. Mathews, p. 259.
5. Ibid.
6. K. Stuart, *The Newspapermen's Guide to the Law*, 4th edn, Durban, 1986, p. 12.
7. Mathews, p. 149.
8. S. 15 (5).
9. Mathews, fn. 16, p. 150.
10. *2 SAJHR*, p. 115 (March 1986).
11. *Cape Times*, 25 October 1985.
12. Stuart, p. 20.
13. Ibid.
14. Mathews, p. 119.
15. S. 47 (1).
16. Mathews, p. 120.
17. S. 47 (2) (d) and (e).
18. S. v Russell 1980(2) SA 459 (E).
19. *S. v. Moroney* 1978 4 S.A. 389.
20. 1985 2 S.A.
21. Mathews, fn. 190, p. 121.
22. Ibid., p. 123.
23. *S. v. South African Associated Newspapers* 1970 (1) SA 469 (W).

24. See for example those by Breyten Breytenbach in *True Confessions of an Albino Terrorist*, Faber & Faber, 1986.
25. See Mathews, p. 151; Stuart, pp. 147 and 148.
26. Stuart, p. 150.
27. Mathews, fn. 26, p. 152.
28. Ibid., p. 154. See also p. 122.
29. Ibid., pp. 155–6.
30. *Weekly Mail*, 28 August/3 September 1987, p. 1.

7 Freedom of Association

Banning of organizations

The Minister of Law and Order has the power to proscribe an organization in terms of Section 4 of the Internal Security Act 1982. Before the passing of this Act, an organization could be banned under the Unlawful Organization Act 1960, which the Internal Security Act 1982 has repealed. But the banning of organizations that took place under the repealed legislation remains in force. In 1977 eighteen organizations were banned. Most were black groups, such as the South African Students Organization (SASO), but there were also white organizations, including the Christian Institute headed by Dr Beyers Naudé.[1]

The Minister may declare any organization unlawful if he is satisfied that it engages in activities which endanger the security of the state or the maintenance of law and order, or that it propagates the principles or promotes the spread of communism, or that it engages in activities for the achievement of any of the objects of communism, or that it is controlled by an organization which is committed to any of these objectives, or that it carries on (or which is established to carry on) the activities of an unlawful organization.[2] The banning, or declaration of unlawfulness, must be by notice in the *Government Gazette* and will not be invalidated because the organization in question is dissolved before the notice takes effect.[3] The words 'is satisfied' give a typical subjective discretion: the Minister's decision can only be attacked if he can be proved to have acted improperly. Actually, 'organizations may be banned not for what they do, but for what the Minister says they are doing'.[4]

Prior to banning, the Minister of Law and Order has to take advice of an advisory committee of three members appointed by the State President on the recommendation of the Minister of Justice.[5]

The right of the organization to be heard by the committee depends on the discretion of the committee itself, which can decided that a hearing would be contrary to the public interest. The advisory committee operates in secret, legal representation before it is prohibited and 'no Court of law shall have jurisdiction to pronounce upon the functions or recommendations of an advisory committee.'[6]

An organization declared unlawful ceases to have legal existence. All its property, including rights and documents, vests in a liquidator designated by the Minister of Justice.[7] The liquidator is required to take possession of all property vested in him, to determine whether the assets are sufficient to pay the debts of the organization, and thereafter to wind up the organization either as a solvent or insolvent organization according to that determination.[8] Any balance remaining after the payment of debts must be paid into the State Revenue Fund.[9]

It is a criminal offence to carry on the activities of a banned organization or to perform certain proscribed acts which would constitute a continuation of its affairs.[10]

The prohibited acts and activities are numerous:

(a) Becoming or continuing to be an office-bearer, officer or member of the organization or performing the act in such capacity;
(b) Carrying, possessing or displaying anything indicating membership of the holding of office or association with the organization;
(c) Contributing or soliciting anything for the direct or indirect benefit of the organization;
(d) Taking part in any activity of the organization or carrying on, in its direct or indirect interest, any activity in which it could have engaged;
(e) Promoting or encouraging the achievement of any of the objects of the organization or any similar objects, or any act likely to further such objects.[11]

These prohibitions apply to members, past or present, and to non-members.[12] They also have a cumulative effect. They indiscriminately punish a host of major and minor acts as serious crimes whose penalty is imprisonment for up to ten years. A single act may be a breach of several prohibitions, and each prohibition covers a large number of specific offences. In *S* v. *Xoswa* the court demonstrated that becoming a member, pinning on a badge and soliciting a small donation for a banned organization could condemn the accused to thirty years in prison.[13]

The banning of an organization also affects individuals connected with an organization by means of the 'listing' procedure of Section 16. The Director of Security Legislation, an officer appointed by the Minister of Law and Order must draw up and keep up to date the 'consolidated list' of all persons whose names appear on lists compiled by the liquidator of a banned organization or of lists compiled by an authorized officer on investigation by him of any organization prior to its banning.[14] Those on the list are 'office-bearers, officers, members or active supporters of the organization' or who were so 'at any time before the commencement of the Act'.[15] These large definitions may cover any person working or having worked 'even in a menial capacity' for the organization.[16]

The disabilities imposed on listed persons are severe. Such a person may not be elected, or if elected, may not sit as a member of a house of Parliament unless the prior written aproval of the Minister or the leave of the house has been obtained.[17] A listed person is disqualified from being admitted to practise as an advocate, attorney, notary or conveyancer, and provision is made for the striking-off of any such person from the appropriate roll of practitioners.[18]

The Minister of Law and Order may also decide that listed persons are prohibited from being office-bearers, officers or members of a fairly long list of specified organizations, of any organization which engages in activities which are calculated to promote any of the objects of such specified organizations, or any other organization 'which in any manner propagates, defends, attacks, criticises or discusses any form of State or any principle or policy of the Government of a State or which in any way undermines the authority of the Government of a State'.[19]

Control and restriction of organizations

The main purpose of the Affected Organizations Act 1974 is to prevent organizations which are declared 'affected' from receiving financial assistance from foreign sources. The State President has the power to declare an organization 'affected' by notice in the *Government Gazette* if he is satisfied that politics are being engaged in by or through an organization 'in co-operation with or under the influence of an organization or person abroad'.[20]

It is an offence to ask for or canvass foreign money for an organization declared 'affected' by the State President, to receive or deal with money from abroad with the intention of handing it over or causing it to be used by the organization, or to bring or assist in bringing money from abroad with a like intention or purpose.[21] Foreign money in the possession of an affected organization, whether received before or after the commencement of the Act, may not be disposed of except by donation within one year to a charitable or other organization *designated by the Minister*.[22]

Major organizations declared affected are NUSAS (13 September 1984), the Christian Institute (30 May 1975, before it was declared an unlawful organization in 1977) and the United Democratic Front (9 October 1986).

We agree with Professor Mathews' conclusion: 'The most disturbing feature of the Act is that the Governing Party, itself a participant in the political process of the country, decides which other groups shall be declared affected without the control of safeguards to ensure a fair, rational and independent judgment.'[23]

The banning of individuals

The restrictions imposed on a banned person affect all the basic liberties; freedom of the person, of association, of movement, of assembly and of speech. They amount 'to a civil death and to a large extent a personal and social death for the victim of the banning order'.[24]

The Minister of Law and Order may impose these restrictions:

If he is satisfied that the person in question is engaging in, or likely to promote, activities that endanger State security or the maintenance of law and order; or if that person is on the consolidated list or has been convicted of specified offences and the Minister has reason to suspect that he will engage in or promote the said activities; or if the Minister is satisfied that the person in question is causing, or likely to cause, feelings of hostility between the different population groups (or parts of population groups) in the Republic.[25]

The Act requires the Minister to disclose only so much of the information which leads to the banning as he deems consistent with the public interest.[26] 'This authorises him to withhold all the relevant information'.[27] In the case of the extension of the ban on Dr. Beyers Naudé in 1982, the Minister gave 'reasons' in one sentence, restating the statutory grounds on which the banning decision was based, without any information to support it. In *Alexander* v *Minister van Justisie* the banned person had been restricted immediately after serving a long prison sentence for furthering the objects of communism while a political prisoner in a maximum security jail. The Appellate Division 'reaffirmed the rule that the Minister's power to ban may be exercised despotically'.[28]

The Minister can prohibit a banned person from attending gatherings by serving a written notice. The Reverend Beyers Naudé was prohibited from attending any gathering anywhere in the Republic, including any social, political or educational gathering. A prohibited gathering may consist of as few as two persons, including the banned person, according to the Appellate Division, which so interpreted the words 'any number of persons' in Section 1 (vii) of the Internal Security Act.[29]

As an automatic consequence of the prohibition on attending gatherings, there is an additional restriction: no speech, utterance, writing or statement made by a person prohibited from attending any gathering may be published without the consent of the Minister unless it is required for purposes of proceedings in a court of law.[30] This 'silencing clause' is applicable to a person who sends material out of the country for publication in a foreign newspaper if the newspaper is one that is imported into South Africa for local distribution.[31] It is a criminal offence punishable by imprisonment for up to three years. The Minister may grant a limited exemption from the silencing clause covering the *bona fide* use in a library of the material in question by members of staff of a university or by registered post-graduate students of a university.[32] But the use of the material must be in accordance with regulations made by the Minister which has provided for the material to be locked in a separate book-case or room, for a catalogue of the material to be kept in the library and for a register of users.[33]

Section 19 authorizes the Minister of Law and Order to impose, singly or in combination, the following restrictions:

(1) Prohibit the person in question from being within or absenting himself from any specified place or area.
(2) Forbid the said person from communicating with any person or category of persons specified.
(3) Place a ban on that person receiving visitors.
(4) Prohibit the performing of any specified act by that person.

The Minister is empowered to act on the same basis as he may prohibit attendance at gatherings, and by written notice signed by him and addressed to the person concerned. The confinement to a place may mean a magisterial district, a house, flat or even room. The area means generally a magisterial district, but both larger and smaller areas might be specified. Breach of the confinement or exclusion from a place or area is a criminal offence.

After having been subjected to various prohibition orders since 1962, Winnie Mandela was banished in 1977 to Brandfort in the Orange Free State, a village she had not previously visited and with which she had no connection. In August 1985 Mrs Mandela's Brandfort lodgings were attacked and set alight resulting in extensive damage. Following this incident, Mrs Mandela decided to remain in Johannesburg in the house that she had occupied before her banishment to Brandfort. In December 1985 she was served with an amended banning order, the effect of which was to preclude her from entering the magisterial districts of Johannesburg and Roodepoort. Her presence in her Soweto home was thus illegal. She was subsequently arrested and held in custody on two occasions for being within the magisterial district of Johannesburg.[34] The prohibition on communicating with another person appears to cover all forms of communication, whether direct or indirect. Communication in writing, by telephonic or other technical means, appears to fall under the prohibition. In *S* v. *Mandela*,[35] the court appeared to accept that communicating indirectly (e.g. sending a message) is within the prohibition.[36] A banned person has been convicted of communicating with her fiancé.[37] The prohibition is absolute with the only exception of being visited by an attorney or advocate who manages his or her affairs and whose name does not appear on the consolidated list and who is not banned.[38] Another *Mandela* case has ruled that the banned person must have intended to receive the visitor in question and where the visitor was entertained by the daughter of the restricted person and had no communication with a restricted person, so prohibition was not contravened.[39]

The Minister may effectively exclude the banned person 'from participation in all significant organizational activity of society'.[40] He may require any person to comply with such conditions as are prescribed in a ministerial notice, while he is an office-bearer, officer or member of an organization of public body specified in the notice or while he holds a specified public office; or to resign his functions and refrain from taking part in any of the activities of the organization; or to refrain from taking part in the activity of any organizations specifying the notice; or to refrain from becoming a member of a public body or to resign from it.[41] The Minister of Law and Order may require a banned person to report to an officer in charge of a police station at such times and during such periods as may be specified in the notice.[42] Failure to do so constitutes a criminal offence for which the penalty is imprisonment not exceeding ten years.[43]

Winnie Mandela had to report weekly to the police station of Brandfort. However, in 1986, after a court challenge, her banning order was quashed, and she is no longer subject to any special restrictions.

Notes

1. Mathews, p. 120. 'On 28 August 1985 the Minister of Law and Order banned the Congress of South African Students (COSAS) in terms of S.4 (1) of the Internal Security Act 1982. Prior to the banning, commentators had suggested that the state of emergency was primarily directed at young black South Africans. The importance of COSAS for young people is clearly indicated in the number of COSAS members who were detained without trial. More than 500 were detained between the declaration of the state of emergency on 21 July and the banning of COSAS on 28 August. Approximately one detainee in five was a member of COSAS. The banning of COSAS is likely to make many thousands of students offenders in terms of S.13 of the Internal Security Act. In terms of that section, for example, it would be an offence to wear a COSAS T-shirt' See also p. 90.
2. Internal Security Act 1982, S. 4 (1). And see p. 66.
3. S. 4 (5).
4. Mathews, p. 103.
5. S. 7.
6. S. 8 (11).
7. S. 13 (1) (b).
8. S. 14.
9. S. 14 (3).
10. S. 13 (1) (a) and S. 56 (1) (a).
11. S. 13 (1) (a).
12. *S*. v. *Mbele* 1964 4 SA 401 N.
13. 1964(2) SA 459 (C).
14. S. 16 (a).
15. Ss. 14 (10) and 6 (2).
16. Mathews, p. 110.
17. S. 33 (2).
18. S. 34 (1).
19. Mathews, p. 114.
20. S. 2 (1).
21. S. 3 (2).
22. S. 3 (3).
23. Mathews, p. 116.
24. Ibid., p. 125.
25. S. 20.
26. S. 25.
27. Mathews, p. 126.
28. 1975 (4) SA 350 (A) *SAJHR*, p. 203, (July 1985).
29. Internal Security Act 1976 (1) S.A. 703 A.
30. Internal Security Act 1982, S. 56 (1) (p).
31. *S*. v. *Laurence* [1975] 4 S.A. 285 A.
32. S. 56 (5).
33. *Government Gazette*, 17 September 1982.
34. 2 *SAJHR*, p. 119 (March 1986).
35. 1974 4 S.A. 878 A.
36. Mathews, fn. 323, p. 136.
37. Ibid., fn. 325.
38. S. 19 (1).
39. *S*. v. *Mandela* 1979 1 S.A. 284 O.

40. Mathews, p. 138.
41. S. 18 (1).
42. S. 21.

8　Freedom of Assembly

The Minister of Law and Order has wide powers to prohibit a gathering 'if he deems it necessary' in the interest of state security or for the maintenance of the public peace. The prohibition may be made for any place or area in the Republic and indeed for the entire Republic.[1]

There is no limit on the duration of the prohibition, and he may issue blanket prohibition on all gatherings or particular kinds of gatherings.

Since 1976 the Minister has annually issued a government notice prohibiting all outdoor gatherings save for bona fide sporting and religious gatherings. Persons wishing to hold an outdoor gathering, for example a funeral, are required to obtain permission for such a gathering from a magistrate. Furthermore, in terms of s 46 (1) magistrates have expressly prohibited specific indoor gatherings. Leaving aside the criticisms of the manner in which the discretion to prohibit gatherings has been exercised, it is clear that the right to gather has been extensively eroded, leading to a situation in which the law is unintentionally broken daily. This, in turn, has allowed the authorities to embark on a policy of selective policing of outdoor gatherings, which, to the minds of many blacks, appears capricious and arbitrary. The police do not disperse each and every gathering that takes place outdoors in South Africa, but when patrolling the townships they may select and disperse with force such gatherings as they choose. In this light the right to use firearms to disperse gatherings is converted into a power to enforce by firearms an informal indoor curfew by day and night.[2]

On other occasions, freedom of assembly is restricted by other means:

It was reported in March that at least 35 minors from Aliwal North, some as young as 11 years, were detained under s 50 of the Internal Security Act 74 of 1982. It was alleged that the detentions were carried out to prevent the children attending a planned funeral for a victim of alleged police action. Shortly thereafter the water supply to the township was cut off for two days. It was claimed that this is a common occurrence and usually precedes police action in the townships. On this occasion, however, it was regarded as 'punishment' for a work stayaway called in protest against the detentions (*Weekly Mail* 21 March 1986). Residents later marched into Aliwal North to demand the release of the children. After negotiations with members of the police, 24 were released and the remainder were charged (*Weekly Mail* 27 March 1986).[3]

The use of force to disperse a gathering is specifically authorized by Sections 48 and 49 of the Internal Security Act 1982. A police officer of or above the rank of warrant officer is empowered to use force including the use of firearms and other weapons, to disperse particular kinds of gathering. The following conditions have to be met:

(1) The gathering has been prohibited in terms of Section 46 of the Act or the persons attending a gathering kill or seriously injure any person, or destroy or do serious damage to any valuable property, or attempt to do any of these deeds or show a 'manifest intention' of doing so.

(2) A police officer of or above the rank of warrant officer has called up on the persons attending the gathering to disperse within a specified time and the persons have not obeyed his instruction.

Force used to disperse the gathering should not be 'greater than is necessary for dispersing the persons assembled, and the force used shall be moderated and proportionate to the circumstances of the case and the object to be attained'.[4]

Section 49 requires that non-lethal weapons should be used first, and only if the gathering is not dispersed, or unless or until persons at the gathering commence or show a manifest intention of attacking persons or valuable property, may firearms or other lethal weapons be used.[5]

Section 49 (2) requires that:

firearms or other weapons likely to cause serious bodily injury or death shall be used for the purposes aforesaid with all reasonable caution, without recklessness or negligence, so as to produce no further injury to any person than is necessary for the attainment of the object aforesaid.

The events at Uitenhage illustrate the way the police can act in dispersing gatherings. The facts are drawn from the 'Report of the Commission appointed to inquire into the Incident which occurred on 21 March 1985 at Uitenhage', by Mr Justice Kannemeyer,[6] and from Haysom.[7]

On 21 March 1985 a police patrol in two armoured cars confronted a crowd marching from Langa, near Uitenhage, to the neighbouring township of KwaNobule to attend a funeral, in contravention of a magisterial prohibition imposed on the gathering. The Commissioner, Mr Justice Kannemeyer, found that the police had behaved improperly in soliciting the prohibition and in attempting to thwart the community's attempts to hold the funeral in the first place. The police patrol fired a volley of SSG shot into the crowd of mourners. Twenty people were killed and over twenty-seven seriously injured. Of those killed nineteen were shot in the back or from the side. Only one, a 16-year-old boy, was shot directly from the front.[8] Many of those killed died as a result of the penetration of a single SSG pellet into the cranium or spine.[9] The police patrol had been deliberately refused equipment such as teargas, rubber bullets, loudhailers, and birdshot.[10] The SSG shot is a heavy calibre shot. Each pellet can penetrate a sheet of heavy metal at seven paces. SSG shot spreads 1 metre in 30. When fired at a crowd, SSG shot will injure, maim or kill all in its path.[11] It will not discriminate between man and woman, adult or child, passer-by or member of an unruly crowd.[12] Two days before the incident, on 19 March 1985, the Senior Deputy Commissioner of Police had sent a telex which stated that 'when acid or petrol bombs are thrown at police or private vehicles and/or buildings an attempt must be made under all circumstances to eliminate the suspects'.[13]

The Commissioner also found that the police had fabricated their version in regard to the extent to which the crowd was threatening or armed. Although the commanding officer claimed to have fired a warning shot, even on his own evidence it appears that the warning shot could not have served to 'warn' the crowd that the police would shoot. The order to fire came almost immediately after the warning shot. The Commissioner expressed the following opinion of current police crowd-control methods:

One was left with the unhappy feeling that in some police circles the prevailing view was that teargas and, in particular, birdshot were not effective enough.... If Major Blignaut's complaint that birdshot used at a range of more than 50 metres is not effective to put a person out of action is typical of police thinking, it is indeed disturbing.... [S]urely when one has to deal with a large mob of rioters, the aim should be to cause the crowd to disperse and not to render the members thereof incapable by shooting them with ammunition such as SSG.[14]

The final chapter in this story typifies the relentlessness of the system: all the members of a peaceful procession to Parliament to present the government with a petition of concern after the shootings at Uitenhage in April 1985 were arrested and charged with contravening the Gatherings and Demonstrations Act 1973, which prohibits those gatherings and demonstrations in the precincts of Parliament.[15]

Notes

1. Internal Security Act 1982, S. 46 (3).
2. N. Haysom, 'Licence to Kill: The South African Police and the Use of Deadly Force', in 3 *SAJHR*, p. 23, (March 1987).
3. 2 *SAJHR*, pp. 268–9, (July 1986).
4. S. 48 (2).
5. S. 49 (1).
6. RP 74/1985 n. 1 pp. 58–62.
7. See note 2.
8. Kannemeyer Report, pp. 77, 87 and 89.
9. Haysom, p. 4.
10. Kannemeyer Report, pp. 91–113.
11. Ibid., pp. 91–2.
12. Haysom, p. 4.
13. Kannemeyer Report, p. 95.
14. Ibid., pp. 108–12.
15. A. Mathews, *Freedom, State Security and the Rule of Law*, Cape Town and Johannesburg, 1986, p. 147.

9 Trade Unions

Trade union law is one area in which the industrial bargaining power of black workers, coupled with the desire of the government to make South Africa attractive to overseas investment, has led it paradoxically to extend the rights of black people. In 1981 discrimination in industrial relations law was largely removed in the amended Labour Relations Act of that year. However, the use of the security laws and the powers of the state of emergency appear to be used extensively to influence the collective bargaining process, and we conclude that black workers remain at a considerable disadvantage in the bargaining process as compared with white workers. The continuing huge income differential between black and white workers demonstrates this.[1]

Following the election of the Nationalist government in 1948, a large number of black trade union leaders were arrested or banned. Black trade unions, which had been allowed to develop during the 1930s and 1940s, were identified with opposition to apartheid. By 1961 the membership of black trade unions was reduced to 64,000.[2] Mixed trade unions had already been banned in 1956 and 'job reservation' protected white workers from competition in many areas.

In the 1970s there were widespread strikes by black workers notwithstanding the limitations on union organization. The government established the Wiehahn Commission to examine industrial relations law and practice. In its 1979 report it concluded that freedom of association for all workers irrespective of race would be beneficial to industrial relations. The Commission also recommended the abolition of job reservation, the autonomy of unions in deciding membership criteria, and a new system of adjudicating on disputes between employer and employee.

The government largely accepted these recommendations, and remedies for unfair labour practices (including unfair dismissal) were provided in a new industrial tribunal framework. The former racially segregated dual system was abolished with the repeal in 1981 of the Black Labour Relations Regulation Act.

Under the current Labour Relations Act workers retain the right to strike, and strikes are lawful unless they are in breach of an agreement or in an essential service or prior to a thirty-day 'cooling-off' period following a reference to a conciliation board. Recently, there has been a further rise in the number and scale of disputes, probably as a consequence of the increasing confidence of black people in their ability to overcome the apartheid system, and their increasing unwillingness to accept discriminatory wages and working conditions. The government has evidently reconsidered the liberalization recommended by the Wiehahn Report and has introduced a new Labour Relations Bill on which we comment below.

The launching of the Congress of South African Trade Unions (COSATU) in November 1985 also demonstrated the growing self-assurance of black workers. The member unions comprise almost entirely black workers, but their standpoint is non-racial. In its early days COSATU limited its activities to strictly industrial matters and devoted its energies chiefly to building up its affiliates and encouraging them to amalgamate to form industry-wide unions. It has been extremely successful in achieving these objectives. It is already the biggest federation of trade unions there has ever been in South Africa. Its total membership has grown from 430,000 paid-up members in thirty-three unions at the date of the launch to 769,000 paid-up members in thirteen unions or sectors by July 1987.[3] Recently, however, it has taken a more openly political stance by announcing its support for the Freedom Charter, thereby aligning itself with the UDF.

The government seems to have had little hesitation in treating COSATU as a political organization throughout, as it has treated the individual black unions. There have been widespread arrests and detention of union leaders under the emergency powers. We were also told on several occasions of interventions by the security forces in industrial disputes. It is widely believed that employers call the police to help them—and we are satisfied that this often happens—but on other occasions it appears that the police take action on their own initiative or on the instructions of the government.

In October 1986 one member of the mission was told by a young shop steward at a store of OK Bazaars, a leading multiple store chain, that following a stoppage of work at his store, the police arrived and arrested all the workers involved. No reason was given, but the powers relied on were evidently the emergency regulations. Most were released after a few hours, but the shop steward was detained for three months.

On a much larger scale was the strike by employees of South African Transport Services which lasted three months from February 1987 until a settlement was reached which, according to the union, met all its demands (including reinstatement of no less than 16,000 who had been summarily dismissed).[4] On 28 March 1987 the police and army surrounded the COSATU headquarters and then broke up a meeting taking place there of 3,000 SATS workers. Many workers were arrested. On 22 April a meeting of the union was broken up at Germiston and three workers were shot dead. Again, the police laid siege to COSATU House, and 400 workers were arrested. Finally, bombs were exploded at COSATU House, causing such damage that the building became unsafe for use. It cannot be concluded that the government or police were responsible for this attack, but none of the culprits has been identified.[5]

Most recently, in August 1987, a strike called by the National Union of Mineworkers, the largest affiliate of COSATU, has led to police raids of union offices and the arrest of a large number of union officials.

Clearly, where industrial action leads to violence the police may properly be called upon to keep or restore the peace. In our opinion, however, what emerges from recent reported incidents of police intervention on the industrial scene is a pattern of deliberate repression of the trade unions, who are no doubt perceived by the government as a threat to minority rule at least as dangerous as the UDF. Such a policy cannot be reconciled with the right of free collective bargaining conferred by international human rights law.

The right of free collective bargaining is also under threat from the new Labour Relations Bill, which seems to reflect the government's desire to draw back from the Wiehahn reforms. Under the bill the government will be able to extend the 'cooling-off period' indefinitely so as to prevent a lawful strike; the bill also proposes to ban sympathy strikes and secondary action of other kinds, and it will also allow the government to amend at will the range of unfair labour practices. There will be a new Industrial Court staffed by judges of the Supreme Court.[6]

We deal more generally with the 'homelands' elsewhere (see Ch. 15), but it is appropriate to comment here on labour legislation in the homelands because it is significant for the whole South African industrial scene. Ironically, as has been pointed out in a study of homelands labour laws,[7] the abolition of a dual system for whites and blacks by the Wiehahn reforms was followed by a new dualism between the homelands and the rest of South Africa. The relative underdevelopment of the homelands has led their governments, no doubt with the encouragement of the South African government, to attempt to attract investment by imposing tough restrictions on the rights of workers and thereby keeping wages at a low level. In some cases these restrictions have been so severe as to deny the possibility of any real collective bargaining, for example in Venda and Transkei.

Legislation in Bophuthatswana has excluded all non-resident trade unions from operating there, and legal strikes are virtually impossible. In Kwazulu trade unions are allowed to affiliate to Inkatha, though in South African law a union may not affiliate to a political party. The relationship between South African laws and homeland laws on labour relations is confusing and workers in the homelands seem in many respects to be virtually denied the protection of the law.

Notes

1. Race Relations Survey (Institute of Race Relations), 1985, p. 131.
2. M. Finnemore & R. van der Merwe, Introduction to Industrial Relations in South Africa, Johannesburg, 1986, p. 6.
3. *Weekly Mail*, 10/16 July 1987, p. 14.
4. *Work in Progress*, no. 48, p. 38 (July 1987).
5. Ibid.
6. Labour Relations Amendment Bill (B118–87 GA).
7. A. Whiteside and N. Haysom, 'A Separate Development: Labour Legislation in the Homelands', 5 *Industrial Law Journal* (1984), p. 251.

10   The Right to Personal Freedom

The security laws: developments before 1982

The policy of separate development begun after the election of the first Nationalist government in 1948 was accompanied by the introduction and systematic refinement of a body of legislation designed to suppress extra-parliamentary opposition—presented as if orchestrated by a communist conspiracy. This legislation remains substantially unchanged today, though now largely embodied in the Internal Security Act 1982.

It was perfectly evident, however, that the objection of the ruling party to 'communism' was equally applicable to any movement which included racial equality among its aims: it was the threat it posed to white domination. The Suppression of Communism Act 1950 was therefore drafted in extremely wide terms, so wide as to make it illegal to advocate a wide range of anti-apartheid policies, including those which could not possibly fall within any intelligible definition of communism. The definition in the Act covers acts or schemes which 'aim at bringing about any political, industrial, social or economic change within the Union of South Africa by the promotion of disturbance or disorder, by unlawful acts or omissions or by means which include the promotion of disturbance or disorder'. It also included doctrines or schemes 'which aim at the encouragement of feelings of hostility between the European and non-European races of the Union'.[1]

Furthermore the definition of 'communist' to whom the Act was applied included not only those who professed to be communist or who were associated with any communist group, but anyone who encouraged in any way the achievement of any of the objects of communism, or who at any time had been a supporter of any organization which in any way furthered any of the objects of communism.

The first substantive provision of the Act declared the Communist Party of South Africa to be an unlawful organization. The State President was given power by proclamation to declare any other organization with any objects comprised in the wide definitions mentioned above to be likewise unlawful. No appeal was permitted, but the State President had to consider before issuing a proclamation a report from a committee of three persons appointed by him to examine the facts. The Appellate Division held by a majority of three to two[2] that an organization had no right to make representations to the committee before it completed its report. By excluding the principle *audi alteram partem* the court rejected an overriding duty to observe natural justice in security cases—an attitude they have regrettably maintained up to the present time. It has thus unfortunately been established law in South

Africa since 1967 that the State President may declare an organization unlawful without notice to the organization and without affording it an opportunity to be heard. The life of an organization comes to an end upon its being declared unlawful and any attempt to continue its activities is a criminal offence—even, perhaps, if it is done unintentionally.[3]

Individuals associated with a banned organization may suffer penalties even though they do not seek to continue its activities. The liquidator appointed to administer the affairs of the organization may be directed to compile a list of people who were active within it. These 'listed' persons continue to be subject to severe inroads on their personal freedom. They may be prevented by ministerial decree from taking part in the activities of any other organization. It becomes a criminal offence to record, reproduce, print, publish or otherwise disseminate any of their speeches or writings. A listed person is disqualified from practice as a member of the legal profession. A listed person cannot change his or her address without notifying the police.

When, after Sharpeville in 1960, the government wanted to outlaw the African National Congress, which had become a widely popular movement, seen by the government as a thorn in its side, it was discovered that even its wide definition of communism could not be stretched to cover all forms of opposition to apartheid. Hence the Unlawful Organizations Act authorized the banning of any organization which in the opinion of the Minister threatened public safety or the maintenance of public order. This Act was used to ban the ANC, the Pan-Africanist Congress and later a number of other organizations. The consequences for the members of being declared unlawful were similar to those under the Suppression of Communism Act.

Trade unionists were a particular target; by 1965 six trade unionists had been listed as communists,[4] and the reduction in industrial disputes during the ten years following the passage of the Act was attributed to the impact of the law on the unions.[5]

As the nationalists proceeded with their policy of imposing a strict legal framework on existing customary patterns of segregation, resistance also grew. The passing of the Population Registration Act and Group Areas Act in 1950 was followed in 1951 by a bill to remove coloured people in the Cape from the common voters' roll. This provoked a 'defiance campaign' in which large numbers of people systematically violated the apartheid laws. It led the government to introduce yet tighter measures of control. The Criminal Law Amendment 1953 imposed drastic penalties on any person convicted of an offence which had been committed 'by way of protest or in support of any campaign for the repeal or modification of any law or the variation or limitation of the application or administration of any law'. The effect was to make minor offences into serious ones if committed with a political motive.[6] The Public Safety Act 1953 empowered the Governor-General (later the State President) to declare a state of emergency if he was of the opinion that public order was seriously threatened.

After the defiance campaign (which the Criminal Law Amendment Act brought to an end),[7] the ANC again became a focus for opposition to the apartheid system, in 1955, with the publication of the Freedom Charter. This was followed by large-scale arrests and the trial of 156 people on charges of treason. The trial lasted for four years until 1961 and ended with the acquittal of all defendants, the court finding it impossible to conclude that the ANC had adopted a policy of seeking to overthrow the state by violence. (It was only after that date that the ANC felt itself forced to adopt a military posture in the face of the government's total refusal to abandon apartheid.)

Unrest, however, continued to occur as the government pursued its policy of separate development. Two parallel struggles were conducted in the late 1950s and early 1960s: the struggle in the rural areas over the government's Bantustan policy, and the urban struggle centred in the black townships. The latter erupted at Sharpeville in March and April 1960, when sixty-nine people were shot dead by the police and many others injured.

For the first time the government used its powers under the Public Safety Act by declaring a state of emergency. Any commissioned police officer was authorized to arrest and detain any person indefinitely if in his opinion it was desirable in the interests of public order or of the person concerned. Another provision allowed indefinite detention of those suspected of having committed offences endangering public order or safety for the purpose of interrogation. Only when the officer was satisfied that all questions had been satisfactorily answered could the detainee be released, and access to a legal adviser was expressly prohibited without the permission of the Minister.

The 1960 emergency only applied to selected magisterial districts — not to the whole country. It lasted only from March to August, but while it was in force 11,382 people were detained of whom only eighteen were white.[8]

After the emergency the government strengthened its permanent security legislation. The General Law Amendment Act 1962 created the offence of sabotage, aimed at 'subversive elements and communists'.[9] It prohibited a wide range of actions mainly involving intentional damage to property but including virtually any act deemed to endanger the maintenance of law and order. The Act shifted the burden of proof to the accused to show that any such action was *not* done with the intention of causing damage to the state. (This summarizes a typically long and wordy list of instances.) Professor Mathews says, 'Just as it can easily be demonstrated that the sabotage provision embraces activities of an entirely non-subversive nature, so too can it be shown that the measure is incredibly broad and vague in its sweep.'[10] The most horrifying fact about this new offence, however, was that it could carry the death penalty (see p. 80).

1963 saw the government for the first time introducing permanent legislation to authorize detention without trial.[11] Section 17 of the General Law Amendment Act 1963, designed to 'break the back' of the armed wings of the ANC and PAC,[12] empowered any commissioned police officer to arrest without warrant and detain incommunicado for up to ninety days any person whom he suspected on reasonable grounds of having committed or having intended to commit an offence under the Suppression of Communism Act, the Unlawful Organizations Act or the crime of sabotage, or *having any information regarding such offences*. In effect the new law allowed detention for 180 days because the Appellate Division (true to form) held that the original detention could be renewed for a similar period.[13] The reality of the ninety-day law was acknowledged in 1965 by the enactment of an explicit 180-day detention law in the Criminal Procedure Act 1965. Although, ostensibly it did not permit interrogation, as the ninety-day law did, because its intention was presented as the protection of state witnesses, in practice detainees were regularly questioned and many were subsequently charged with offences. The plight of such detainees held in solitary confinement has been described in heart-rending detail by the former South African lawyer Albie Sachs.[14]

Further provisions for detention without trial were introduced in the General Law Amendment Act 1966 and the Terrorism Act 1967. The former provision contained the relatively mild power for a police officer of or above the rank of lieutenant-colonel to arrest any person suspected of terrorist activities and detain them for a period of fourteen days. The Terrorism Act in effect rendered it obsolete by allowing *indefinite* detention by order of an officer of that rank with a view to obtaining information or on suspicion of offences under the Terrorism Act. Those offences were even broader than sabotage, which at least required the commission of a 'wrongful and wilful' act. The offence of terrorism seems to be capable of commission by a lawful act, even one committed outside South Africa. It covers an act done in order to encourage the achievement of social change in co-operation with an international body or institution. Professor Mathews suggests that a man who writes to an agency of the United Nations asking for financial assistance for a depressed community in South Africa would be guilty of terrorism. The definition of terrorism, like that of sabotage, is bewilderingly complex. Professor Mathews says 'it is quite needlessly (but perhaps intentionally) complicated'.[15]

In spite of the obscurity of its definition and the fact that it brought 'virtually every criminal act within the statutory scope of terrorism',[16] like sabotage, it may also be a capital offence.

Indefinite detention under Section 6 of the Act for the purpose of questioning could be continued until the detainee had satisfactorily replied to all questions or no useful purpose would be served by further detention. However, applying these criteria was entirely a matter for the police in their highly subjective judgment. Fortnightly visits were to be made to detainees by a magistrate, but even then only 'if circumstances so permit'. The government always refused to disclose the number of detainees held under Section 6, but in 1983 the Minister of Law and Order said that 4,104 people had been detained under Section 6 from its introduction until 1 July 1982.[17] The effect of the plethora of security legislation, combining a series of broadly defined offences with virtually unlimited detention powers, may well have contributed to a period of relative political calm until the early 1970s. Thereafter there was a steady rise in organized resistance within the industrial sphere but no changes in the operation of the law.

After the Soweto violence in 1976, further provision was made in Section

10 of the Internal Security Amendment Act 1976 for preventive detention of persons apparently engaged in activities calculated to endanger the security of the state or the maintenance of public order. This time a review committee was established to investigate detentions ordered by the Minister under this power not later than two months after the commencement of the detention. Since the committee was appointed by the Minister, met in camera and made recommendations which the Minister was not obliged to follow, its value as a safeguard for detainees was minimal. Eventually these provisions (like most others discussed so far) were incorporated into the Internal Security Act 1982.

By the late 1970s the government had come to rely heavily on its detention powers to contain opposition to apartheid. In order to justify measures which openly flouted international legal norms it labelled the opposition as communist-inspired and threatening violence. Such measures were presented as necessary to secure the safety of the state, but in defending systematic repression, the government failed to acknowledge that those who opposed the state rejected its legitimacy, by reason of the disenfranchisement of the black majority of the population.

'Reform' of the security laws

Anxiety about the security laws increased among the white population, however, as more and more reports emerged of brutal treatment of detainees, culminating in the death of Steve Biko in 1977. At the same time business-men were calling for reform as they faced industrial unrest and saw South Africa increasingly held up to condemnation by other countries with whom business links became more problematic. In keeping with his promise of a new reformist approach, P.W. Botha on his accession to power appointed a Commission of Inquiry under Mr Justice Rabie (subsequently Chief Justice), to investigate the security laws. In explaining the appointment of the Commission the Minister of Justice enumerated the following reasons for a reappraisal:

1. Threats against security change, and some measures necessary in the past may no longer be necessary.
2. For the same reason new measures may be needed
3. It has been alleged that some measures are unfair especially in the absence of adequate judicial supervision. The Commission would be able to make recommendations as to this.
4. The measures were spread over a number of Acts with the result that they are not easily identifiable and manageable; they have therefore as a group become an unwieldy instrument and on the other hand the mere number of security measures has become handy anti-South African propaganda material. Some of the measures resulted from emergency situations and were therefore drafted in haste with the result that they were perhaps not so elegantly formulated. The Commission will thus be

able to consider the possibility and desirability of reformulation and consolidation.[18]

Apart from a brief nod in the direction of judicial supervision, the government evidently did not intend more than a tidying up exercise. Nor did the Commission of Inquiry disappoint them. Many South African judges do not consider that upholding the rule of law is their responsibility. In an extreme statement of the 'positivist' position, the late Mr Justice O.D. Schreiner said that a complaint that the rule of law had been infringed was a political and not a legal complaint.[19] Professor Mathews comments that this statement encouraged the Rabie Commission to discard the rule of law as a helpful guide in framing a new security policy.[20] He also points out that the appointments to membership of the Commission excluded anyone who would challenge the basis of white political thinking on the function of the security system, namely the protection of the power and privilege of the ruling minority from all forms of attack.[21]

The Rabie Commission carried out a detailed survey of the legislation and heard evidence about security legislation in other countries, in particular Israel and Northern Ireland. In its report it made some positive recommendations. For example, it recommended the abolition of the death penalty in cases where no violence was established; it recommended the abolition of a mandatory five-year sentence required under the Terrorism Act and the provisions relating to the offence of sabotage; it recommended the abolition of the shifting of the onus of proof in some of the statutes to the accused to rebut presumptions of guilt with proof 'beyond reasonable doubt'. It considered that proof by the accused on the balance of probabilities was sufficient.[22] These improvements in the position of those accused of security offences pale into insignificance when set in the context of the oppressive laws which the Commission was prepared to tolerate or even to approve. Indeed, to require the accused to prove that he or she has *not* committed an offence, whatever the standard of proof, is objectionable.

For in essence the body of security laws described above was considered by the Commission to be fit to be left intact, subject only to consolidation of most of the law in more manageable form in a single comprehensive statute.

A seminar was organized by the Centre for Applied Legal Studies of the University of the Witwatersrand chaired by Sydney Kentridge QC following publication of the report. It was attended by nine senior counsel (one of whom is now a Supreme Court judge) and several of the country's most distinguished academic lawyers. The Rabie Report was subjected to detailed analysis and was heavily criticized. A pamphlet subsequently published by the Centre gives the views of those present and contains a trenchant critique of the approach of the Commission of Inquiry and its report.[23]

The importance of the Rabie inquiry is that it is the only recent occasion when a government-appointed body had a real opportunity of examining the operation of the security laws and recommending changes which could have brought them into line with international human rights law. It may be doubted whether the government would have been prepared to accept such recommendations even if they had been made, but the Commission's failure is a serious condemnation of its chairman, who at the time was a Judge of Appeal. He is now Acting Chief Justice, having served as Chief Justice until he reached the statutory retirement age.

In carrying out its work the Commission made no effort to interview detainees or former detainees, or any of the lawyers who represent them. It relied heavily on the evidence of the police, which it appeared willing to accept without question; it ignored the inquiries into security laws carried out in other countries (including the series of reports commissioned by the British government into security laws in Northern Ireland, of which evidence had been put before them); and it ignored relevant provisions of international human rights law, decisions of the European Court of Human Rights and the Supreme Court of the United States, and findings even of South African courts and inquests in which appalling abuses by the security forces towards detainees were exposed. It failed to carry out any investigation of the physical and psychological effects of such detention, even though much medical evidence was readily available. It is hard to resist the conclusion that the Commission was deliberately set up to endorse the government's policies for that is exactly what it did.

In his conclusion to the Centre critique, Professor John Dugard acknowledges that harsh security laws have had some effect in deterring certain persons from engaging in politically motivated acts of violence. But, on the other hand, he points out, 'it is equally certain that these laws and their implementation have alienated large sections of the community and have engendered an hostility to the authorities which has often been translated into violent acts against the State.'[24] The sense of alienation to which he refers is, not surprisingly, especially marked in the black community, which, no doubt correctly, increasingly see the apparatus of the law as the white man's method of maintaining his dominant position. But Professor Dugard also points to the evidence of racial discrimination in the administration of the security laws (not considered by Rabie though brought to his attention). At the time when he wrote, forty-five blacks but only one white had died in detention. (The figure is now said to be over eighty.[25]) Many whites as well as blacks have lost confidence in the system, and international opinion has, he says, become alienated. He draws attention to Resolutions 417 and 418 unanimously adopted by the Security Council of the United Nations in October and November 1977 condemning the implementation of the security laws, in particular in relation to the death of Steve Biko. Professor Dugard concludes by suggesting that over-stringent security laws may be counter-productive even in terms of their own objectives.

The Internal Security Act 1982

Notwithstanding these powerful criticisms, the government accepted the recommendations of the Rabie Report and enacted the Internal Security Act 1982 in virtually the very terms drafted by the Rabie Commission. That Act remains in force today subject only to some amendments which have made it even stricter. At the same time as the Internal Security Act, the government passed three other Acts which embodied other recommendations of the Commission; namely the Protection of Information Act, the Intimidation Act and the Demonstrations in or near Court Buildings Prohibition Act.

The principal offences under the Internal Security Act are terrorism, subversion, sabotage and advocating any of the objects of communism. Terrorism, like the common-law offences of treason and murder, carries the death penalty, though it is not a mandatory sentence.[26] The characteristics of these offences have already been described above.

There are many other offences outside the Internal Security Act which are also used by the prosecuting authorities in security or political situations. Murder and treason have already been mentioned, but charges of sedition and intimidation are not unknown. In recent months the government has launched prosecutions for sedition against certain residents of black townships who are accused of organizing 'alternative structures' for local self-government.[27] While the promotion of such structures has been made an offence under the state of emergency regulations,[28] the use of this much more serious charge is a disturbing development. Most frequently used of all is the common-law offence of public violence with which very large numbers of people, especially young men and children, have been charged in connection with allegations of unrest in the townships.

In addition to re-enacting the criminal offences mentioned above, the Internal Security Act repeats the measures from earlier legislation empowering the Minister of Law and Order to declare an organization to be unlawful; prohibit a publication; authorize the investigation of any organization, (including powers of search and seizure); direct a list of persons associated with a banned organization to be prepared (making them 'listed persons')[29] impose a banning order on any person 'who the Minister is satisfied engages in activities which endanger or are calculated to endanger the security of the state or the maintenance of law and order or propagates or promotes or is likely to propagate or promote such activities.' The Minister may restrict publication of the utterances of such persons. He may also restrict attendance at gatherings, and order any person subject to the Act to report at police stations.

These indeed are only some of the extraordinary powers given to the Minister by the Internal Security Act. Even more drastic are the detention powers now set out in Sections 28 to 31 and Section 50 of the Act:

(1) *Section 28* replaces Section 10 of the Internal Security Amendment Act 1976 and authorizes the Minister of Law and Order to impose preventive detention on any person who in his opinion is likely to commit the offence of

terrorism, subversion or sabotage or if he is satisfied that a person will endanger the security of the state or the maintenance of law and order. There is no limit on the period of detention and no court of law may review the Minister's decision. Access to legal advice is allowed only for the purpose of preparing written representations to the Minister. However, the Appellate Division has held that a Section 28 detainee is entitled to be given reasons for his detention such as to afford him a fair opportunity to make representations.[30] Such representations must be made within fourteen days of the detention, and the Minister must thereafter give reasons for the detention to a Review Board (appointed by himself). The Minister is not obliged to accept their recommendations. The detainee may have his case resubmitted to the Review Board at six-monthly intervals. There is yet another 'safeguard', however, if the Minister does not accept recommendations of the Review Board and thereby the detainee is worse off. The Minister must submit all the papers to the Chief Justice of South Africa, who may set the detention order aside *if* he finds that the Minister exceeded his powers or acted in bad faith. This review procedure is manifestly useless if it is seriously intended to provide any safeguard for the detainee. No doubt it is intended to delude the public into thinking that a real safeguard exists. In 1985 fifty-four cases came before the Review Board but it did not recommend release in a single case. Thus the Chief Justice was not even called upon.[31]

(2) *Section 29* provides for detention for the purpose of interrogation, replacing Section 6 of the Terrorism Act 1967. Similarly, it allows any officer of or above the rank of lieutenant-colonel to arrest without warrant any person believed to be connected with subversion or terrorism. Such a person may be held until the police are satisfied that 'the said person has satisfactorily replied to all questions at the interrogation or that no useful purpose will be served by his further detention'. The authority in writing of the Minister is required to extend this period for more than thirty days (though we were told of one case in which a judge was prepared to overlook the absence of the Minister's written authority). The Commissioner of Police must furnish reasons to the Minister justifying the continued detention, and after six months a Review Board must consider whether there are still reasons justifying the continued detention. Again, the Minister is not bound to accept any recommendations from the Review Board and this time there is no further review by the Chief Justice. The Act provides for Section-29 detainees to be visited in private not less than once a fortnight by a magistrate and by a district surgeon. There is also a government official called the Inspector of Detainees who is required to visit detainees as frequently as possible to satisfy himself as to their well-being. We comment below on the evidence as to the effectiveness of these supposed safeguards.[32]

(3) *Section 30* is not strictly a provision for detention but has the same effect. It allows the Attorney-General to order that a person who has been arrested on a charge of having committed a security offence should not be released on bail if he regards his detention as necessary in the interests of the security of the state or the maintenance of law and order. Generally, bail is in the discretion of the court. This section permits the state to override that

discretion by issuing what is in effect a veto. In *State* v. *Ramgobin* (the Pietermaritzburg UDF treason case) the Attorney-General's attempt to prevent bail for the accused failed on the technical point that the Attorney-General's order pre-dated the formulation of the indictment. In Pretoria, the Transvaal Division were faced with the same facts in September 1985 in relation to the other UDF treason trial (still in progress at the time of writing). They followed the Natal decision on the law but exercised their discretion against granting bail (though later all but three of the twenty-two accused were released on bail). One member of the mission was in court when Mr Justice Eloff, the Judge President, accepted the Attorney-General's evidence that the release of the accused would be against the interests of the state even though the Attorney-General declined to disclose the evidence supporting his claim on the ground that its disclosure would likewise be against the interests of the state.

(4) *Section 31* is the remarkable provision which permits the Attorney-General to order the detention of potential prosecution witnesses. He may arrest such a person if he is of the opinion that he or she may be tampered with or intimidated, or may abscond, or whenever he deems it to be in the interests of that person or of the administration of justice. The detention will continue until the conclusion of the proceedings in question, save that if no indictment is served within six months of his arrest he is entitled to be released forthwith. Such witnesses may be held incommunicado and indeed no one else has to be informed of such a detention. A member of the mission was informed by the Attorney-General of Transvaal (Mr Brunette) that it was necessary to refuse access to Section-31 detainees by family and legal advisers because visitors might discourage them from giving evidence. It is widely acknowledged that in fact potential witnesses are subjected to severe pressure from the police while detained, and any statement or evidence of such a person would seem to be of highly doubtful reliability. Nevertheless, in many political trials the conviction rests solely on the evidence of such witnesses which judges often accept.[33]

In some cases it also happens that the witness goes into the box at the trial and refuses to incriminate the accused claiming that a statement was extracted under torture. In *R* v. *Baleka* and others (the Transvaal UDF treason trial) the judge (Van Dijkhorst J.) excused the witness from giving evidence on this basis but refused to allow the defence to cross-examine the police on their treatment of this and other witnesses. In a terrorism trial at Pietermaritzburg part of which two members of the mission observed,[34] we were informed that a witness who made a similar claim and refused to incriminate the accused was sentenced by the judge, Thirion J., to a term of imprisonment for refusing to testify. It should be pointed out that though not allowed visits from family and lawyers, Section-31 detainees are supposed to receive fortnightly visits from the district surgeon and the magistrate. We comment below on the apparent ineffectiveness of such visits.

The treatment of detainees

Unfortunately we are forced to conclude that the system of safeguards against abuse of the detention process is little more than window-dressing. The Biko inquest and its aftermath showed the extent to which some district surgeons are prepared to subordinate their professional duty to the requirements of the police, and the Aggett inquest showed that access to detainees pursuant to the statute is not always allowed.[35] Members of the mission were told by former detainees that visits by magistrates were perfunctory and there was reluctance to listen to complaints. Even when complaints were noted, nothing was done about them.

Section 29 detainees may not receive visits from family or legal advisers except with the permission of the Minister. The number of persons detained is inevitably speculative because the government can so easily conceal information. However, the DPSC estimated that 280 persons were detained under Section 29 during 1984, a further 406 during 1985 and 1197 during 1986.[36]

Two posts of Inspector of Detainees were created in June 1978 following the international outcry over the death in detention of Steve Biko. The initial appointees were retired officials of the Department of Justice.[37] In the same year instructions were issued by the Commissioner of Police for medical treatment, nutrition, sleeping and exercise facilities of detainees. They were, however, unenforceable, having only the status of administrative guidelines.[38] On 24 November 1982 the Minister of Law and Order issued new directions for treatment of Section 29 detainees.[39] Paragraph 15 states, 'A detainee shall at all times be treated in a humane manner with proper regard to the rules of decency and shall not in any way be assaulted or otherwise ill-treated or subjected to any form of torture or inhuman or degrading treatment.'

These directions provided for detainees to be informed of their rights, for their families to be informed of their detention, for the speedy investigation of complaints, for the conduct of interrogation, for visits by doctors and magistrates and for records to be kept of such visits. But much of the document is expressed in vague and ambiguous terms and is made subject to what may be 'practicable' in particular circumstances. Worst of all, no independent check or check on behalf of the detainee was provided and there appears to be no means of enforcing the directions.[40] The directions did not include any guidance as to the conduct of interrogations save to state that 'the investigation . . . shall be concluded as rapidly as possible so as to limit the period of detention to the minimum'.[41] Also, firearms were prohibited from the interrogation room 'unless there are compelling security reasons', but following the death of Mr Paris Malatji at the hands of the security police on 5 July 1983, a police sergeant was convicted of culpable homicide for shooting him at point-blank range through the head during interrogation. The policeman was sentenced to ten years imprisonment.[42]

Foster describes provisions for detainees' protection as characterized by attempts to shield and protect the system of interrogation from exposure rather than to grant real protection to its victims.

The justification for this assessment is well established by the empirical study which was conducted under the auspices of the Institute of Criminology at the University of Cape Town which is the basis of Don Foster's book. Foster and his colleagues carried out a series of personal interviews with former detainees over the whole of South Africa between mid-1983 and November 1984. The sample consisted of 158 persons, some of whom had been detained on more than one occasion, making a total of 176 cases. The date of detention ranged over the period since 1974, but seventy-eight cases occurred between 1981 and 1983. The interviewees were questioned about the length and condition of interrogation. Most had been subjected to several sessions lasting more than five hours each. Nineteen per cent claimed that they had been interrogated for periods exceeding nine hours. Only 17 per cent of the detainees said that they had *not* been subjected to physical torture. Of the remainder, 75 per cent said they had been beaten, including punching, kicking and whipping as well as being attacked with a number of implements; 50 per cent forced to stand for long periods; 34 per cent forced to maintain other abnormal postures; 25 per cent had bags put over their heads; 25 per cent received electric shocks; 21 per cent food deprivation; 18 per cent strangulation by means of a cloth or towel; 14 per cent suspension in various forms. Twenty-seven per cent reported other forms of physical torture including manacling and chaining, pulling out hair, genital abuse, beating on the soles of the feet, burning and other hideous tortures. Notably, a significantly smaller proportion of the thirteen white ex-detainees among those interviewed reported torture: 69 per cent of the whites said they had not been tortured whereas only 7 per cent of the Africans said so.

The investigators also explored the use of psychological forms of torture. A large majority of the interviewees said that they had been subjected to false accusations, solitary confinement, verbal abuse and threats of violence. No less than 41 per cent claimed that they had been threatened with execution. During and following detention most of those interviewed reported a variety of health problems. More than half complained of difficulty sleeping and headaches during detention and many complained of weight loss, loss of appetite, difficulty in concentration, nightmares, memory difficulties and depression. After release the same problems appeared to persist and many said they had difficulty in relating to their family, friends and other people.

The report of the investigation also contains a number of graphic descriptions by former detainees of their own particular experiences during detention. The members of the mission did not, so far as they are aware, meet any of those who took part in the Foster study, but they talked to other former detainees who recounted very similar experiences. This leads the mission to find the conclusions of the Foster study entirely credible. They reveal an appalling state of affairs in which torture and brutality are virtually routine for the security forces, and lack of supervision by the government so universal as to establish beyond question that torture of detainees who have been convicted of no crime at best condoned by the government.

One member of the mission was able during a visit to South Africa in October 1986 to meet a group of prisoners awaiting trial on terrorism charges. All save one of the accused had been held in prison awaiting trial since their arrest in December 1985; the sole woman defendant, who was pregnant, had been released on bail. One accused described his arrest and subsequent interrogation, which began shortly after his arrest at 11.15 p.m. and continued all night and until 4 p.m. the next afternoon. He said that during the whole of that time he was not allowed to visit the lavatory, and that over the next few days he had been repeatedly assaulted, pummelled all over and kneed in the groin. He did not allege electric shocks but other accused claimed that they had received electric shocks on hands, feet and genitals. There were allegations from all the accused (save the one woman) of violent beatings, and kicking over several weeks. The accused were detained initially under Section 29 until they were subsequently charged with offences. The first accused described his experiences in great detail and with powerful effect. He explained that the police constantly made clear that they had the power of life and death over detainees. He described the constant assaults as scientifically planned, so as to leave no scars, but continued relentlessly so as to destroy resistance.

He claimed that he reported the assaults to the Inspector of Detainees who visited him after one month. The Inspector apparently referred the matter to the uniformed branch to investigate. The detainee was asked to lay a formal charge but he refused. He was without legal advice and was afraid that if he laid a charge he would be victimized. (The same explanation was given to us by other ex-detainees for their failure to lodge complaints.) He said that he was detained under Section 29 for five months, and during the whole period he was not let out of his cell except for interrogation. He had no contact with any other person except his captors; he received no visits, no newspapers and had no communication with the outside world at all. He did not see the sunlight for the whole five months. When he saw it again for the first time, he felt blinded and could not see properly for several hours.

Another of the prisoners found out subsequently that his family did not learn of his whereabouts until he had been detained for four months. He complained that the food was totally inadequate and that he had lost 14 kg in five months. He said that his wife was detained and separated from their four-month old baby in order to induce him to respond to the interrogation. He said he submitted finally to pressure to sign a confession statement, though in fact what he signed was the invention of the police. The view of all the accused was that any statement made under Section 29 is worthless because it is made under duress. There is constant pressure to 'co-operate'. The detainee struggles constantly to resist but his need for food and minimal comfort forces him to make a statement just to survive.

All the accused were kept in isolation until they made statements. They were then charged and brought together at the prison, where they shared a large cell. As 'awaiting trial' prisoners, their conditions were significantly better, but even then they were locked up for twenty hours a day. Members of the mission met other former detainees in all the parts of the country they visited. Their stories were consistent with each other and with the findings of the UCT study. Other studies have been carried out by the DPSC in

September 1982, in which seventy-two former detainees alleged widespread torture, and by the National Medical and Dental Association in April 1987. The latter concluded that 'torture in detention is a continuous process'.[43]

If further evidence is needed, it is supplied by Dr Wendy Orr and the many co-plaintiffs and witnesses who supported the action which she brought in September 1985 against the Minister of Law and Order and a number of police officers in the Port Elizabeth area. Dr Orr had been employed since January 1985 as a medical officer in the District Surgeon's office in Port Elizabeth. One of her duties was to attend prisoners at the local prisons and in particular to examine them on admission and release. She estimated that from July 1985 about 1,800 men and a number of women as well had been detained under the emergency regulations. At the beginning of August, she said in a sworn affidavit, she was seeing about twenty newly admitted prisoners a day, of whom a large proportion complained that they had been assaulted by the police. They exhibited consistent symptoms, including severe multiple weals, bruising and swelling. She mentioned some cases of severe injuries and one case in which the detainee complained that he had been forced to eat his own hair, which she was able to some degree to confirm by diagnosing an intestinal obstruction. On one day she says she had to examine about 170 detainees of whom roughly half complained of assault by the police and most showed consistent injuries. In one case of severe injuries, Dr Orr directed that she wanted to see the prisoner again a few days later, but he was not brought to her, and when she enquired she was told he had been released. She says this must have been done in breach of the rules and she considered that in view of his condition she would not have certified him as fit to be moved. Dr Orr also stated in her affidavit that she was discouraged by her superiors from recording the complaints or from completing forms which would normally lead to an investigation. She said that it had become 'apparent to me that the police apparently believe that, under the emergency regulations they cannot be held responsible for the abuses and that the Departments of Prisons and Health are apparently unconcerned and have turned a blind eye'.

Many other affidavits were filed by relatives of detainees and detainees themselves confirming that they had been violently assaulted and tortured. The government made no serious attempt to contest the allegations, and an interdict was granted prohibiting the police from continuing their assaults or threatening assaults. The court order was read out to all emergency detainees at the prisons. Wendy Orr resigned from the Department of Health.

Unhappily, the treatment of detainees in general has evidently not improved as a result of the brave and persistent efforts of Wendy Orr.

Capital punishment

Although the death penalty is not as such prohibited by the main inter-national human rights conventions and declarations, there is general con-demnation of inhuman or degrading treatment or punishment which, according to modern notions, would include the death penalty. Amnesty International has long campaigned against the death penalty, and few countries which claim to respect civilized values continue to impose it. The United States ackowledges the right of individual states to permit the death penalty, and after several years when the legal position was uncertain, some executions for murder have taken place.

In South Africa the death sentence may be imposed on those convicted of several offences, many of them political.[44] In recent years there have been more than 100 executions annually. Apart from any general objection which may be taken on moral grounds to the deliberate taking of life by the state, serious criticism has been made of the use of the death penalty in South Africa because:

(1) All but a very small number of those executed are black, suggesting that the imposition of the death penalty is racially discriminatory.
(2) The procedures at 'political trials' are unfair and convictions therefore unreliable.
(3) Those convicted of offences committed in the course of the political struggle should not be treated as criminals but under the international law governing armed conflict between an unlawful government and those who seek to overthrow it.

The fact that the death penalty is disproportionately and unequally used against black people is readily established. In 1984, 131 people were hanged of whom only two were whites. In 1985, 161 people were hanged, but the number of whites was the same.[45] Ironically, in 1970 Professor van Niekirk of the University of Natal was charged with contempt of court for alleging in an academic article that blacks were more likely to be sentenced to death than whites, yet his allegation was supported by the opinion of a large number of lawyers as well as such demonstrable facts as the absence of any white person sentenced to death for rape of a black woman up to that time, while 150 blacks had been executed for raping white women.[46]

There are many instances where lenient sentences have been imposed on white persons for offences which for black people would certainly have attracted the death penalty. The case referred to earlier of the policeman who shot dead an unarmed detainee is an example. Another case brought to our attention is that of the white farmer who was only fined when he killed an unarmed black man whom he found unlawfully squatting in one of his farm buildings.

Second, in political trials the procedures are weighted very heavily against the accused, who in most cases is black. Sydney Kentridge SC is reported to have said:

Now, a visitor walking into a court in which one of these trials is going on will see a trial being conducted with all the customary decorum of our courts. He will see a judge obviously exercising the utmost judicial care, and he will have the impression he is watching an ordinary trial at law. But of course he is not. He is watching a procedure in which all our cherished rules and maxims, or many of them, have gone by the board. There is an onus on the accused; there is a form of hearsay evidence which is admissible beyond anything that the reformers of the law of evidence have ever thought of. The state witnesses are all under pressure and, I think it must be said, the lawyers appearing are perhaps under some pressure themselves.[47]

He might have added that the state witnesses had probably been detained by the police incommunicado and subjected to torture for many months before the trial, as indeed might be true of the accused. In the recent murder trial of the 'Sharpeville Six' the accused were convicted and sentenced to death largely on the evidence of witnesses who had been so held.[48] This is the pattern for virtually all the thirty persons on death row for 'political' murders at the time of writing.

The so-called political cases seem to be of two kinds: those in which persons are charged with offences which have arisen out of political conflict, for example as in the case of the Sharpeville Six, where a community councillor or government agent has been killed in the course of protests at rent increases imposed in accordance with government policy, or where violence has erupted in response to police provocation or brutality; and those in which the accused are identified as ANC combatants. In the former type the provocation or unjust treatment of the accused should mitigate the offence or exonerate the accused entirely, and in no such case could execution be justified.

In the second type it has been argued that ANC combatants are entitled to the protection of the Geneva Protocol I of 1977.[49] Not surprisingly the court in Cape Town rejected the argument. International lawyers have also argued that the apartheid policy violates the UN Convention on the Protection and Punishment of Genocide, and that judicially ordered executions pertinent to that policy may constitute crimes against humanity for which judges may be personally liable under the Nuremburg principles.[50]

Other forms of oppressive conduct

The South African government employs or condones several forms of harassment of those whom it perceives as its opponents, in addition to the enforcement of the security laws and the powers available under the emergency regulations.

One related form is what was described to us as 'harassment by process'. It is common for prosecutions to be launched for which there is little or no evidence; whether or not a conviction is achieved, the accused may suffer deprivation of liberty and other serious damage over a long period of time. For example, we were informed by the Black Sash in Cape Town of a survey they had carried out of public violence and similar charges against young people in the area. Those charged are often refused bail or bail is set at a high figure which is a serious burden on the family or friends. There are long delays before the cases are brought to trial. Yet in 83 per cent of cases in the Cape Town and Boland area from January to October 1986, the charges were withdrawn or the accused were acquitted. Many of the accused thus were punished and had their lives disrupted by what can only have been the improper use of legal procedures.

Another striking illustration is the notorious 'Trojan Horse' case. The killing in September 1985 in the 'coloured' township of Athlone of three children by policemen concealed in boxes on what appeared to be a civilian truck was followed not by the arrest of the policemen but by the rounding up of a large number of local youngsters who were later charged with public violence. The purpose seems to have been to support the police explanation of the killings that they were in self-defence against a hail of stones thrown at the truck. Nearly a year later, however, when the public violence cases came to court, the prosecution failed to produce any evidence of any substance at all and the magistrate had no option but to throw out the cases without even calling on the defence to answer the charges.[51]

This case also illustrates the almost total failure of the government to discipline or punish its agents who commit the grossest abuses. At the time of writing the killers have not been prosecuted in spite of repeated demands by lawyers representing the families of the deceased, and the Attorney-General has even failed to authorize the families to bring their own prosecution.

Other examples of harassment by process are the treason trials of mainly United Democratic Front leaders at Pietermaritzburg and Delmas (the latter now transferred to Pretoria). Members of the mission have observed part of both trials. The Pietermaritzburg trial involved sixteen defendants accused of treason by advocating the armed overthrow of the state. Several of the accused were detained as early as September 1984 and the Attorney-General exercised his veto to prevent bail.[52] It was not until the middle of 1985 that bail was eventually granted following an application to a full bench of the Supreme Court in Natal.[53] Bail was then granted on conditions which prevented the defendants from engaging in political activity and from leaving the area of their residence. The trial finally collapsed in February 1986, and all defendants were acquitted—but meanwhile their liberty had been severely infringed for some eighteen months.

The position of most of the twenty-two defendants in the similar trial in the Transvaal has been even worse. They were refused bail altogether until after the trial started in early 1986, having been in custody awaiting trial for at least a year. Three defendants were discharged altogether after the conclusion of the prosecution case, and three other defendants are still without bail. The trial still continues and could last another year. During all this time the defendants, though convicted of no offence, are excluded from lawful political activity. The enormous advantage to the government in using (or rather abusing) the courts in this way is that they can hope to stifle international as well as domestic criticism by the plea of 'sub judice' and by relying on the past reputation of the judicial system for independence and impartiality.

These and other treason, terrorism and sedition trials illustrate not only a form of harassment involving the abuse of the trial process, but the government's particular hostility towards the UDF, the National Education Crisis Committee and—especially in recent months—the Congress of South African Trade Unions, notwithstanding the unchallenged legality of these organizations. Emergency detentions have been systematic against leading members of these organizations. Almost the whole national executive of the NECC have been detained (so we were informed by one member remaining at liberty). Many leading members of the UDF are in detention. Raymond Suttner, a senior lecturer in law at the University of Witwatersrand has been detained without charge since July 1986. Azhar Cachalia, National Treasurer of the UDF and also a lawyer has been detained and harassed in other ways. Murphy Morobe, National Publicity Secretary, and Mohammed Valli, another national official were detained only recently under the emergency regulations. Many trade union officials have been detained. Moses Mayekiso, General Secretary of the Metal and Allied Workers' Union, is detained and on trial for treason and sedition. COSATU has also been subject to harassment in the form of arson and bombing of its premises. It is impossible to prove that such harassment has been carried out by members of the security forces, but it is disturbing that no one has been arrested or charged with such serious offences.

In the last paragraph we noted that two lawyers were among those detained. While in those particular cases the government might argue that their status as lawyers was incidental and that their detention was based on other grounds, we came upon several cases in which lawyers were detained in circumstances which could only be interpreted as a deliberate interference with their professional duties. The most striking of these was the case of the advocate Anwar Albertus and the attorney Trevor de Bruyn, who were detained for several days after being arrested by the police at a magistrate's court in the Western Cape where they were seeking to interview clients immediately before their trial. Mr Albertus informed a member of the mission that he was seized by the police while telephoning the office of the Attorney-General in the magistrate's office. The case is the subject of a complaint to the Attorney-General of the Western Cape, but we have received no evidence of any disciplinary action against the police concerned. In another case, a Johannesburg attorney, Prakash Diar, was detained outside a court in the presence of his clients and held without charge for a month, after which he was released. We were also told of frequent minor instances of harassment of lawyers, for example by not informing them of the arrest or trial of their clients or by failure to inform them until it was too late for them to arrange representation. In another case we were shown a listening device found by a well-known defence lawyer in the wall of his office.

We have mentioned the 'Trojan Horse' case as an example of failure to discipline or prosecute members of the security forces who appear to have engaged in plainly illegal actions. We came upon many other examples. One of the most striking is the case of the massacre by security forces of about twenty persons taking part in a funeral procession at Langa on 21 March

1985, of whom seventeen were shot in the back. A more detailed account of this case will be found in Chapter 7.[54] In 1987 civil claims were settled by the government in favour of fifty-one persons injured in the same incident by payments totalling R.1.3 million. Liability was no longer contested. Nevertheless, no disciplinary action has been taken against the police officers responsible for the killing and injuries.

Similarly, the police officers responsible for assaulting Steve Biko, who died as a result of his injuries in 1977, far from having been punished, have all subsequently been promoted. So has one of the doctors, Dr Ivor Lang, who was found guilty of improper conduct in his treatment of Biko by the South African Medical and Dental Council. He is now Senior District Surgeon for Port Elizabeth and the surrounding areas.[55] As such he was responsible for the examination of those detainees whose condition in 1985 led Dr Wendy Orr to take legal action.[56] In many other cases following arrests, detentions and allegations of violence against the security forces, civil actions have been brought by the victims against the government, who have frequently accepted responsibility and offered compensation.

Vigilantes

The government has evidently found it convenient to enlist the aid wherever possible of black people to implement its strategy of repression in the townships. It has been able to do so by using its power to allocate jobs, housing and other resources (including money), by condoning or actively assisting violence or oppression by favoured black groups against those seen as dissidents (often by inflaming traditional suspicion or hostility) and by direct recruitment of black people into police forces.

The obvious targets for these protests were the community councillors— township residents who had accepted lucrative office under the new devolved and pseudo-democratic arrangements for township administration. They and their supporters were naturally helped by the government to defend themselves and to counter-attack. The pro-government black groups developed in different ways in different parts of the country and their one common characteristic is that consciously or unconsciously they are acting on behalf of the government.

In the Western Cape, vigilantes (there known as 'witdoeke' in reference to their white arm-bands) have been particularly active in the squatter camps of Crossroads. It has long been the aim of the government to remove the tens of thousands of black people occupying these camps, either to relocate them at Khayelitsha—a windy and dusty place far away from the white suburbs of Cape Town but far also from the prospect of employment—or to send them to the homelands of Transkei or Ciskei. But the lack of jobs in the homelands drives even more people to take their chance at Crossroads.

In May and June 1986 a series of squatter camps were demolished and their inhabitants rendered homeless:

In a period of less than four weeks, an estimated 70,000 squatters from Portland Cement, Nyanga Bush, Nyanga Extension, and nearby KTC became refugees in their own land as hundreds of 'witdoeke' with the uncontested support of members of the security forces declared war on these communities. Countless sworn affidavits from the residents of these areas, reporters, clergymen and other eye-witnesses, bear testimony to the fact that this was not spontaneous. From the evidence, it appears that the systematic destruction of these squatter camps took place in two separate, but related, operations which were carefully planned and executed with military precision.[57]

We have seen many of these affidavits and were able to chart the subsequent legal developments with the assistance of the Legal Resources Centre in Cape Town. The affidavits indicate that police vehicles were standing by while the attacks took place and that police officers were actively assisting the attackers. Lawyers from the LRC immediately applied to the court for and were granted on 26 May 1986 an interdict restraining the South African Police, the South African Defence Force and vigilante leaders from mounting further attacks. The judge rejected government arguments that an interdict would 'limit and seriously hamper the activities of the security forces . . . and could lead to the necessary withdrawal of all security forces' which would 'result in the collapse of law and order and a bloodbath between rival factions.'[58] Notwithstanding the interdict, however, on 9 June an even fiercer attack was launched, and this time again there was overwhelming evidence of the active participation of security forces on the side of the attacking vigilantes. When the LRC went to court again soon afterwards, the government offered no defence, claiming that the issue was now academic, and that the state could not afford to have many policemen tied up in court to the detriment of their other duties. The state was ordered to pay the LRC's legal costs. Subsequently, the LRC launched a large number of civil damages claims against the government and the police, and some of these are before the courts at the time of writing. This incidentally is another case where plainly illegal conduct by the police in flouting the court interdict has not led to any form of disciplinary action.

Vigilante activity has also been of major importance in Natal, where the vigilante role is filled by members of Inkatha, the Zulu-based organization led by Chief Gatsha Buthelezi, widely regarded as a 'moderate' black leader. The important difference between the *witdoeke* of the Western Cape and the Inkatha *impis* (military-style gangs) is that Chief Buthelezi is also the Chief Minister of the homeland of KwaZulu. Inkatha thus has direct control of government resources and KwaZulu has its own police force, which, though subordinate to the SAP, has recently increased its direct responsibility for policing its area.

We were supplied with much evidence of violent attacks by Inkatha *impis* on those believed to support the UDF and trade unions which are affiliates of COSATU. The pattern was often similar to the vigilante attacks in the Western Cape in that there was evidence of security forces standing by or even positively assisting the *impis*. A Durban attorney whose house was attacked and burned by an *impi* reported that a police vehicle was present throughout but no attempt was made by the police to restrain the attackers. We examined a house in which eight people were killed in January 1987; it was the home of a leading UDF activist. The killers, whose identity is widely suspected, have not been apprehended. We raised the question of Inkatha violence with Mr Rowley Arenstein, a lawyer who represents Chief Buthelezi and who met us on his behalf. He claimed that the violence was not initiated by Inkatha members but was largely the responsibility of UDF supporters. He said he could provide us with evidence through the Inkatha Institute but he did not do so. We approached the Inkatha Institute direct seeking evidence to contradict the overwhelming case that most violence is initiated by Inkatha supporters, but again none was forthcoming. We were also provided with research studies from the University of Natal of violence among black groups in Natal; these also placed the blame on Inkatha for a high proportion of the incidents.

We received information about vigilante activity in other areas which supports the general conclusion that vigilantes are part of the state's armoury against opposition to the apartheid system. We were impressed by the evidence of the situation in thirteen different regions of South Africa contained in 'Mabangalala: A Study of Right-Wing Vigilantes in South Africa' by Nicholas Haysom,[59] which confirms the consistent accounts of lawyers and community workers to whom we talked.

Notes

1. In *R* v. *Sisulu* 1953 3 SA 276 (A)), the definition was extended to cover an innocuous campaign by women who breached municipal bye-laws in the course of a campaign to change marraige laws. A. Mathews, 'The South African Judiciary and the Security System', 1 *SAJHR* p. 199 (November 1985).
2. *South African Defence and Aid Fund* v. *Minister of Justice* 1967 (1) S A263 (A).
3. A. Mathews, *Law, Order and Liberty in South Africa*, p. 59.
4. Don Foster, *Detention and Torture in South Africa*, 1987, p. 17.
5. J.A. Coetzee, *Industrial Relations in South Africa*, 1976.
6. Mathews, p. 184.
7. Mathews, ibid.
8. Foster, p. 22.
9. Mathews, p. 164.
10. Ibid., p. 166.
11. General Law Amendment Act 1963, S. 17.
12. Foster, p. 23.
13. *Loza* v. *Police Station Commander, Durbanville* 1964 2 SA 545 (A).
14. *The Jail Diary of Albie Sachs*, (London), 1967.
15. Mathews, p. 171.
16. J. Dugard, *Human Rights and the South African Legal Order*, Princeton, NJ, 1978, p. 119.
17. Foster, p. 29.
18. Quoted in Rabie Report, p. 5, para 3.2.
19. *The Contribution of English Law to South African Law*, Hamlyn Lectures, London, 1967, p. 100.
20. A. Mathews, *Freedom, State Security and the Rule of Law*, Cape Town and Johannesburg, 1986, p. xviii.

21. Ibid., p. 281.
22. J. Dugard, in Centre for Applied Legal Studies, University of Witwatersrand, *Report on the Rabie Report: An Examination of Security Legislation in South Africa*, March 1982, p. 6.
23. *Report on the Rabie Report*. See previous note.
24. Ibid., p. 95.
25. Foster, pp. 217–8, lists 81 up to the end of 1985.
26. s. 54 (1).
27. *Weekly Mail*. Major trials are now in progress of residents of Alexandra township, including Moses Nayekiso. See p. 83.
28. See Chapter 11.
29. See Chapter 7.
30. *Nkondo & Gumede* v. *Minister of Law and Order* 1986 2 SA 756 (A).
31. Mathews, *Freedom*, p. 73.
32. See p. 76.
33. The 'Sharpeville Six', condemned to death for murder in 1985, were convicted largely on such evidence. In December 1987, the Appellate Division rejected their appeals.
34. *S* v. *Buthelezi and others*. Unreported.
35. Lawyers for Human Rights Bulletin No. 2, June 1983, cited by Foster, p. 34. One of the ironies of the Biko case is that the doctor and police officer involved in his death were subsequently promoted. *Weekly Mail*, 11–17 September 1987 p. 15.
36. 3 *SAJHR* p. 126 (March 1987).
37. Foster supra, p. 36.
38. Lawyers for Human Rights Bulletin No. 2.
39. *Government Gazette*, No. 8467 of 3 December 1982.
40. Professor Mathews argues that they could be enforced but no attempt at enforcement has apparently yet been made. See A. Mathews, *Freedom, State Security and the Rule of Law*, p. 86.
41. Foster, p. 38.
42. Ibid.
43. *Weekly Mail*, 28 August/3 September 1987, p. 4.
44. The full list appears to be: murder, treason, rape, robbery and housebreaking with aggravated circumstances, sabotage, receiving training that could further the objects of communism etc., kidnapping and child stealing, terrorism. See Dugard, *Human Rights*, pp. 124–30.
45. R. Omond, *The Apartheid Handbook*, Harmondsworth, 1985, p. 144, and *SAJHR*, 2, 1986), 3: 349.
46. Omond, p. 148.
47. Quoted in Foster, p. 44.
48. See 'Save the Sharpeville Six', Southern Africa – The Imprisoned Society, London, April 1986 and February 1988.
49. Roberts & Guelff, Documents on the Laws of War, 1982, p. 387.
50 Kader Asmal, Rights of Children under International Law, Harare Conference, September 1987.
51. Information supplied by a defence lawyer.
52. Under S.30 of the Internal Security Act 1982.
53. *S* v. *Baleka* 1986 1 SA 361 (T).
54. Report of the Commission Appointed to Inquire into the Incident which Occurred on 21 March 1985 at Uitenhage, RP74/1985.
55. *Weekly Mail*, 11/17 September 1987, p. 15.
56. See p. 79.
57. J. Cole, *Crossroads*, Johannesburg 1987, p. 131.
58. Ibid., p. 141.
59. Centre for Applied Legal Studies, Occasional Paper No. 10, 1986.

11   The State of Emergency

As if the permanent powers enshrined in the Internal Security Act and the common law were not enough to give the government all the weapons it could possibly need to suppress dissent, the Public Safety Act 1953 empowers the State President to declare by proclamation that a 'state of emergency' exists in any part of the Republic. A proclamation under this Act is not subject to any legal challenge. Having proclaimed that an emergency exists the State President is automatically empowered to issue by proclamation such regulations as appear to him to be necessary or expedient for maintaining public safety or public order and terminating the emergency or dealing with circumstances pertaining to the emergency. The Act authorizes him to make different regulations for different areas and classes of person, and, importantly, to delegate authority to make orders, rules and bye-laws.

Before 1985 these powers had been used only once, after Sharpeville in 1960. On 21 July 1985 they were used to proclaim a state of emergency in certain areas. It was lifted on 7 March 1986, but a new state of emergency covering the whole country was proclaimed on 12 June 1986. Under the statute a state of emergency expires automatically after twelve months if not previously withdrawn. On 11 June 1987 a further state of emergency was proclaimed to take effect immediately on the expiry of the previous one.[1]

It may be wondered, nevertheless, why the government should take the trouble to assume these extra powers, especially as the open acknowledgement of a situation of national danger could be expected to produce more alarm than reassurance. As Professor Anthony Mathews of the University of Natal has remarked:

'Ordinary' and permanent legislation has already brought about ninety per cent destruction of the rule of law and put the country into a permanent state of emergency. When, on top of this, an emergency is declared under the Public Safety Act of 1953, the tattered remnants of the rule of law are stripped away for the duration of the crisis.[2]

It is nevertheless true that the extra powers which the government has been able to give itself under the state of emergency have added enormously to its ability to mount an all-out assault on those who oppose its policies. Most importantly, it has been able to use those powers to bypass both Parliament and the courts.

The government of course controls Parliament and can win any vote. Nevertheless, unpopular measures which violate human rights take time to get through the Parliamentary process and their passage is likely to be accompanied by vociferous opposition and Press publicity under the protection of parliamentary privilege.

Bypassing the courts is an even more valuable benefit for the government. Already the security legislation goes far to exclude judicial intervention, but the emergency regulations go further still, and the courts have upheld regulations which exclude even the principles of natural justice.[3] But even if the judges do 'interfere', the government has the enormous advantage that a loophole found in the regulations by an astute judge can quickly be blocked (even the same day[4]) whereas a loophole in legislation has to stay open until the whole legislative process can be gone through again.

Nevertheless, it is plain that the government in early 1986 was anxious to bring an end to the partial state of emergency then in force, intending to secure the same powers by means which were less provocative and which were at the same time free of some of the mildly irksome concessions to parliamentary control which the 1953 Act imposed, such as the need to table regulations in Parliament within fourteen days of their promulgation.

The Public Safety Amendment Act 1986 renders superfluous the need for a state of emergency to be proclaimed by the State President by authorizing the Minister of Law and Order to declare any area (or indeed the whole country) to be an 'unrest area' and in those areas apply such regulations as he deems necessary. This power is broadly similar to that of the State President under the 1953 Act but can obviously be exercised with less publicity. The Minister's declaration lapses after three months unless renewed, but it may be renewed an indefinite number of times with the consent of the State President. Second, the Internal Security Amendment Act authorized a new form of preventive detention for up to 180 days.

The government met an obstacle when it introduced the bills to bring about these amendments: the 'coloured' and 'Indian' houses of Parliament were not willing to pass them. Accordingly, the State President had to summon his President's Council to put these would-be legislators back in their place, giving a practical demonstration of a fact which some of them had previously been reluctant to acknowledge, that their votes would only be counted if the government allowed them to be.[5]

The time needed to complete this process was too long for the government to wait to regain the emergency powers which it wanted, and the State President therefore proclaimed the second national state of emergency on 12 June 1986. The regulations issued by the State President at the same time were wider in scope than those issued under the previous emergency.[6] They included a power of arrest and detention by the most junior soldier or policeman for up to fourteen days, infinitely extendable by the Minister of Law and Order. Section 3 (1) of the regulations said:

a member of a Force may, without warrant of arrest, arrest or cause to be arrested any person whose detention is, in the opinion of such member, necessary for the maintenance of public order or the safety of the public or the person himself, or for the termination of the state of emergency and may, under a written order signed by any member of a force, detain, or cause to be detained, any such person in custody in a prison.

The regulations prohibited the making, possession or dissemination of subversive statements—defining 'subversive' so widely as to cover virtually any criticism of the status quo; they gave power to outlaw and seize any publication deemed by the State President to threaten the interests of the state; they prohibited the publication of any information about police activities in relation to any 'unrest' incident; they granted an indemnity to members of the security forces against criminal or civil liability arising out of unlawful acts (provided only that they could not be proved to have been done in bad faith!); and they purported to oust the jurisdiction of the courts to adjudicate on the lawfulness of the regulations or anything done in reliance on them.

A bewildering profusion of local regulations were issued by divisional police commissioners under delegated authority including:

> detailed restrictions on funerals;
> banning possession of T-shirts and emblems of forty-seven named organizations in the Eastern Cape;
> imposing curfews;
> prohibiting pupils from being outside their classrooms in school hours;
> prohibiting the dissemination of statements made by 119 named organizations in the Western Cape;
> prohibition of gatherings convened by named organizations in Witwatersrand;
> prohibition of loitering anywhere in Kwandebele.[7]

Breach of any of these regulations is a criminal offence punishable by a fine not exceeding R.20,000 or imprisonment for a period not exceeding ten years. Few prosecutions are known to have been brought for breach of emergency regulations because detention without charge for an indefinite period is simpler—and it avoids the need to prove a case against the accused before a court. Plainly, a major advantage of the emergency regulations is that they can provide virtually unlimited legal authority (or the pretence of legal authority) to the security forces while at the same time removing their activities from public scrutiny.

As previously stated, the state of emergency declared on 12 June 1986 lapsed on 11 June 1987, but on that day the State President proclaimed a new state of emergency accompanied by fresh regulations replacing those made under the previous emergency. Surprisingly, the government chose not to take advantage of the powers in the Public Safety Amendment Act 1986 which were now available having gone through all constitutional stages.[8] Perhaps they thought that international opinion had now got so used to the state of emergency that any further public outcry would be short-lived, or as they had shown in other ways, they no longer cared what others thought of their contempt for human rights.

The new regulations were essentially the same as the previous ones. Both impose the same three forms of control: restrictions on access to news and control over publications; the extension of delegated powers to enable the police to issue their own regulations of the kinds exemplified above; and powers of arrest and detention which are wider even than those already contained in the Internal Security Act. One significant extension in the new regulations is that detention may now be ordered by any member of the security forces (even the rawest recruit) for up to thirty days on the merest suspicion. Under the 1986 regulations the limit was fourteen days. This period remains, of course, infinitely extendable on the authority of the Minister, and there are many detainees who have remained incarcerated without charge or trial since the beginning of the 1986 emergency.[9]

Although, as has been pointed out, the State President has sought to exclude judicial intervention by stating in the regulations that the jurisdiction of the courts is ousted, many challenges have been brought before the Supreme Court and the Appellate Division during the emergencies, and some of them have been successful, at least initially. The ouster clause itself was given short shrift by judges who held that an ouster clause could not exclude the responsibility of a judge to determine the meaning and validity of regulations.[10]

Media censorship

In relation to the media and the publication of information about 'unrest', there has been a series of challenges to the regulations of 12 June 1986 and to the subsequent regulations of 11 December 1986, which imposed further restrictions.

The 12 June regulations prohibited, in the absence of permission from the Commissioner of Police or other authorized officer, the making or broadcasting of any film or other representation of any public disturbance or of any person present on such an occasion. These regulations also prohibited the making, possession or dissemination of any 'subversive statement'. The definition of 'subversive statement' was quite extraordinarily wide, covering many statements which advocated or encouraged actions which were entirely lawful. For example, it included any statement likely to have the effect of inciting any member of the public to take part in any protest procession (regardless, apparently, of the object of the protest), or which could incite a person to oppose the government or any Minister or official in connection with any measure relating to the maintenance of public order or in connection with the administration of justice.

The 11 December 1986 regulations expanded the definition of 'subversive statement' even more widely, to cover a statement inciting the public to take part in any boycott or unrest or civil disobedience or to take part in any illegal strike or to take part in any informal administrative or judicial structure or procedures. The latter issue had become increasingly disturbing to the government as black people sought more and more to establish their own forms of self-government within the townships in the absence of acceptable forms of official administration and growing disillusionment with the judicial system.[11]

The 12 June 1986 definition had already been successfully challenged.[12] Several parts of the definition had been struck out for uncertainty, and the prohibition on the mere possession of such statements had been set aside. The 11 December regulations restored the substance of the original definition as well as expanding it. They laid down a comprehensive code of restrictions prohibiting the media from reporting events considered by the government to affect the security of the state.

In addition to making and publishing 'subversive statements', it was now illegal to report virtually any form of activity by the security forces—or indeed any matter connected with any form of public protest. The reporting of any reference to alternative structures was likewise prohibited. Even the presence of journalists at scenes of unrest, restricted gatherings or security action was banned—and likewise the taking of pictures of such events. Wide powers were given to the security forces to seize any material believed to contravene the regulations, and for this purpose wide powers of entry and search were also provided.

This account of the regulations as they affect the media is by no means complete, but it gives the flavour of the scope and complexity of the rules. The government were evidently determined to forestall all possible legal challenges and limitations on the powers of the Executive while at the same time, characteristically, maintaining the formal framework of legality.

The State President had already made clear to the Press early in December 1986 that he was dissatisfied with the way in which they were reporting unrest. He sought to persuade the Newspaper Press Union to agree voluntary restraints on reporting such matters. The Cape Town branch of the Southern African Society of Journalists unanimously passed a resolution expressing concern over the attempts, as they saw them, by P.W. Botha to co-opt newspaper management into siding with him against those who opposed apartheid. It was not altogether surprising therefore that when the 75th anniversary of the ANC was marked by the publication in several newspapers of an advertisement calling for its unbanning and the release of Nelson Mandela, the police seized copies of the newspapers, and the Commissioner of Police issued an order under the emergency regulations prohibiting the publication of any advertisements promoting the public image of a banned organization or justifying its activities.[13]

The Argus newspaper group brought an application challenging both the order of the Commissioner and a notice directed by him to the group purporting to outlaw support for unlawful organizations. The Supreme Court declared the order invalid because the Commissioner had no power—as the regulations were worded—to make orders with effect over the whole country; he could make orders for particular areas only. The notice to the applicants was also declared void for uncertainty.[14]

At midnight on the day the judgment was delivered[15] the Commissioner issued a fresh notice and a fresh order revoking the ones questioned in the Argus case in terms which avoided the court's objections. On the same night the State President issued a proclamation amending the 11 December media regulations. The amendment empowers the Commissioner of Police to prohibit nationally or locally the issue of any news, comment or advertisement which he considers a threat to public safety. Thus the government responds to defeat in the courts: it simply changes the law, widening its powers yet further—in this instance, as the *South African Journal of Human Rights* commented[16]—making the Police Commissioner the country's chief censor.

The 11 December regulations were themselves in turn challenged in the courts in actions brought by the UDF and the Release Mandela Campaign. These cases make clear that whatever changes and twists the government may make by amendments to the regulations, they remain subject to the power of the courts to determine their validity. Again, many regulations were set aside and suddenly journalists were again at liberty to report unrest incidents. This at any rate was true in Natal. The government claimed the decision was not effective in any other province pending an appeal to the Appellate Division, which remains to be determined.[17]

Nor was the government deterred by the prospect of losing the appeal from repeating the same invalidated regulations in those published on 11 June 1987. Their optimism about the attitude of the Appellate Division is understandable in the light of past experience.[18]

Delegation of powers

The South African courts have accepted that the powers given to the State President to promulgate such regulations as appear to him to be necessary or expedient for the purposes identified in the Public Safety Act include the power to delegate power to issue orders which may themselves have the character of regulations. The June 1987 regulations authorize the Commissioner of Police to issue orders for the purposes permitted by the Public Safety Act, including orders which may prohibit any person from being anywhere except his own home; orders which may prohibit any gathering or impose any conditions on any gathering; and orders which may prohibit any publication, television, film or sound recording containing any news comment or advertisement on or in connection with any matter specified in the order to be published.

As was demonstrated in the Argus Newspapers case,[19] the order is invalid if beyond the powers which have been delegated, but the breadth of these delegated powers leaves little scope for challenge. It is also important to note that the powers given to the Commissioner of Police are not restricted to the holder of that office at the national level. The regulations allow the powers granted to the Commissioner to be exercised by divisional police commissioners in relation to their division. But there cannot be further sub-delegation of the power to make orders save where specific powers have been conferred directly on more junior officers.[20]

Nevertheless, the grant of power to make orders to divisional police commissioners accounts for the profusion of detailed orders of which examples have already been given. Within a week of the issue of the 1987 regulations, separate sets of restrictions on funerals had been ordered in fifty-four townships and in other cases on the funerals of specified individuals.[20]

Detention

In terms of personal liberty, the powers of arrest and detention are the most drastic of those given to the security forces by the emergency regulations. Those given under the regulations of 11 June 1987 are substantially similar to those of the previous June. The regulations of 11 December 1986 do not affect arrest and detention, and although there have been some successful court challenges in the intervening year, the government has felt no need to introduce substantial variations save for the extension of the initial detention period to a maximum of thirty days.

The number of emergency detainees under the 1986 emergency is believed to be about 25,000, of whom it is said that about 40 per cent were children under the age of 18.[21] Many of these were held throughout the whole one-year period, and many have been redetained under the 1987 emergency. While in some instances reasons have been given for the detention, it must be stressed that even where, in the minority of cases, reasons have been disclosed or hinted at, the law gives no opportunity for those reasons to be challenged in any form of independent hearing. There is no firm basis, therefore, upon which it can be said that even a single case of emergency detention is justified by the conduct of the detainees.

There are five elements in the arrest and detention process at which the possibility of legal challenge arises:

(1) When the arrest takes place.
(2) When a person is detained.
(3) At the end of the initial detention period (if the detainee has not by then been released).
(4) After the Minister has exercised his discretion to extend the initial detention period.
(5) In relation to treatment while in detention.

As to (1), the arresting officer is required, as a precondition of exercising his power of arrest, to form the opinion that the detention of the arrestee is necessary for the safety of the public or for the safety of that person himself, or for the termination of the state of emergency. Unlike Section 29 of the Internal Security Act,[22] where the detaining officer must have 'reason to believe' (held to be an objective requirement subject to judicial review[23]) the courts have accepted the notion that they cannot interfere unless they can conclude that the officer's opinion was not honestly or genuinely formed.

Some judges have been prepared to reach the latter conclusion. In *Dempsey* v. *Minister of Law and Order*,[24] Marais J. ordered the release of a nun, Sister Clare Harkin. Following an application to the court, the police filed evidence which made it clear that she had merely intervened to protest when another person was, in her view, wrongly arrested. The judge found that a policeman who regarded detention in these circumstances as necessary for any purpose covered by the regulations could not have seriously applied his mind to the question at all. But in other cases where the arrest was equally arbitrary and absurd, the court declined to interfere with the decision. The case of Makhajane, referred to elsewhere in this report,[25] is a blatant example. There have been other cases in which courts have added other qualifications to the inviolability of the policeman's opinion: his discretion must be exercised in a manner which excludes irrelevant considerations and takes account of all relevant considerations. In practice, such a test is not seriously applied by many South African judges, and the prospect of securing release of a detainee by persuading a judge to go behind the officer's decision is so remote that few detentions have in fact been challenged on this ground, even where no plausible basis for detention could conceivably be advanced.[26] Nor does it appear that the judges will even require the security forces to comply with the normal formalities of a valid arrest, such as the obligation to give a reason for the arrest.[27]

As to (2), once the detention has been validly carried into effect, it remains valid only so long as the necessity for it continues—so the detaining officer must, in theory at least, maintain continuous supervision over the case of each detainee to ensure that, as soon as the detention ceases to be necessary, the detainee is released.

However, the implementation of this principle is rendered virtually impossible by the extreme difficulty of obtaining access to a detainee or any information about the reasons for his arrest or the conditions of his detention. Regulation 3 (8) of the 1987 detention regulations provides that no one other than the Minister of Law and Order or other state official is to be entitled to access to any detainee (except with the consent of the Minister) or 'to any official information relating to any such person, or to any other information of whatever nature obtained from or in respect of such person'. On the face of it, this prevents a detainee even from obtaining legal advice as to the validity of his detention without the Minister's approval (the Minister having a contrary interest to that of the detainee). In *Momoniat* v. *Minister of Law and Order* and *Bill* v. *Minister of Law and Order*, the refusal of the Minister to allow legal consultations was held by two different Supreme Court judges to be unlawful on the ground that the legislature could not have intended in the Public Safety Act to have authorized the exclusion of so fundamental a right. In effect, the court asserted a power to declare subordinate legislation to be *ultra vires* if it seemed to the court to be wholly unreasonable. In doing so, they followed the well-established English precedent of *Kruse* v. *Johnson*, which defined the jurisdication of the court to review local government bye-laws.[28]

Some of the judges have shown great courage and independence of mind in striking down regulations. Goldstone J. was the judge in the Momoniat case. In *Metal and Allied Workers Union* v. *State President*,[29] Didcott J. struck down regulations on two other principles: that subordinate legislation is void if it is vague and uncertain, and if it goes beyond the objectives for which the statute (in this case the Public Safety Act) authorizes regulations to be made.

Stage (3) also had to be considered in the Momoniat case. The Minister had ordered the period of detention to be extended beyond the fourteen-day initial period. The regulations require such an extension to be authorized by a notice in writing addressed to the head of the prison, but the Minister is not required to give notice to the detainee or to give him an opportunity to make oral representations. This requirement in itself was an addition to the regulation as it had appeared in the 1985 version. In *Nkwinti* v. *Commissioner of Police*,[30] Kannemeyer J. held that further detention beyond the initial fourteen days was invalid because the detainee had not been given the opportunity of being heard. The change in the 1986 regulation stopped up this loophole. As it happens, Kannemeyer J. had in Nkwinti expressed the view that the State President had no power to exclude a hearing by regulation, but this did not deter the State President asserting this in the new regulation. As it turned out, his confidence that his power would be upheld was not misplaced.

In Momoniat, interpreting the 1986 version of the regulation, the court was prepared to hold that the exclusion of a legal adviser was *ultra vires*, but it was not prepared to accept the Kannemeyer view that the refusal of a hearing (in breach of the *audi alteram partem* principle of natural justice) prior to a decision to extend the period of detention was beyond the State President's powers. The judge did say, however, that it would be beyond them to exclude a right to make representations *after* a decision to extend the period. In *Fani* v. *Minister of Law and Order*, the 1986 amendment was even held by a different judge to exclude the right to make representations in writing.[31]

If it is 'wholly unreasonable' for the legislature to grant delegated powers which violate natural justice, as is the most obvious rationale of the part of the Momoniat decision which upheld the right to legal advice, it is difficult to see why the refusal of a hearing—let alone the refusal to accept written representations, as in the Fanie case—should not be equally unacceptable.

The Appellate Division has now removed this anomaly but, regrettably, by extending the denial of fundamental rights. After Momoniat, the same issue arose in the case of Abdullah Omar, a leading advocate in Cape Town who has also been a prominent supporter of the United Democratic Front. This time the refusal to allow him access to an attorney was upheld by the Supreme Court, as was the refusal to allow him an oral hearing before the Minister decided whether or not to extend the period of his detention.

The *Omar* and *Fani* cases, together with the case of *Bill* in which similar issues arose, were considered together by the Appellate Division.[32] Chief Justice Rabie and the majority of his colleagues had little difficulty in deciding that there was no basis for assuming that Parliament and the State President intended that the Public Safety Act and the regulations made under it should be subject to any implied preservation of natural justice or fundamental human rights. They ruled that the Minister was not required to give reasons for detentions; that detainees were not entitled to make representations to the Minister; that if representations were in fact made the Minister was under no obligation to consider them; and that detainees had no right of access to a legal representative. The Appellate Division thus lived up to its 'positivist' tradition, declining the opportunity to mitigate the usurpation of arbitrary power by the Executive. These decisions have, in the view of many lawyers, closed the door to effective challenges to the emergency regulations.

As to (4), it has already been pointed out that some lower courts before the decision of the Appellate Division just described accepted that a detainee would have a right to make representations to the Minister *after* he had extended the detention period. It is not clear whether any judge thought a detainee would be entitled to an oral hearing; certainly we have been told of none that has taken place. In those cases in which a challenge has been made to continued detention in the courts, it has faced the refusal of the court generally to go behind the subjective opinion of the detaining officer.

As to (5), in keeping with the intense legalism of the South African government, detention conditions and arrangements are themselves governed by detailed regulations which are likewise issued under the authority of the emergency regulations promulgated by the State President. The Minister of Justice proclaimed new rules for the conditions of detention of emergency detainees on 11 June 1987, the day on which the current emergency was declared. These were almost identical to the two sets of rules under the previous two emergencies. These rules compare unfavourably with the United Nations Standard Minimum Rules for the Treatment of Prisoners. In particular, provisions for internal discipline and punishment exclude the right to legal representation. They also compare unfavourably with the rules applicable to awaiting trial prisoners.[33]

On 26 June 1987 the Minister's rules were superseded by regulations promulgated by the State President which purported to bring the position of emergency detainees into line with awaiting trial prisoners. This appears to be not entirely the case, in that, for example, the compulsory exercise period is only half an hour for emergency detainees, as against one hour for awaiting-trial prisoners. Furthermore, there are the following special provisions for emergency detainees:

(1) They must be segregated from other prisoners.
(2) Study privileges cannot be granted without the agreement of the Commissioner of Police.
(3) The detainee may not obtain newspapers, foodstuffs and other items from outside the prison.
(4) Detainees may not receive visits from any person, and no information can be obtained about them save under the authority of the Minister. This is the same provision which the courts have held removes the right of access to legal advisers.

This imperfect step towards aligning the position of emergency detainees with that of prisoners awaiting trial indicates a recognition that emergency detention may in practice be long-term imprisonment. Many detainees (though we do not have precise figures) have been held since June 1986. Among these a high proportion are leading members of the UDF. As more UDF leaders have been detained only recently (e.g. the arrests of Murphy Morobe and Mohammed Valli in July 1987) there seems little prospect that leaders held for longer periods will soon be released.

The detention rules provide for regular inspection visits by magistrates and medical officers, and judges of the Supreme Court have an acknowledged right to enter prisons at any time. We have been told by former emergency detainees that these visits are often perfunctory in the extreme and provide no effective restraint on the persistent abuses, often amounting to torture of which we heard complaints from several first-hand as well as secondary sources. We have also seen much convincing medical evidence. Moreover, two members of the mission were eye-witnesses of scars and injuries which appeared compatible only with torture.[34]

At a recent seminar on detainees' rights attended by human rights attorneys from all parts of South Africa and Namibia, it was agreed that a number of proposals should be made for the improvement of conditions for detainees, including the following:

(1) District surgeons should be reported to their professional bodies if they failed to carry out their professional duty to attend and care for detainees.
(2) Detainees have the right to be released in good health and ill-health in detention should be a ground for release.
(3) Diet should be improved to an adequate level and discrepancies between different categories of prisoners (e.g. on racial grounds) should be eliminated.
(4) Solitary confinement should not be permitted except as a punishment for an offence properly charged and investigated.
(5) Legal visits should be permitted as of right and should be conducted out of the hearing of a warder.[35]

We entirely endorse these proposals to mitigate the hardship of detention while it continues. At the same time, of course, we stress our opposition in principle to the whole system of detention without charge or trial as practised in South Africa.

In the now celebrated case of Dr Wendy Orr, a young doctor employed in the Prison Medical Service at Port Elizabeth, her evidence and affidavits of other doctors, former detainees and members of their families led to the Supreme Court being satisfied *prima facie* that torture had taken place on a large scale at the prisons visited by her, and in consequence the court granted an interdict against the government and the prison authorities restraining such conduct. Similar interdicts have been granted in other cases. Indeed, according to Professor Mathews 'they are becoming almost commonplace'.[36]

Unfortunately, there is little reason for confidence that the wide public exposure of brutality and torture towards detainees, including young children—or even the intervention of the courts—has had any noticeable effect on the government's repressive policies or on the conduct of its forces.

Finally, it should be mentioned that the State President also made regulations on 11 June 1987 under his emergency powers governing education. These empower the Director-General for Education and Training to issue orders (without prior notice and without hearing any person) to exercise dictatorial powers over the school system, including the exclusion of any pupil or any other person from any school premises or from participation in any school activities for any period of time, control over school syllabuses, prohibition of any particular form of clothing or any object bearing a specified slogan or emblem, 'regulating or controlling the movement or activities of pupils on any school or (school) hostel premises—and making it an offence punishable by up to two years' imprisonment to disobey any such order. We comment further on government control of the education system elsewhere in this report (see Ch. 5).

Notes

1. See *Weekly Mail*, June 12–18, 1987.
2. A. Mathews, *Freedom, State Security and the Rule of Law*, Cape Town and Johannesburg, 1986, p. 265.
3. E.g. *Omar* v. *Minister of Law and Order* and *Cameron-Bill* v. *Minister of Law and Order*, 1987 (3) SA 859 (A).
4. 3 *SAJHR*, p. 131 (March 1987).
5. See p. 128.
6. 3 *SAJHR*, p. 269 (July 1987).
7. 2 *SAJHR* p. 253 (July 1986).
8. Mathews, p. 214. An unsuccessful attempt has been made to persuade the courts to declare the new emergency invalid on the ground that it was introduced while the old one was still in force.
9. Detainees Parents Support Committee, Report for the year 1986.
10. *Momoniat & Naidoo* v. *Minister of Law and Order* 1986 2 SA 264 (W).
11. *Leadership* magazine, January 1987.
12. *Metal & Allied Workers Union* v. *State President* 1986 4 SA 385 (D).
13. 3 *SAJHR*, p. 131 (March 1987).
14. Ibid.
15. Ibid.
16. Ibid.
17. 3 *SAJHR*, p. 270 (July 1987).
18. E.g. in the cases cited in Note 3 above.
19. See Note 13 above.
20. *Natal Newspapers (Pty) Ltd* v. *State President* (4th September 1986).
20. A. 3 *SAJHR*, p. 294 (July 1987).
21. DPSC report. See note 9 and p. 101.
22. See p. 74.
23. *Hurley* v. *Minister of Law and Order* 1985 4 SA 709 (D).

24. 9 July 1986 (unreported).
25. See p. 106.
26. Ibid.
27. Mathews, p. 201.
28. [1898] 2 QB 91.
29. See Note 12 above.
30. 1986 2 SA 421 (E).
31. See note 3.
32. Ibid.
33. Paper by Nicholas Haysom prepared for international conference on 'Children, Repression, and the Law in Apartheid South Africa' (Harare, September 1987).
34. See p. 135.
35. Haysom, ibid.
36. Mathews, p. 274.

12 Children

South African legislation provides for two separate systems for the protection of children. The welfare system, which is operated through the Children's Courts, is intended to provide for the general welfare and protection of children in South Africa. The Children's Act 1960,[1] and the Child Care Act 1983[2] lay a duty of care and support on the persons who have custody of a child. The Children's Court may conduct an inquiry to determine whether or not a child is in need of care, and if it is, can order that child to be placed in care. One expert on South Africa's welfare system has said that there is 'blatant racism' practised in the field of child care, and that white children have more institutions, better facilities, better staff and better conditions than their black counterparts.[3]

The second system is the criminal justice system for juveniles, which is provided for in the Criminal Procedure Act 1977[4] and which is operated through the Juvenile Courts. The Security Legislation is also applicable to children, but they are not granted any special protection under it.[5]

Under South African common law, children under the age of 7 are deemed to be *doli incapax* and are held not to be capable of acquiring the criminal intent necessary for the commission of a crime, and are therefore deemed not to be responsible for criminal offences. Children between 7 and 14 years of age are presumed to be *doli incapax*, but this presumption is rebuttable, the onus being on the prosecution to show that the accused was capable of forming the necessary intent. In *S* v. *Dyk*[6] the Supreme Court said that when considering whether or not a child is *doli incapax*, the crucial test to be considered by the court is the state of mind and general appreciation of the child at the time the offence is committed. In this case, the court doubted that an 11-year-old child had, in fact, appreciated the wrongfulness of his participation in a crime for which the magistrate had found him guilty. Therefore, when a child under 14 is detained by the security forces, he is denied the benefit of the presumption which he would have if charged with a criminal offence.

Children in detention in South Africa

The number of persons detained under the emergency regulations since 12 June 1986 is believed to be in the region of 25,000, and it is estimated that about 40 per cent of these were children under the age of 18.[7] The Detainees' Parents Support Committee (DPSC) has recently estimated that 10,000 children under the age of 18 have been detained, of whom 8,500 are under 17.

However, it is not possible to calculate the exact number of detainees with any accuracy. The government is obliged to disclose the number of detainees at the beginning of each session of Parliament. Up to 12 February 1987, the government has released the names of 13,194 persons detained since the start of the present emergency.[8] But these figures do not include those who, at the time when each set of figures was released, had been detained for less than thirty days. Furthermore, they do not include those who were detained under the Internal Security Act or who were held in custody awaiting trial or who were serving prison sentences following conviction. The government's figures have been found to be incomplete. We saw a letter from the Minister of Law and Order denying the detention of a named individual, yet a letter from the local police of the previous day acknowledged that he was detained by them. There was also confusion and uncertainty over the identity of detainees listed by the government. The names were often misspelt and no information other than the name of the detainee is disclosed. Many families have extreme difficulties in tracing children who may have been detained, and it can take a considerable time to determine whether or not a child has been detained and the place of detention.

The Detainees' Parents Support Committee's Johannesburg office recently published statistics relating to the detention of children in the district which they cover up to 5 February 1987. They record 885 children under 18 who have been detained since the start of the emergency. In Southern Transvaal, 537 children aged 17 and under remain in detention. Of those detained in this area, only three are known to have been charged with any criminal offence. Among children who have been detained, there are several aged 10, 11 and 12. At least four 12-year-olds, who are identified in the DPSC Report, have remained in detention since the start of the emergency and are still detained.

The number of children who have been held in police cells awaiting trial is much larger. The Minister of Law and Order told Parliament that in 1986 58,962 children aged 17 or under had been so detained. Many of these may have been subsequently released on bail and either acquitted or given non-custodial sentences. On 15 October 1986, the Minister of Justice said that 2,677 children under the age of 17 were being detained in prison, of whom 254 were aged 15 or under. These figures do not include 2,280 small children (of whom 1,880 are black) who were staying in prison during 1986 with their imprisoned mothers.

In a survey conducted on 22 May 1984, it was found that there were fifty-seven sentenced juveniles between the ages of 15 and 17, and 142 unsentenced juveniles between the ages of 11 and 17, in Pollsmoor Prison in Cape Town, together with nineteen children under 4 years of age, five of whom were under three months old, who were imprisoned with their mothers.[9]

Assaults and abuse of children

Black children hold a special position in the political struggle which is taking place in South Africa, which results in their prominence among the detainees.

Children are often at the forefront of resistance to apartheid in South Africa and are seen by the government as being the 'cutting edge' of community action. What has been described as 'the war against children'[10] stems from their vigorous resistance to discrimination in the segregated school system. The disturbances which took place in Soweto in 1976, ruthlessly quelled by the police, who took many lives, arose from the refusal of pupils to accept an inferior curriculum imposed by the government. Because the segregated educational system is a corner-stone of apartheid, the movement to change the structure of education and place control of schools in the hands of the community is seen as an attack on the whole political system. The government feels that if the community is allowed to gain control of the schools that it will not stop there, and that it will demand control of all political institutions.

Children have therefore been a particular target of violent oppression by the security forces, and they are treated as if they were adults. The security forces patrol the townships in armoured vehicles, which is provocative and solicits stone-throwing from the children, who are extremely frustrated and are unable to express their opposition in any other way. The response of the security forces is frequently excessive and violent. The initial response is usually with so-called 'non-lethal' weapons, such as rubber bullets, tear-gas or bird-shot. Even these weapons have caused injury or death. In the worst cases, shotguns and rifles are used. This was so at the Langa massacre of 21 March 1985, when twenty people were killed by the police, nineteen of whom were shot in the back or side, and 13 of whom were between 11 and 17 years old.[11]

Following what the police call an 'unrest' incident or a school boycott, there are frequently arrests, sometimes of very large numbers. In one incident on 12 September 1985, the police arrested 745 members of the Hlengiwe High School in Soweto, and detained them for a day and a night at Johannesburg's Diepkloof Prison, before releasing them without charge, following an application to the Supreme Court for their release.[12]

Physical abuse and torture of children is widespread in South Africa. Assaults on children tend to be at two levels. First, children are assaulted at the hands of the police, who try to extract information, at the time of arrest and afterwards at the police stations. The DPSC state that assaults on children at this level tend to be for three reasons:

(1) to elicit a confession from the child;
(2) to obtain information on other children;
(3) to strike fear and terror into the children.[13]

Second, there is a great deal of abuse of children in prison. We have been told of a huge increase in the use of electric shocks and tear-gas. The Minister of Law and Order has even acknowledged in Parliament that twenty incidents of tear-gassing had taken place in prisons in South Africa in 1986. Even the existence of electric shock machines in police vehicles has been established.

The assaults on, and torture of, children have been vividly documented in four recent reports on the plight of children in South Africa,[14] and in vast numbers of affidavits which are used to ground applications to the Supreme Court for the release of children. These reports give details of many statements and affidavits recording assaults and torture of children. They show that the abuse is widespread. When we were in South Africa in February 1987 we saw nothing to indicate any change. We were assured that such assaults were continuing on the same scale as before.

While we were in South Africa, an application was made to the Witwatersrand Local Division of the Supreme Court on the 10 February 1987, seeking an interdict restraining the torture of children.[15] The affidavits grounding the application gave evidence of assaults on children by prison warders at the new Johannesburg Prison at Diepkloof. The children said that they were subjected to severe beatings, sjambokking, kicking, being subjected to tear-gassing, and being forced to do painful exercises. The assaults resulted in broken limbs, and one boy had to receive surgery as a result of the injuries sustained. The application was adjourned upon the respondent's undertaking that there would be no 'common law infringement of the rights of the persons listed' in the application or any breach of the 'prison regulations in relation to them'.

More recently, the police appear to have become more sophisticated in their assaults on the children, and are better able to hide the results. As a result of the recent successful applications for interdicts, and the more recent successful applications for Anton Piller search orders,[16] the security forces are now using electric shocks and tear-gassing more frequently, as well as torture which inhibits breathing. The police know that their victims will be in detention for long periods and therefore confine their abuse to the early periods of detention, allowing the latter part of the detention for the wounds to heal. There is also an increasing use of psychological torture, particularly by the security police.

Two members of the Mission witnessed in the Supreme Court in Ciskei the result of police torture eight months after police interrogation.[17]

In public statements, the South African police have said that large numbers of 'mobs' responsible for violence and unrest consisted of children, and that they are forced to take drastic action to deal with these mobs. The police have expressed concern about the violence that children witness and participate in, but say they cannot be expected to allow arsonists or stonethrowers to roam free just because they are youths. They conclude that the arrest of youths is 'unavoidable'.[18]

Conditions of detention

There appeared to be huge dissatisfaction with the conditions of detention among the commentators that we spoke to in South Africa. There is vast overcrowding, the food is monotonous, badly cooked, unhygienic and insufficient. Ther were very poor washing and toiletry facilities, the exercise facilities are inadequate and there are very.few recreational facilities. There are far too many people crowded into one cell. In cells, which are no larger than 7 metres by 6 metres, up to forty people were commonly held. In Diepkloof Prison, forty-two children were detained in one cell, whereas the number was forty-eight in Moderbee and twenty-five in Pollsmoor. The children sleep on rubber mats on the floor, and in many incidences, due to overcrowding, they are required to share mats and blankets. The diet is wholly inadequate for growing children. In one case, a Supreme Court Judge ordered the amount of food given in one prison to be increased after a dietician found that the diet was 'a strict weight-reduction diet'. Medical treatment is also wholly inadequate, and there have been frequent reports of pregnant women receiving inadequate or no medical attention or treatment.

A spokesman for the South African Prison Department said that it was prison service policy that imprisoned juveniles be kept separate from adults, but that 'circumstances may prevail where exceptions have to be accommodated, but this is handled with the utmost responsibility'.[19] The Prisons Act of 1959 provides that unconvicted prisoners under 18 must not be kept with someone who is over 21, unless he is a co-accused or the association would not be detrimental to the child. The Act defines a juvenile as being a person under 21. Despite this policy, we heard numerous reports of young children being kept in the same cells as adults. There were frequent reports of children being beaten up, sodomized and having their food stolen by such adults. Even if the older persons are under 21, there are many hardened gang members under 21 who could have a detrimental effect on young children.

It is highly undesirable that children should be kept in the same cells as adults. This places additional pressure on children in an already pressurized environment, and can have adverse psychological effects on the children. The Deputy Minister of Law and Order told us that he would take action if he found that adult prisoners were being kept in the same cells as children. He said that he would much prefer if the children could be held in rehabilitation centres, but none were provided for black children, only for white.

Sentences and alternative punishments

Frequently, children are charged with public violence, a common-law crime, which carries a maximum sentence of ten years' imprisonment when tried before a Regional Magistrate. There are estimated to be many hundreds of public violence cases being conducted throughout the country against children and young persons. Black Sash in Cape Town have recently monitored such cases and have supplied us with the results of their work. Those charged with unrest-related sentences are often refused bail, and there are long delays before cases are brought to trial. In a very large proportion of the cases, the charges are withdrawn at or shortly before the trial, or the accused is acquitted. Black Sash say that of 234 cases in the Cape Town and Boland areas from January to October 1986, only 17 per cent of those charged were convicted in court. The remaining 83 per cent, who must be presumed to be innocent, have suffered severe hardship, with little hope of redress. They are punished and their lives disrupted by what in many cases is a gross abuse of the criminal process. In this manner, the government can keep people out of circulation without the accompanying embarrassment of placing them in detention without trial.

We were given many examples of this abuse of the prosecuting process. In one case a 16-year-old boy was charged with thirty-two counts of sabotage and seven counts of arson, was not granted bail and was remanded in custody. The child was subsequently acquitted, but only after he had spent seven months in jail. In another case, an 8-year-old boy was arrested in Middleburg in connection with the offence of 'intimidation' and was refused bail.[20] And in yet another case, an 11-year-old boy spent two months in jail, and was refused bail twice, before being acquitted of all charges.[21] These are not isolated cases, and are occurring on a large scale throughout South Africa.

Where children are convicted in the courts of security-related offences, they receive what we regard to be excessively harsh sentences. A four-year sentence is not unusual in a public violence case, even where the child is a first-time offender, for whom an alternative non-custodial sentence could easily have been found. The Minister of Law and Order has decreed that there is to be no remission of sentences in public violence cases, thus making it clear that it is seen as a political offence. One member of the Mission was in court in Cape Town in October 1986 when two Supreme Court Judges refused to vary sentences of seven years' imprisonment on a number of youths who were aged between 16 and 20 years of age, all of whom were first-time offenders, for an offence of punching a man and causing bruises, setting fire to curtains and breaking windows.

One case which particularly disturbed us was that of the 13-year-old Zachariah Makhajane, who was detained without charge under the emergency regulations on 21 August 1986. A Supreme Court judge refused to order the child's release in a judgment which made no reference to the boy's age, though he clearly must have known it. An appeal to a full Supreme Court bench of three judges, which included the Judge President of the Transvaal and another judge, who is generally regarded as the most liberal of the Transvaal judges, was dismissed on strictly legal grounds. The applicant's papers were deficient and arguments which were raised in court were not evidenced in affidavits.[22] It is very difficult to understand the conduct of any judge who authorizes the continued imprisonment of a 13-year-old child in these circumstances.

The South African courts have recognized the undesirability of sending children to prison 'to herd with hardened criminals',[23] and have recognized that the legislature has been careful, where punishment and detention follows on conviction, 'that children should not come into contact with other criminals and life in an ordinary gaol'.[24] The Appellate Division stated in 1975 that 'the interests of society cannot be served by disregarding the interests of the juvenile, for a mistaken form of punishment might easily result in a person with a distorted or more distorted personality being eventually returned to society'.[25]

The South African legislature has provided for alternatives to imprisonment in their legislation. A juvenile may be sent to a reformatory or to a place of safety instead of a prison.[26] The Criminal Procedure Act 1977 also provides for the placing of a child in the care of a person in whose custody he is,[27] and the custodian is then obliged to secure the child's attendance at court. Sentences may be suspended or postponed,[28] and juveniles may be placed on probation under the supervision of a probation officer.[29] However, these alternatives are apparently not used by magistrates in political cases. The magistrates most frequently sentence a child in such circumstances to a whipping and/or a term of imprisonment.

Psychological effects

It is clear therefore, that incarceration is a common threat to children in South Africa, whether on conviction or under the emergency, and a child can expect considerable abuse while so detained. Psychologists have expressed considerable concern about the effects of such treatment on children, particularly young children. The experience of detention has been seen to be disturbing for all detainees, but it is seen as being far more traumatic for a child. Psychiatrists estimate that as many as 70 per cent of detained children develop post-traumatic stress disorder, and detained children are particularly susceptible to anxiety disorders and psychotic episodes. The symptoms commonly exhibited by children are insomnia, nausea, lack of concentration and memory deficiencies, relationship and sexual disorders, and many children will often be depressed and will frequently exhibit acute feelings of fear, guilt and isolation, and will find it extremely difficult to integrate back into society after their release.

In August 1985 the Johannesburg Child Welfare Society said that the fact of imprisonment alone, without the attendant abuses, would have 'terribly warping effects on young children'. The Society gave an example of a 15-year-old boy who, after two weeks in detention, had to be admitted to a psychiatric hospital because he had become psychotic.

We conclude this chapter with the following quotation:

We therefore record that, at present, children are imprisoned without trial in our country, under the following statutory regime:

*   No person other than the Minister or a state official may have access to the detainee, except with the consent of the Minister or a person authorized by him;
*   No detainee may communicate in writing with any person outside the prison, except with official permission;
*   A detainee is not entitled to have any reading matter except the Bible or other holy book of religion or selected magazines supplied through the person in command of the prison;
*   A detainee may not receive any articles or foodstuffs or potables from persons outside the prison;
*   A detainee is not entitled to study, except with official permission;
*   A detainee may not receive any radio, record player, tape recorder, musical instrument or television set from persons outside the prison;
*   A detainee must clean his/her place of detention, including the ablution facilities;
*   A detainee commits a criminal offence if he or she: is idle, careless, or negligent; leaves his or her sleeping or eating place without permission; or sings, whistles,

or causes unnecessary trouble, or is a nuisance. The penalty for contravention can include deprivation of meals, being placed in solitary confinement for up to 30 days, or being subjected to up to six strokes.

This is the statutory regime under which children are imprisoned without trial in our country.

Any comment would be superfluous.

Notes

1. Act No. 33 of 1960.
2. Act No. 74 of 1983.
3. Fiona McLachlan, 'Children: Their Courts and Institutions in South Africa', Institute of Criminology, University of Cape Town, 1986.
4. Act No. 51 of 1977.
5. See Fiona McLachlan, 'Children in Prison in South Africa', Institute of Criminology, University of Cape Town, 1984.
6. 1969 1 SA 601.
7. Estimate of the Detainees' Parents Support Committee.
8. *Weekly Mail*, 20/6 March 1987.
9. See McLachlan, note 5.
10. Lawyers' Committee for Human Rights, *'The War Against Children: South Africa's Youngest Victims'*, New York, 1986.
11. Kannemeyer Report, see p. 61.
12. *Mabobe* v. *Minister of Law and Order*, WLD, unreported, 13 September 1985. See 1 *SAJHR* p. 300 (November 1985).
13. Detainees' Parents Support Committee, 'Abantwana Bazabalaza: A Memorandum on Children under Repression', October 1986.
14. (a) Lawyers' Committee for Human Rights note 10; (b) Update of *'The War Against Children'*, Lawyers' Committee for Human Rights; (c) DPSC note 13; (d) Black Sash, 'Memorandum on the Suffering of Children in South Africa', April 1986.
15. *Mokone and others* v. *Minister for Justice and others*, WLD, 10 February 1987.
16. See p. 112 and footnote.
17. See p. 134.
18. Race Relations Survey, 1985, Institute of Race Relations, 1986.
19. Ibid., p. 443.
20. *Sunday Tribune*, 9 February 1986.
21. Ibid., 2 February 1986.
22. *Makajane* v. *Minister of Law and Order*, TPD, Case No. 1871/86, 16 October 1986, unreported.
23. Wessels J.P. in *R* v. *Smith* (1922) TPD, 199 at 201.
24. *Attorney General, Transvaal* v. *Additional Magistrate for Johannesburg* (1924) AD 421 at 436.
25. *Per Botha JA, S.* v. *Jansen* [1975] 1 SA 425 (A) at 427–8.
26. We were informed by the Deputy Minister of Law and Order that there are, however, no such places provided for black children.
27. S. 72 (1) (b).
28. S. 279.
29. S. 290.
30. Budlender, *3 SAJHR*, p. 2 (March 1987).

13   The Administration of Justice and the Judicial System

The judiciary

Until recently, the South African judiciary enjoyed a high reputation for independence from the Executive. The government has been condemned for imposing discriminatory laws and a repressive legal order, whereas the judiciary has been singled out as being 'a liberal institution in an illiberal community'.[1] One judge told us that the South African judiciary did not need an introduction as they were regarded world-wide as being 'the strongest bastion of human rights'.[2] However, since the 1950s, reservations have been expressed about the independence of the South African judiciary, and in 1968 the International Commission of Jurists declared that they were 'as establishment-minded as the Executive'.[3]

The 1950s saw a period of confrontation between the new National Party government and the judiciary. The response of the government to judicial opposition was to 'pack' the courts with its own supporters rather than appointing the most senior advocates to the bench, as had previously been the tradition. The size of the Appellate Division was increased from five to eleven judges for the hearing of constitutional cases,[4] thus providing an instant government-supporting majority in the Division. As a result of this action, the court took a much more pro-government stance during the 1950s and 1960s. The judiciary, however, retained the good reputation of their predecessors, and gave the appearance of being surrounded by an 'aura of infallibility'.[5]

From 1962 onwards, the government reverted to the traditional method of appointing judges on merit. At the same time, however, the government introduced more laws to limit the powers of the judiciary, and thus, as one commentator suggested, 'could afford the luxury of political opponents on the bench'.[6]

We were constantly reminded by the judges whom we met that 'we declare what the law is, we do not make it'.[7] The South African judiciary has a strong tradition of positivism, and the constitutional system, which makes Parliament supreme, allows no judicial review of legislation passed by Parliament. The judges said that they saw their role as giving effect to the true intention of the legislature as expressed in statutes. The judges deny that they have any choice, and they claim that they merely do what the legislature has commanded them to do through legislation.

We accept that the South African judiciary operate under limitations, that in many cases they have no choice and merely enforce the clear terms of the law. However, it is clear that in many cases the judges have a choice, and it is seldom that the court retains no power at all. There is invariably some 'residue of jurisdiction'[8] and freedom of judicial action. The judges are free to interpret legislation (as distinct from reviewing it) in the light of the common-law rules of interpretation, which embrace presumptions in favour of liberty and equality. Administrative powers can be reviewed in accordance with the principles of natural justice, and the judges can review subordinate legislation and test it by common-law standards of reasonableness and certainty. The common law can be developed so as to keep pace with contemporary society, and the judiciary retain a wide discretion in sentencing. Through the use of these powers, a judge can still mitigate the harshness of the system.

In recent times judges, especially in Natal, have demonstrated that they do have choice in many cases. A judge can choose one interpretation rather than another, or elect to adopt one precedent and distinguish another. A judge cannot be said to mechanically declare the law where there are competing interpretations, precedents and authorities. The judge has a choice, and in making that choice he creates a new precedent and develops a new law.

It is important to measure the performance of the South African judiciary bearing in mind the limitations that are placed on them by the Executive, but ignoring self-imposed limitations. Given the evident intention of the government of South Africa to deny human rights to the majority of its citizens, the question we must ask is how far do the judiciary exercise their freedom of choice and powers, albeit limited powers, to mitigate the harshness of the system and to protect human rights?

The judges see themselves as belonging to the same tradition as the English and American judges, in which a high degree of technical competence and independence from the Executive are valued. Their positivist approach to their functions leads them to exclude overt political influences and to assume an obligation to give effect to the intention of Parliament, regardless of their personal view of its wisdom or morality.

Two recent academic studies of the Appellate Division from 1910 to 1980 have criticized its excessive readiness to support the policies of the government at the expense of individual freedom.[9] The studies found that, although the courts seldom associated themselves with government policy directly, the decisions of the court substantially facilitated the implementation of government policy by failing to keep the Executive within the law. The authors conclude that the court has abandoned its role as guardian of individual liberty against the might of the state. In most cases, the judges preferred harsh and pro-Executive interpretations even where there were persuasive legal grounds for a more liberal interpretation.

Perusal of the South African Law Reports for the years 1960 to 1982 reveals a large number of cases where the Appellate Division decisions were very Executive orientated. In many of these cases there was a clear judicial choice open to the judges, but generally the judges chose the course most favourable to the government. The cases are too numerous to set out in full, but we feel that a few examples illustrate the point clearly, though we acknowledge that they are highly selective:

(1) Where a statute was silent on the right of a detainee to receive reading and writing materials, the Appellate Division said that these articles were 'luxuries' and were to be impliedly excluded because they would alleviate the tedium of solitary confinement, and thereby interfere with the purpose of the statute, which was to induce detainees to talk.[10]

(2) The Appellate Division has refused to allow a detainee to testify in court on the grounds that it would interfere with the interrogation process and 'negative the inducement to speak'. The statute was silent on the matter and the court held that its jurisdiction to interfere had been implicitly excluded.[11]

(3) The Supreme Court has accepted the evidence of a detainee who had been detained in solitary confinement for over 500 days, and thereby failed to recognize the coercive effect of long-term detention on the voluntariness of a statement.[12]

(4) Even where the Appellate Division has rejected confessions as being inadmissible on the ground that there was clear evidence that the accused had been tortured, the Division did not comment adversely on the torture by the police, and thus, while they may have done justice between the parties, they did not stem the tide of widespread police abuse and torture.[13]

Many judges do not apply any presumption in favour of personal freedom when the release of detainees is sought. Indeed, the Appellate Division has in effect told them not to do so.[14] Moreover, it is quite obvious from the expressed attitudes of many judges that they support apartheid and the policies of the government towards those who oppose it. Thus a claim to independence is not wholly justified. We accept that judges are now more generally appointed on merit, but the predominance of Executive-minded judges ensures that the court will generally reach decisions which accord with the government's wishes.

Even where there are judges on the Bench who give decisions adverse to the Executive, the government can ensure that their impact in the security area is kept to a minimum by appointing only government supporters to the position of Judge President. The Judge President is the administrative officer of each division and organizes the allotment of judges to the various courts. He is thus in a position to ensure that only government supporters hear security cases. A large number of lawyers to whom we spoke felt that Judge Presidents deliberately assigned security cases to government supporters. However, the judges that we spoke to said that this could be equally explained by the fact that such cases were allotted to the most senior judges on the Bench. The most senior judges on the Bench are also those who were appointed during the era when mainly government supporters were appointed to the Bench. But no matter what the explanation, the result is the same. The notable exception seems to be the Judge President in Natal, Mr Justice Milne, who was appointed in 1982 and who shows no partiality towards the government. This is one reason why we see so many decisions adverse to the government coming from Natal. It has recently been announced, however, that he is to be promoted to the Appellate Division.

Once judges are appointed, they have the potential to be totally independent, because they cannot be dismissed. Recently, there has been a tendency, especially in Natal towards more overt opposition by the judges to curbs on individual freedom. The following are examples of court decisions which, at least temporarily, have reduced the impact of the emergency and security laws:

(1) The Natal Supreme Court, whose decision was affirmed by the Appellate Division, ruled that a police officer's decision to arrest and detain indefinitely for the purpose of interrogation is subject to judicial review. Leon J., at first instance, held that there must be a factual basis for the police officer's reason for arrest, and that the objective existence of such a jurisdictional fact was justiciable in a court of law. In the Appellate Division, Rabie J.A., held that it was most unlikely that the legislature could have intended that the reason that was required for an arrest under Section 29 of the Internal Security Act need not be founded on reasonable grounds.[14]

(2) The Appellate Division upheld two previous Natal decisions in holding that the Minister for Law and Order was required to furnish proper reasons for the preventive detention of individuals. Rabie J.A. said that it was the legislative intent that a defendant should have a fair opportunity of dealing with the Minister's reasons for detaining him, and it was consequently not sufficient merely to repeat the statutory reason for detention.[15]

(3) The Natal Supreme Court has ruled that the regulations purporting to inhibit a detainee's access to a lawyer were invalid. This decision has, however, been overruled by the Appellate Division. The court also held that the emergency regulations did not prevent the court from considering whether regulations (which are subordinate legislation) are void for vagueness.[16]

(4) The Cape Supreme Court has held that the power of arrest under the emergency regulations is not an unfettered power which may be exercised capriciously or arbitrarily. Marais J. said that an honest opinion must be held that the detention is necessary and not merely desirable. The exercise of the power of arrest was held to be justiciable. The court held that the ouster clause in the regulations did not apply where an act was not done in accordance with the legislation. If the detention is not in accordance with the regulations, the court can review it.[17]

We noted much ingenuity by lawyers in South Africa in using the law to challenge the Executive. The interdict (or injunction) has been used to restrain police from torturing detainees and is a doubtful clog on abuse of police powers. The Supreme Court has also held that torture victims may have the right to search police stations for torture equipment without notice to the police concerned.[18] In June 1986 the Cape Supreme Court granted an Anton Piller order to four alleged torture victims to search two police stations where they had been held, and held that an inventory of items found therein was to be filed in court.[19]

Unfortunately, some of these liberal decisions have been reversed by the Appellate Division, and others have been reversed by the government amending the law. It seems that the government would not allow an adverse decision to stand if it inhibits its freedom to detain whoever it wishes to detain. One judge said to us that the judiciary has acted as *ad hoc* legal advisers to the Executive, in that each time the judiciary strike out a particular act or regulation, it is improved by the government.[20] It is therefore obvious that judges, however courageous and independent, can mitigate only marginally the impact of the security laws. However, many of the judges that we spoke to believed that their decisions could make an impact. One judge that we spoke to said that the pit was bottomless and that he only had a small shovel, and whereas he could never fill the pit in, he would do what he could.

We were impressed by the assurances by judges that we spoke to that they would in no circumstances be prepared to accept instructions from the government, except in the form of enacted legislation. We were also impressed by their obvious awareness of the fundamental injustice of the system of which they were a part. All the judges felt that they were justified in continuing on the Bench, and they emphasized that questions of individual liberty were not a regular part of their work.

Most of the black lawyers and political leaders with whom we spoke thought that 'the liberal' judges should resign, but it was generally acknowledged that resignation would have little impact unless it was accompanied by a public exposure of the reasons for resigning. Two judges are believed to have resigned in recent years in protest against the government action, but have not acknowledged this publicly. Other leading advocates are believed to have refused judicial appointments. However, whether or not a judge should continue to hold office under the present South African regime is a moral question for each individual and we express no conclusions on the issue here.

Many South African judges are open to criticism not only on account of their participation in a legal system which denies basic rights of personal liberty, but also on the ground that, in administering the ordinary laws, they have made decisions which seem inhuman and have imposed excessively harsh sentences, especially in relation to children who are charged with public violence (see Ch. 11). It may be that the climate of violence and repression, interacting with deep-rooted racism and fear which virtually all white South Africans must be prone to, has made it extremely difficult (if not impossible) for a white judge to regard a black person with objectivity.

In conclusion, we were not impressed by the argument that the judges are powerless in the face of government restrictions in the security area. We recognize that the judiciary are operating in a climate of severe government restrictions, but we believe the judges can choose to make an impact. If a judge remains on the Bench in such a repressive regime, there can be no excuse for failing to exercise his choice in favour of individual liberty, and whereas some judges have done justice in such cases in recent times, the majority of the South African Bench have failed to do so. We feel that it is as a result of this failure that the South African judiciary are open to the criticism of their fellow jurists in other countries.

The magistrates

The lower courts in South Africa are staffed by magistrates who are appointed from the ranks of the civil service. They undergo a course of training at a Magistrates' School and are then appointed initially as prosecutors, and are subsequently promoted to the Bench. Once appointed to the Bench, there is the possibility of further promotion to the position of senior magistrate, eventually the possibility of an appointment to the Bench in the Regional Magistrates Courts. The magistrates are government servants and they are not independent of the Executive in the sense that the judges are. The magistrate is often regarded as biased in favour of the state. Magistrates have been said to be 'products of their upbringing and captives of the bureaucracy'.[21]

In South Africa, as in most countries, the vast bulk of court work is done in the Magistrates Courts, and if these courts are executive-minded and unfair, huge injustice will result. It seems to be accepted widely in South Africa that the magistrates are not independent and that they will usually decide in favour of the government.

The judges that we spoke to said that the lack of independence of the magistrates did not have serious effects due to the 'safety valve' that was operated in the review procedure. Any decision of a District Magistrate in a criminal case where a fine of R.100 or a term of imprisonment of more than four months is imposed automatically goes on review to the Supreme Court. Potentially, this procedure can rectify any mistakes made in a Magistrates Court, but this does not happen in practice. Decisions of magistrates who have gained enough seniority do not go on review. The most serious of the cases that come before the magistrates, and in particular charges of public violence, will go before the most senior magistrates.

Legal aid

The rule of law depends not only on the availability of fair legal procedures and independent judiciary and laws which recognize basic human rights, but also requires that citizens have access to the law to defend these rights. This means that those who do not have the means to pay for legal representation in matters where their liberty is at stake must be provided with such representation at the expense of the state.

The provision of legal aid in South Africa is wholly inadequate and the money supplied by the government for this purpose falls far short of the sums provided in comparable legal systems. The need for legal aid is particularly marked in South Africa, where a large number of trials are continuously taking place in which the accused, if found guilty, can face long terms of imprisonment and even the death penalty.[22] The antiquated *pro deo* system provides for legal representation of indigent accused in capital cases. Under this system, junior advocates in their first years at the Bar can take on the case for a nominal fee, which is paid by the Bar. Ironically, most advocates in South Africa have their first experience of conducting criminal cases by defending black people charged with murder. Many advocates claim they are too occupied with other cases to undertake *pro deo* work. Other impoverished defendants must rely on the help of those who are able to represent them without charge or who can be paid from charitable sources, usually from outside the country.

Detention and harassment of lawyers

The Legal Resources Centre, which has offices in the major cities in South Africa, together with a number of attorneys and advocates in private practice, do a huge amount of work in representing persons who do not qualify for legal aid and who cannot afford to litigate by themselves. All these lawyers are willing to risk harassment and even detention to ensure that proper defences are prepared at least in political cases. A measure of the risk involved is that at least five lawyers whose cases were brought to our attention had been detained during the present emergency while engaged in their professional work. One attorney we spoke to was arrested, along with the advocate he was instructing, in a magistrates court when an argument developed with the police as to the right of access to their client. Further, the magistrate was prevented by the police from phoning the Attorney-General to inform him of the situation. After a period in detention, the charges were later dropped, but only after the papers of both lawyers were gone through by the police. The harassment of lawyers so as to discourage them from carrying out their duties is manifestly improper and itself undermines the rule of law.

Particular difficulties are experienced by those who are faced with prosecution in rural areas. There are few lawyers practising in such areas, and those that do exist are dependent on the white property owners for their income. Consequently, they are unable or unwilling to represent black people apparently in conflict with the established order. The progressive lawyers who are prepared to represent black persons in such communities are almost all based in the major cities. Lawyers whom we spoke to said they were prepared to travel large distances to rural areas but they found it very difficult to deal with the obstructions that were put in their way by prosecutors, the police and even the magistrates. Defence lawyers complained of discourteous treatment, being made to wait for local lawyers to have their cases dealt with first, and being summoned to court to make formal applications which could have been dealt with by way of correspondence. Also, when defence lawyers seek to instruct local lawyers to act as agents, they often decline to do so on political grounds. There have also been complaints that attempts to establish local advice centres in rural townships were thwarted by the police, and advice workers have been detained under the state of emergency.

Legal services in rural areas

Because of the fact that most lawyers live in the city, inhabitants of rural areas find it extremely difficult to get legal representation. There have been moves in recent years to establish advice centres in rural areas, and these have proved to be very successful. In general, organizations such as the Legal Resources Centre and the Black Lawyers Assocation have trained para-legals in the type of law that is most sought after in the townships. These para-legals opened advice centres in the townships, and they can deal with the vast majority of the queries that are brought to those centres. The parent organizations, however, are always available to these centres to give legal advice, and lawyers will travel around to visit these centres periodically. The advantage of the para-legal system is that the most important cases can be filtered out and placed before the lawyers, without the lawyers having to waste their valuable time on preliminary matters. When a para-legal identifies a case as requiring the attention of a lawyer, the case is passed on to the lawyer, and he will deal with any court proceedings that are necessary for that particular client.

The Legal Resource Centre tries to concentrate on what it calls 'impact litigation', which is litigation which is aimed at having an effect on the community at large rather than only the parties. The Legal Resources Centre tries to locate patterns of abuse, and then to litigate to prevent this. The Centre in Johannesburg services twenty-three rural offices within a radius of 350 kilometres of the city, and their lawyers saw about 15,000 people last year. The Black Lawyers Association has recently established an *African Law Review* and has reserved two pages to giving information to the advice centre workers and to giving guidelines on the law.[23] The demand for legal services, however, vastly exceeds the supply.

Abuse of the prosecuting process

When an accused person is charged before a court in South Africa, he can apply for bail, and should get it provided that he can satisfy the court that he will turn up for his trial and will not interfere with witnesses. The mere fact that the state opposes bail will not mean that it won't be granted, although the Attorney-General can veto the granting of bail under the Internal Security Act.[26]

A number of lawyers pointed out to us that the prosecuting process was being abused by fixing bail at a sum in excess of that which an accused can afford. Bail in one case of public violence was fixed at R.3,000 for a person under 18, though more usually bail is fixed at between R.100 and R.300. However, this is still greater than the average monthly income of most families in the townships. The lawyers claimed that people were being charged with offences, and bail is set at a figure greater than that which they can afford, and thus they are remanded in custody pending the trial. When the case comes up, in many cases the prosecution offers no evidence against the accused, or their case collapses. In other cases, even where a conviction is secured, a non-custodial sentence is imposed. By abusing the process, the state can ensure that people are kept out of circulation without proving a case against them, or without detaining them under the state of emergency.

This form of harassment by process is a cause for concern. Bail should not be more than the accused can afford; otherwise it is a denial of bail. This is merely a further constraint on the right to individual liberty in a system which places little value on that right.[24]

Alternative courts

The lack of confidence in the court system among black people in the townships of South Africa has led to the creation or development of alternative courts. There is also a strong desire among many black people to challenge and replace official government structures which are identified with the apartheid system. In Soweto, for example, in 1985 the people set up their own form of alternative government as a form of protest against the new tricameral parliamentary system. In addition to the civic associations, which the people set up as their public representative body, there were also set up law and order committees, among whose function was the prevention and punishment of petty crime. The usual form of punishment imposed by the Tribunal was a whipping, though more serious forms of punishment could be imposed. The government re-acted harshly to the introduction of these committees in an attempt to eradicate them. Initially, persons involved in the carrying out of the punishments imposed by the Tribunal were charged with assault, but more recently are being charged with the more serious offence of sedition.

Notes

1. J. Dugard, *Human Rights and the South African Legal Order*, Princeton, NJ, 1978, p. 279.
2. Interview with a Supreme Court judge, Ciskei, 17 February 1987.
3. The International Commission of Jurists, *Erosion of the Rule of Law in South Africa*, Geneva, 1968, p. iv.
4. The Appellate Division Quorum Act, no. 27 of 1955.
5. Corder, *Judges at Work*, Johannesburg, 1984, p. 2.
6. Dugard, p. 285.

7. Interview with Transvaal Supreme Court judge, Johannesburg, 25 February 1987.
8. A. Mathews, 'The South African Judiciary and the Security System', 1 *SAJHR*, p. 199 (July 1985).
9. Corder; Forsyth, *In Danger for Their Talents*, Johannesburg, 1985.
10. *Rossouw* v. *Sachs* 1964 2 SA 551 (A).
11. *Schermbrucker* v. *Klindt* 1965 4 SA 606 (A).
12. *S* v. *Gwala* (1977) NPD unreported.
13. *S* v. *Mogale* reported in Riekert, 'Police Assaults and the Admission of Voluntary Confessions', 1982 99 SALJ 125.
14. *Hurley* v. *Minister for Law and Order* 1986 4 SA 709 (N) and 1986 3 SA 508 (A).
15. See Dugard and others 'Focus on Omar' 3 *SAJHR* pp. 295–337 (November 1987).
16. *Nkondo* v. *Minister for Law and Order* 1986 2 SA 256 (A).
17. *MAWU* v. *State President* 1986 4 SA 358 (A).
18. *Dempsey* v. *Minister for Law and Order* 1986 4 SA 530 (1). See also Basson, 'Judicial Activism in a State of Emergency', 3 *SAJHR* p. 28 (March 1987).
19. Ex Parte Matshini. 1985. EPD, unreported. 'Anton Piller' is a reference to an English case in which powers of search were granted as a preliminary step in legal proceedings.
20. Interview, Johannesburg, 25 February 1987.
21. J. Dugard, 'Judges in a State of National Crisis', p. 9.
22. See p. 83.
23. Vol. 1, no. 1 (Jan. 1987).
24. See p. 74.

14 The Security System

South Africa is sometimes referred to as a police state. If this expression means that the state is run by the police and security forces unrestrained and unfettered by the rule of law, then South Africa comes close to fulfilling the definition. Often the police flout the law, but in any event, the law passed by Parliament gives extraordinarily wide powers to the police and removes judicial safeguards against police action.

A church leader in South Africa said to us that there was an element of uncontrollability in the police and in the army in South Africa, and that this was deliberately created by the government. Before the emergency, it was well known that the police violated human rights and committed atrocities and the emergency gave immunity from liability for some violations. The church leader said that 'The uncontrollability is part of the design because it is only by sheer terror that you can continue to hold people down'. We feel that this is an accurate statement of the position that operates in South Africa today under an emergency which gives to the police and security forces wide freedom from public scrutiny.

The security forces

The security forces have an almost unlimited power to arrest and detain and have little fear from the courts in their pursuit of these objectives. There is very little evidence of disciplinary action being taken against the police in cases where they have been manifestly guilty of gross abuses.

We were given many examples of police abuse while we were in South Africa. In one case, the Legal Resources Centre in Cape Town had obtained an interdict (injunction) against the Minister of Law and Order and the police to restrain further assaults on the residents of some of the squatter camps at Crossroads. Notwithstanding the interdicts, attacks were mounted by both vigilantes and the police, which fact was established by both photographic as well as overwhelming eye-witness evidence. This illegal police action led to the eviction of 60,000 people and the destruction of their property and homes on 9 and 10 of June 1986. When the case came to court for the interdict to be made final, the state conceded the case. However, no disciplinary or court action has been taken against the police, notwithstanding their gross contempt of court.[1]

Another incident in the Cape area received considerable notoriety due to the presence of a television crew to record the incident. In the so-called 'Trojan Horse' incident, three children were shot dead by policemen who emerged from boxes on top of an unmarked police lorry and opened fire. The act of shooting was said to be in self-defence, but the whole incident was set up to solicit stone-throwing on the part of the youths in the area, so that the police action could be justified on the grounds of self-defence. Further, the police proceeded to arrest people in the neighbourhood and charge them with the offence of public violence, alleging that they were throwing stones. When the cases came to court in late 1986, the police were unable to produce any credible evidence and the case was dismissed. Again, no prosecution or any disciplinary action has ever been taken against the policemen responsible for the killings.

In exercising control over the townships, there is compelling evidence that the security forces take advantage of the existence of significant numbers of black people, who for ideological or economic reasons are prepared to assist the authorities to quell the opposition. The government seeks to evade responsibility for much of the violence in the townships by ascribing it to 'black on black' conflict. There are fierce differences in viewpoints between black people, some of which are a legacy of ancient tribal rivalries but appear to be much more frequently the result of the apartheid system, which creates desperate competition for scarce resources. The black groups which generally support the authorities are usually known as vigilantes. The 'Comrades' are the young opponents of apartheid who usually support the United Democratic Front. Government support for those who attack the Comrades may take the very tangible and attractive form of money payments, priority in housing and employment, and the provision of weapons.[2]

A recent tendency has been for the vigilantes to be recruited into the police, either the South African Police or the local township police. Apart from the regular police, another, subsidiary force has been formed called 'kitskonstabels'. They have been recruited in response to what the Deputy Minister of Law and Order called a demand for 'more bodies on the beat'.[2] The kitskonstabels are given minimal training and are sent into townships fully armed. Many are driven to join the police by severe unemployment and there have been complaints that the advertisements for positions are vague. We were told that many believed they were merely applying for positions in private security firms. The community responds badly to the kitskonstabels, because they see them as representatives of the South African government. The community puts pressure on them and their wives and families to resign, and this has caused many families to break up and has caused some officers to commit suicide. Others react violently against the community due to this pressure, and there have been many deaths in the townships due to the recklessness of the kitskonstabels. The increasing use by the government of its economic power over black people to compel them to police each other is another way in which it seeks to perpetuate minority rule.

We have no doubt that the South African police and security forces extensively use torture and beat up those whom they detain. Some people said that torture was not aimed at getting information but was merely a form of harassment. The scheme seems to be that a detainee is tortured at the beginning of his detention, so that the tangible evidence has cleared up by the date of his release. Recent reports indicate that the security police are now getting more sophisticated, and that they are tending to resort more to psychological torture rather than physical brutality. The security police at John Vorster Square are said to use psychological torture to the virtual exclusion of physical brutality now, and they have the capacity to be just as destructive by using this form of torture, if, for example, they keep a detainee in solitary confinement for long periods, isolating him totally from contact with the outside world. One doctor told us of a detainee who was left in a cell for twenty-four hours with a dead body shot through the head by the security police. He was suffering from severe psychological disorders as a result.

Large numbers of people have alleged brutal violence and torture on arrest, in vehicles and in police cells. We have discussed torture in more detail elsewhere in this report.[3]

In carrying out their duties, the South African police use firearms and other deadly weapons, and inflict deadly force too readily and in unacceptable circumstances.[4] The use of firearms in crowd control invariably leads to death and is inexcusable save in the most extreme circumstances. But the South African police now seem to be using them as a first choice in many cases, despite instructions to the contrary.[5] The R1 and R4 rifles which are used by the police are weapons of war, and should not be used for the purposes of crowd control. South African government statistics for 1985 showed that a total of 512 African adults and 187 African juveniles were killed due to police shootings, and a total of 2,312 were wounded.

There are basically three methods of redress against the police in South Africa:

(1) A police enquiry by an internal tribunal. However, this involves the police in investigating, prosecuting and judging themselves, and this is clearly unsatisfactory. Even the Deputy Minister for Law and Order recognized that this is not seen as an effective means of redress by the public.

(2) A criminal prosecution may be brought against police officers. The Attorney-General may do this or authorise a private prosecution, but the latter is rare. Plainly, criminal charges against the police are very hard to prove, witnesses are reluctant to come forward, and it is very difficult to identify specific policemen, particularly in circumstances where there have been allegations that the police remove their identity numbers.

(3) A civil action may be taken against the police. This is probably the most effective remedy, but it is dependent upon the victims knowing their legal rights. Also, people are afraid to issue proceedings against the police. Furthermore, there is a six months' limitation period for the bringing of an action against the police, although the ordinary time limit for the bringing of an action for damages for personal injuries is three years. A summons against the police must therefore be issued within six months, and one month's notice must be given to the police of the intention to issue the summons, which, in effect, means that a person has five months to issue proceedings from the date of the assault, which in

most cases is far too short.

It is important to note that these remedies are only available anyway astride the Emergency regulations under which the security forces have a wide immunity.

Section 27 of the Police Act 1958 makes it a criminal offence to publish any untrue matter about the police without having reasonable grounds for believing the statement to be true. The burden is on the publisher to prove he has reasonable grounds. This is a huge onus, which operates as an inducement not to publish, and is a further example of attempts by the South African government to hide police abuses. However, in a recent prosecution of Mr Tony Weaver, a journalist on the *Cape Times*, the defendant succeeded, by proving that the police abuses which he described had actually taken place.

The South African government has paid out considerable sums in compensation to victims of police abuses in recent years, and in most cases this is done prior to the case going to court. In July 1987 it agreed to pay R.1.3 million in damages to fifty-one victims of the shootings at Langa, near Port Elizabeth, which took place on 21 March 1985, and this is seen as being the biggest unconditional police pay-out in South African legal history. In the Langa incident, police present at a funeral march shot and killed twenty people, including thirteen children who were aged from 11 to 17. The lawyer for the victims said that the Minister of Law and Order agreed to pay the compensation shortly before a court hearing was to begin in Port Elizabeth. This is a further example of the desire of the government to keep disputes of this nature out of the courts.[6]

The state security system

South Africa has always had a well-developed security system, but more recently a much more sinister shadow security structure has emerged. The National Security Management System (NSMS), which consists of over 500 committees controlled by the police or the army, is a shadow state structure which exists alongside and parallels the normal government structures and operates at every level from the individual small community to the Cabinet. The NSMS deals only with security matters, but as it regards every social issue as a potential security problem, it regards every area of life in South Africa as part of its concern. The South African Minister of Defence, in 1986, said that this network acts as both the government's early warning system for internal threats to state security, and also as a 'highly mobile mechanism to defuse revolutionary unrest'.[7]

The NSMS was established in 1979 as a result of a lack of co-ordination between government department and the competing intelligence services, and as a result of the drying up of information from informants, which was the traditional source of intelligence information. The NSMS operates in secret and functions through a complicated structure of committees which is headed by the State Security Council (SSC). The SSC, which is a subcommittee of the Cabinet, is the pinnacle of this security structure. The chairman is the State President and the members are department heads and the heads of the police and army. The SSC makes recommendations on security matters to the Cabinet, and many people feel that it decides security matters and that the Cabinet merely rubber stamps its decisions. There are various working committees, at the level of government departments, which assist the SSC, and decide on the SSC's programme before it meets. The SSC is also aided by a Secretariat, which is made up of thirteen interdepartmental committees of the SSC. Two of the most important of these committees are the Strategy Branch, and the National Intelligence and Interpretation Branch. The Interpretation and Intelligence Branch is a national clearing house for the four intelligence services and collects information gathered by them, processes and interprets it, and then passes it on to the SSC. The Strategy Branch draws up strategies to meet the threats that have been identified by the Interpretation Branch. They develop what they call 'total strategies' to deal with what they see as 'total onslaught'. At regional level there are Joint Management Committees (JMCs), each of which has its own Intelligence Committee. There are twelve of these JMCs, which roughly correspond with the twelve military commands. As well as an intelligence committee, each JMC also has an economic and social committee which takes non-security-type action where this is seen to be warranted. In addition to the JMCs, there are sixty sub-JMCs and 448 mini-JMCs, that all work at local level.

When a problem is discovered at local level, it is passed through the structure to be interpreted, so that a response can be decided upon, approved by the SSC, and then implemented through the structure. Each sub-JMC and mini-JMC is responsible only for security in its region. Information is interpreted and co-ordinated at a higher level with security information from other regions. All JMCs are made up of civil servants and not elected representatives. All chairmen are either members of the SAP or the SADF.

There are two possible forms of response to a problem or recommendation:

(1) Military or police action.
(2) Economic or social action.

There has been increased reliance on the latter in recent times, and there are many cases where food parcels have been passed out and where the army have been involved in delivering water to townships, and in establishing water schemes for areas. The notion behind this latter form of response is to identify and address black people's grievances before they lead to trouble.

The security system is part of the general pattern towards government by bureaucrats and appointees, as opposed to government by elected representatives. A parallel structure is being developed to enable South Africa to be governed without elected representatives. The power of the JMCs is enormous. If they fail to get their decisions implemented through the normal channels, they can do it through their own shadow structure.

Great stress is placed on secrecy. All members swear an oath of secrecy, and all documents are secret and are delivered by armed couriers. All members have to go through a security clearance before they can join. It is therefore impossible for the community to know what these committees are doing.

The structure is controlled by the military. If they took over government, they would find a ready-made administrative structure in place. But the whole point of the structure is that the military do not need to take over. They have found a way of getting what they want without taking over direct power. They have pushed Parliament aside. It is clear that a secret parallel system of government has been created which can operate independently from the formal constitutional structure. Albeit concealed behind a smoke-screen of disinformation, censorship and legal formality, the apparatus of the police state is already well established in South Africa.

Prisons

The Prison Act 1959[8] makes it a crime to publish any false information concerning the experience in prison of any person or concerning the administration of any prison. It is clear that the state will only tolerate 'ineffectual criticism' of the prison system,[9] and even where publishers have made attempts to verify information, they have been convicted of an offence under this section, the courts having held that they did not do enough.[10] The effect of this provision, plus the courts' interpretation of it, and their placing of a heavy onus on the publisher, has been to insulate the prison system not only from false criticism but also from any form of hard-hitting criticism. One commentator has said that 'freedom to publish that is made conditional on the truth of what is published, is no real freedom at all'.[11]

Many people whom we spoke to who had been in prison said that conditions were deplorable. The food was very bad and the cells were grossly overcrowded. One group of prisoners said that nineteen had been forced to sleep in a cell which was no bigger than 25 feet by 10 feet, and had to share one toilet in the cell.[12] Many prisoners are forced to sleep on rubber mats on the floor, and the toilet is often either a bucket or an outlet into an open sewer which is not partitioned off from the main cell. Medical treatment is unsatisfactory, and prisoners have complained of long delays in receiving treatment, and even when they get treatment it is often inadequate. One prisoner who served a sentence on Robben Island said that he waited for two days to get a broken leg treated, and others have said that it often takes months to see a dentist.

A major problem in South African prisons is the gang system which is a nation-wide organization.[13] These gangs have a structure, ranking and disciplinary code which has its roots in South African history. The gangs are organized in a quasi-military manner, and each gang enforces its own disciplinary code and imposes its own punishment. Between 1974 and 1978, in the Western Cape alone, forty-one prisoners were killed in gang murders, and seventy-seven people were sentenced to death for gang murders.[14] The situation is so severe that the prison officials say that they cannot guarantee the safety of inmates.

The Prisons Act 1959 and the regulations promulgated in terms of it, with the exception of the racially discriminatory provisions, were designed to be 'a conscious and positive response' to the United Nations standard minimum rules for the treatment of prisoners of 1955.[15] The Act provides that white and non-white prisoners shall be kept in separate parts of the prison, so as to prevent whites and non-whites from 'being within view of each other'.[16] The prison regulations further provide that each prisoner is to be provided with food 'according to the prescribed diet scale applicable to his race group'.[17] It is clear that the food supplied to white prisoners is of a far higher standard than that supplied to blacks.

An internal complaints procedure was set up by the Prison Regulations,[18] but its observance is not enforceable by the courts.[19] Also, prisoners are deterred from complaining by the threat of conviction for a disciplinary offence if their complaint is held to be 'false, frivolous or malicious'.[20] Under the regulations, Supreme Court judges have access to all prisoners[21] and the right to visit any prisoner at any time. Potentially, this is a valuable safeguard, but the visits are not frequent enough or well enough organized to amount to a major form of control, and it depends for its effectiveness on the interest of each Supreme Court judge. The 1984–5 Report of the Department of Justice reveals that there were ninety-five visits to prisons by Supreme Court judges during this period, but many of these were made by one Transvaal judge, thus many Supreme Court judges never visited a prison.

The Minister of Justice has established rules governing the condition of detention of detainees under the emergency regulations.[22] By virtue of these regulations, a detainee is in a worse position than awaiting-trial prisoners or sentenced prisoners. Emergency detainees cannot receive food, drink or cigarette parcels, they have to seek special permission to write letters, to study or to see legal advisers; access to reading material is restricted, and when they appear before a disciplinary hearing, they require the permission of the Minister of Law and Order to be legally represented.

We heard many reports of brutality in prisons. We were given examples of the use of tear-gas in enclosed cells, the use of dogs to break up protests, and reports of continuous brutal beatings by warders. We also heard reports of children being kept in the same cells as adults and of children being beaten and sodomized by gang leaders in the cells. However, despite the harshness of the treatment received in prison, many prisoners saw the prison as a place of refuge from the security police, because it is only when a detainee was taken from the prison by the security police that he was subjected to torture.

There is some evidence that prison abuses lead to disciplinary action. The head of Barberton Prison, who was found guilty of common assault in 1984 for issuing instructions that prisoners be assaulted, was demoted and placed in charge of a storeroom. In 1983, six prison warders, who had acted on his instructions, were found guilty of assault and sentenced to jail terms ranging from one to eight years for the deaths of three prisoners and the assault of thirty-four others.[23] Whatever complaint one may have about the adequacy of the punishment received by the officers, at least the authorities took some form of action in this case. However, it seems that these are among the few exceptions to the general rule, and that the authorities will only act when compelled to do so by overwhelming evidence.

Conclusion

When the National Party came to power in South Africa a series of 'draconian' security laws were passed, commencing with the Suppression of Communism Act 1950, which were designed to preclude almost all forms of extra-parliamentary opposition. The flow of enactments in a similar vein became a flood by the 1960s, and by the end of that decade a state security apparatus had been fully constituted.[24] The irony of the South African security system is that when the Suppression of Communism Act was introduced South Africa was a peaceful society. The growth and rigorous application of the security laws in subsequent years was paralleled by a huge increase in crime. The South African security system thus fails, in spite of all its brutality, even to achieve its own objective: the maintenance of peace and order in South Africa. One commentator has said, 'The misuse of the security machine by its operators is converting it into a major engine of divisiveness and strife in South Africa.'[25]

Notes

1. Civil actions for damages were subsequently brought by victims against the government and others but are still in progress at the time of writing. See p. 81.
2. See p. 84.
3. See p. 76.
4. S. 49 (2) of the Criminal Procedure Act 1977 (no. 5 of 1977), allows a police officer to use deadly force where a subject resists arrest or flees from an impending arrest.
5. S. 49 of the Internal Security Act 1982 (no. 74 of 1982), allows a police officer to use force, including the use of firearms and other weapons, to disperse particular kinds of gatherings, but non-lethal weapons should be used first. See also p. 61.
6. ibid.
7. Race Relations Survey, 1985, Institute for Race Relations, 1986, p. 464.
8. Act no. 8 of 1959, S 44 (1) (f).
9. A. Mathews, *Freedom, State Security and the Rule of Law*, Cape Town and Johannesburg, 1986, p. 132.
10. *S* v. *S.A. Association of Newspapers* 1970 1 SA 469 (W).
11. Mathews, p. 153.
12. At Modderbee Prison.
13. See N. Haysom, *Towards an Understanding of Prison Gangs*, Institute of Criminology, Cape Town, 1981.
14. Haysom, op. cit.
15. Dirk Van Zyl Smit, 'Normal Prisons in an "Abnormal" Society?'
16. S 23 (1) (6).

17. Regulation 132 (4).
18. Regulation 103 (1).
19. *Goldberg* v. *Minister for Prisons* 1979 1 SA 14 (A).
20. Regulation 99 (1) (0).
21. Regulation 104 (2).
22. *Government Gazette* 10281, 12 June 1986 and see pp. 97–9.
23. Race Relations Survey, 1985, p. 501.
24. See Chapter 9.
25. Mathews, p. 156.

15   Political Institutions

Before the coming to power of the National Party in 1948 there had been some limited non-white representation in government. The new government was evidently determined to end it and soon tackled the constitutional problem presented by the presence of 'coloured' voters on the common electoral roll. Their franchise was preserved by an entrenched provision of the Constitution which could not be altered save by a two-thirds majority vote of a joint sitting of both houses of Parliament. The government contended that such a majority was not required, but legislation passed by a simple majority establishing a separate roll for coloured voters was successfully challenged before the Appellate Division.[1] The government subsequently achieved its object by packing the Appellate Division with its supporters. In a fresh challenge the newly constituted Appellate Division reversed the previous ruling.[2] The corollary of the exclusion of all non-whites from the government of South Africa was the homelands policy, which aimed to remove South African nationality from all blacks and give them ostensible citizenship rights in territories which were nominally self-governing. Thereafter until 1983 all non-white people were effectively disenfranchised.

In November 1983 the white voters endorsed a new constitution providing for the creation of three legislative chambers: a House of Assembly for whites; a House of Representatives for 'coloured' people; and a House of Delegates for Indians. The members were to be elected from separate rolls and each house was to have virtually exclusive legislative power for its own electorate and community in matters classified as 'own affairs'. All other matters, called 'general affairs' (e.g. matters affecting the economy, security or foreign affairs) were to fall within the purview of the Parliament as a whole, and the overall Cabinet, led by the State President, was the executive authority and the initiator of general legislation. The State President has sole authority to decide what are general affairs. The Cabinet has had only two non-white members, one of whom has recently resigned.[3]

In the event of conflict between the houses, a President's Council, established simultaneously, has the deciding voice. Its membership is chosen in proportion to representation in the separate houses. The House of Assembly has 178 members, the House of Representatives has 80, and the House of Delegates has 45. There is thus a built-in, pro-government white majority on the President's Council which ensures that the non-white houses cannot defeat the decisions of the government-controlled House of Assembly. This is illustrated by the conflict over the Internal Security Amendment Act 1986, which both non-white houses rejected but which was later passed by decree of the President's Council. In any case, such disputes are likely to be uncommon because the non-white legislators are people who have already compromised with the government by defying the overwhelming opposition of black people to participation in this constitutional system. This was demonstrated in the response to the campaign by the United Democratic Front to dissuade coloured and Indian voters from taking part in the election for their respective houses. The polls in the election were extremely low, averaging about 30 per cent in the coloured election and 24 per cent in the Indian.[4]

Thus we find that the attempt by the government in the 1983 Constitution to achieve greater democracy—or to present the appearance of so doing—has not in reality conferred any significant rights on members of the coloured and Indian communities. There has been some degree of delegation to those communities of administrative responsibility for some matters deemed to be their exclusive concern. These matters include education and housing, but within strictly defined limits. The chief restraint is that financial control is kept in the domain of the Parliament as a whole. The overall effect is to leave minority white domination essentially intact. The apartheid system is not significantly relaxed by what is little more than a charade, designed to mislead the naïve into believing that there has been a real shift of power in favour of two minority communities.

Of course, the major glaring undemocratic feature of the 1983 Constitution is its total omission of any participation by black Africans who comprise about 72 per cent of the population of South Africa. Manifestly, the creation of an African house of parliament with proportionate representation to population would have made any pretence of democratic decision-making impossible without surrender of white domination. Thoughts of surrender are evidently far from the minds of those who are dominant in the National Party and the government.

The unique feature of South Africa is the exclusion from any participation in government of the great majority of its citizens. This is so even if one regards as valid the 'homelands' policy, which has led the government unilaterally to replace for some 8 million people their South African citizenship with a dubious homeland citizenship. The denial of the franchise has led some black defendants in treason and other trials to reject the jurisdiction of the courts, and we have considerable sympathy with their attitude. However, while we believe the legitimacy of the South African government to be seriously in question, it is plainly in *de facto* control of the country. It cannot escape responsibility for meeting the requirements of international law in relation to human rights as if it were a democratically elected government.

Notes

1. Harris v Minister of the Interior 1952 (2) SA 428 (AD).
2. Collins v Minister of the Interior 1957 (1) SA 552 (AD).
3. Mr Allan Hendrickse, following his attempt to bathe at a whites-only beach.
4. Davenport, *South Africa – A Modern History* (3rd edn., 1987), p. 471.

16 The Homelands

The 1970 Bantu Homelands Act (now the National States Citizenship Act) provides for the establishment of ten so-called homelands to which eventually all 20 million black South Africans are to belong as citizens according to their ethnic, linguistic and cultural affiliation. This policy of denationalization, often referred to as 'Grand Apartheid', was pursued by South African governments well before the enactment of the Bantu Homelands Act and, to some extent, may be traced back even before the National Party came to power in 1948.[1] Ten homelands have been created: Transkei, Bophuthatswana, Ciskei, Venda, Lebowa, Gazankulu, Qwa-Qwa, KwaZulu, KwaNdebele and KaNgwane.

Only the first four of these, with a population of around 8 million people have opted to become 'independent' states. However, their statehood is not recognized by any other state save South Africa, and the United Nations has repeatedly denounced their independence as unacceptable under international law.[2] Some 13 per cent of the territory of South Africa has been set aside for these homelands, and, in fairness, it should be noted, that not all of them are devoid of agricultural or mineral resources potential, though the infrastructure in most is grossly underdeveloped and the living conditions are squalid. It is therefore not surprising that most blacks prefer to remain South Africans than to accept an independence which makes them aliens in their country of birth and deprives them of the economic opportunities, however meagre, which South Africa may offer. It is the leaders of the homelands that mainly profit from independence and often force it on their people in collusion with the South African government. In one instance the government of KwaNdebele requested independence, but after mass protests, their initiative was overturned on 12 August 1986 by the KwaNdebele Legislative Assembly. The case of KwaNdebele also exposes the hypocrisy of the South African government's claim that it wishes to set up 'self-governing' structures along ethnic and language lines to avoid tribal strifes between blacks: on 12 January 1986 it incorporated the 120,000 people of Moutse against their will into KwaNdebele, although most of them speak Pedi rather than Ndebele.[3]

Also, when Bophuthatswana became independent, large numbers of non-Tswana people living in that area were incorporated into that homeland without receiving the citizenship of Bophuthatswana, and the Bophuthatswana authorities are said to have waged a fairly systematic campaign of persecuting those non-Tswanas and discriminating against them by, for example, excluding them from access to the state's pension scheme and certain social services.[4]

Joseph Lelyveld, in a scathing attack on Pretoria's homeland policy, vividly describes how spurious the government's claim remains that it wanted to regroup territorially black people along ethnic lines and what nightmarish bureaucratic consequences the implementation of this policy led to.[5]

It was the bureaucrats in Pretoria, finally who determined that there were ten black nations. They could just as easily have counted two, or three, or twenty. Black nationalists, of course, count only one. Two, or three would have meant the surrender of large amounts of white land and the creation of black power bases, plausible states, from which a successful challenge to white dominance might have been mounted. Twenty would have been unmanageable. Ten was an arbitrary compromise, a way of diffusing the demand for black political rights without being any more ridiculous than necessary.[6]

It is not surprising that the government's homeland policy has recently become more and more controversial even within government circles. It is, indeed, difficult to imagine how homelands, such as Bophuthatswana, consisting of seven separate territories scattered over three provinces, or KwaZulu, fragmented into forty-one territorial segments across one province (Natal), are able to develop politically into statehood or survive economically. The latter homeland, understandably, has so far adamantly refused to accept a meaningless 'independence'. In vain also were the government's attempts, through an international treaty, to cede large chunks of South African territory bordering Swaziland, a UN member, to that state, although the Swaziland government would probably have accepted such aggrandisement since Pretoria had promised also to cede another portion of South African territory in such a way as to give land-locked Swaziland a long-sought access to the sea. It would have allowed South Africa to rid herself of hundreds of thousands of its black citizens, mostly Swazis, but the Supreme Court of South Africa annulled that treaty as unconstitutional.

Our mission focused its attention mainly on two homelands, both 'independent': Ciskei and Bophuthatswana. Constraints of time allowed us to visit only these two homelands to examine the state of human rights and the administration of justice.

Ciskei, together with Venda, has the worst reputation among the homelands in this respect. It became independent in December 1981. Its inhabitants are almost entirely Xhosa speaking and they have no different identity from the Xhosas of Transkei, the much larger neighbouring homeland to the north, though the Ciskei government frantically tries to pretend that there is a special Ciskeian national identity. The two homelands' leaders idiosyncracies occasionally lead to bizarre antagonistic political manoeuvres, culminating recently even in the threat of war, although military hostilities are difficult to imagine since the two homelands are separated by a small patch of South African territory. Ciskei's Parliament consists of twenty-two elected representatives and thirty-two tribal personages, mostly appointed by the President and therefore loyal to him. He is thus assured of a parliamentary majority even in the unlikely event that his party, the Ciskei National Independence Party (CNIP), should not win all the twenty-two seats among the elected members. Any political opposition is ruthlessly suppressed. In addition, any Act of Parliament requires the assent of the President to become the law of the land.[7] Lennox Sebe, said to be a cunning and shrewd politician, was elected 'President for Life', although Section 24 of the Constitution provides for a period of office of only seven years.

This mockery of a parliamentary democracy is mirrored by the provisions of Chapter III of the Constitution, titled 'Declaration of Fundamental Rights'. It contains a number of human rights and freedoms not much different from many Western-styled constitutions, but in Section 19 (para 3), there is an exclusionary clause virtually nullifying their value: 'No law made by the National Assembly or which continues in force in Ciskei under any provision of this Constitution shall be declared invalid by any court of law by reason only of the fact that it contravenes or is in conflict with any provision of this Chapter'.

Under these circumstances, it is not surprising that the Ciskei government has little to fear from the courts, and if the courts should rule against government abuses and issue orders to stop them, the authorities often simply ignore them. The events surrounding the infamous 1983 bus boycott may serve as an example. They have been described in some detail by Nicholas Haysom in a paper which he appropriately called 'Ruling with the Whip'.[8]

In May 1983 the Ciskei Transport Corporation (CTC) announced an increase of its fares by at least 11 per cent. The company, 50 per cent of whose shares are owned by the Ciskei government, operates approximately 650 buses to transport nearly 50,000 persons daily, mostly Ciskeians commuting between Mnandantsane, a black township of about 350,000 inhabitants close to East London but within the Ciskei, and East London, where most of them work. In a community meeting summoned by various civic organizations, a committee of ten members was elected to make representations to the company; since they were unsuccessful in these attempts, another meeting on 17 July 1983 decided to call a boycott of the CTC buses. The boycott was immediately followed to the extent that the occupancy rate in CTC buses dropped by some 80 per cent the second day after the boycott call. Most commuters preferred to switch to the South African run railways for transport to their places of work though it meant for most of them considerable delays. Many used taxis, shared private cars or simply walked across the border.

The Ciskeian authorities immediately reverted to various means of harassment, intimidation or outright violence against the boycotters or those that were presumed to participate in the boycott. Eight representatives of the Committee of Ten were detained, which made peaceful negotiations even more difficult. The police set up road blocks forcing cars to wait for extensive periods of time, asking passengers why they were not taking the buses, mishandling passengers including women and children. Beating passengers and whipping them with sjamboks became common abuses, and many victims reported to the hospitals with injuries ranging from broken bones to wounds caused by shots. In one instance, soldiers tried to force people about to board the train to use the buses; they refused, some stones were thrown, people were shot at by Ciskeian soldiers, allegedly to defend themselves against 'an unprovoked attack by a rowdy crowd'.[9] When at a subsequent trial fifty-nine persons were charged with that assault, the magistrate, when the prosecution introduced its third witness, asked the prosecution to admit defeat of its case, saying, 'They are obviously not guilty'.[10]

In another instance, six commuters applied for an interdict to restrain the police from assaulting them on their way to and from work and forcing them to use buses. The Ciskei Supreme Court granted the interdict—to little avail: the harassment of commuters continued unabated.

Police and government sponsored brutality actually increased after a state of emergency was declared on 4 August 1983. Particularly infamous became the treatment experienced in the Sisa Oukashe stadium where hundreds of Ciskeians were detained for days, often rounded up at random, on unfounded allegations, from their houses and at public places. Whipping, beating and various forms of torture were common practice; those injured did not receive any medical treatment, neither food nor water nor blankets were provided. This 'concentration camp' was run by so-called vigilantes, a kind of unofficial police reserve composed of members of the Ciskei National Independence Party, mostly loyal to Lennox Sebe. The vigilantes were often the most ruthless when it came to harassing and assaulting their fellow citizens, usurping executive powers they do not have under the law. However, they act more or less in open collusion with the police and are backed up by the authorities. Thus it is not surprising that the police have consistently refused to accept allegations of assaults taking place in the stadium, and the Minister of Justice, D.M. Tahane, equally denied any knowledge of such facts, although these excesses were public knowledge in Mnandantsane and reported to the police by various victims.

The assaults on bus boycotters took a heavy toll in life and limb: it is estimated that there were over ninety fatalities, though the official figures are considerably lower.

We have so far followed the account given by Nicholas Haysom, who made his investigations on the spot. It is revealing that the Ciskei government threatened him with a libel suit but eventually decided not to pursue it. However, our mission is able to confirm his allegations that there is a persistent pattern of violations of human rights on a massive scale. Two of our members were present in Ciskei's Supreme Court on a day when thirty-nine young people were brought in for trial for the first time. From what we could gather from interviews with some of the accused and their lawyers, the facts of the case are as follows.

The state claims that in the Wittlesea area (Ciskei), during the night of 24 April 1986, rioting occurred in the course of which various homes and possessions of persons were burnt and destroyed, some persons assaulted and two persons killed by 'necklacing'. One of the killed was a schoolteacher who was said to be a member of the ruling party in the Ciskei, the other a potential state witness in a criminal case.

Since the police had no clues as to the assailants, the police during that night and for several days later arrested many people; at one stage a total of 158 people were in custody, as one of the advocates found from the charge sheet in the Magistrates Court. Thirty-nine persons, most of whom were minors under 18, the youngest a girl of 14, were eventually charged with two counts of murder and nine counts of public violence. Most of the accused had remained in custody until the day of the first court hearing. Many of the potential witnesses had also remained in protective custody for more than eight months by virtue of an order by the Attorney-General, until they were called to testify for the state during the court hearing. Neither the accused nor the witnesses were allowed to have access to legal representation while in custody; they were practically kept incommunicado, under Section 26 of the Ciskei Internal Security Act; their parents were able to visit them only twice during that period. Lawyers were able to speak to the witnesses only after the first of the four state witnesses was sworn in by the court and requested to speak to her attorney. When the witnesses were allowed to do so—in the presence of two members of the security police who were investigating the case—they withdrew their incriminating statements given previously against the accused to the police, alleging that they were forced to sign them under duress after being tortured by the police. In court the first witness exhibited marks from injuries allegedly caused by a sjambok. The second witness said that a rubber tube was put over her head which almost suffocated her. The third witness, also a young girl, showed weal marks allegedly resulting from assaults by the police. The fourth witness also described various injuries inflicted on his body. One of the state witnesses described an assault on another state witness whereby some plastic tube was tied around her legs and set on fire; it appeared that her toes had been fused together as a result.

It was not our mission's task to ascertain whether the charge laid against the accused was justified or not. But we do express our profound shock about the barbarities inflicted on the accused and witnesses in this case. It is revealing how one of the Supreme Court justices whom we interviewed—he was, however, not judging this case—responded to the question of credibility of such statements given in police custody:

Apparently from what I heard, it seems that there was a number of witnesses who were present at the time, who gave statements in the normal course of giving statements to the police who were investigating. They must have told what occurred, saw what happened—vital witnesses. We now come to the trial some months later and what happens? The AG consults with them the morning before the trial because the police took the statement and he and the barrister must now hear from the mouth of this witness what he intends to say. He finds that they confirm basically what is in their statements. He has now called some four of them, and each one has immediately after taking the oath told the court that he knows nothing about this, he was not there. If you look at what occurred and the repetition of it, there can be no doubt in anybody's mind that these people were subjected to something—call it possibly intimidation, coercion whatever—but clearly these people have decided that they know nothing. This happens in Northern Ireland all the time, where groups do this to frustrate the workings of justice. I mention this to you as an example where people committed killings—political or otherwise. Committed crimes are being protected by coercion from somewhere—gives you an example of the situation one is living with. . . .

The judge's bias speaks for itself. There are, however, South African judges who appear more sceptical about confessions made in police custody and who claim that they disregard them as evidence. For example, Stewart C.J. of Bophuthatswana told us that he would never allow statements made to the police to be introduced in court.

We saw the accused that same day, nineteen of whom showed us marks of bodily injuries which were clearly visible even eight months after they were alleged to be inflicted upon them—a horrifying experience. Most had stripes on their back, allegedly caused by whippings with sjamboks and sticks. Some also had scars on their heads due to beatings with sticks. One claimed that boiling water was poured over his left foot—we noticed that the black pigmentation was replaced by velvet spots on his flesh. One had lost his sight in his left eye; he said a policeman had hit it with his fist. Many of the accused alleged that, at some stage during their incarceration, they were admitted to the Mulder Drift prison (Ciskei) and complained about and exhibited their injuries to a certain Chinese doctor; however, he seems to have ignored the injuries and made no record of them.

The lawyers of the torture victims intend to request the Attorney-General to prosecute the policemen involved. In the light of past experience, this will prove difficult. A civil suit for damages is also unlikely to succeed: a case against the Minister of Police must be lodged within six months after the cause of the action; but the witnesses and accused were able to see their lawyers only more than eight months after the injuries were inflicted upon them. Limitation therefore bars any civil claims against the government, and a civil case may be instituted only against the individual policemen; neither they nor their colleagues are likely to co-operate in any investigations by the prosecution.

It may be surprising that these and other glaring excesses of police powers remain largely ignored by the international community; however, the homelands, being not recognized internationally, rarely face the consequences of being in the public eye. Thus President Lennox Sebe could openly declare that 'potential insurgents should expect to be tortured', without risking a public outcry.[11] Only occasionally the human rights situation in Ciskei is taken note of by a foreign country. So notorious is the lawlessness in Ciskei, that some time ago the US Embassy to South Africa strongly advised US citizens not to travel to that homeland because of a total breakdown of the rule of law.

Compared with the Ciskei, the independent homeland of Bophuthatswana may appear almost a sanctuary of the rule of law, though a closer look will soon reveal a rather less glowing picture. Bophuthatswana, more familiarly referred to as simply 'Bop', is a unique feature of the landscape of South Africa. It consists of seven parts, separated from one another, looking like a patched rug on the map of the northern regions of South

Africa, not dissimilar to some of the scattered states in eighteenth-century Germany.

The Bophuthatswanas Constitution (Act no. 18 of 1977, as amended) in its Chapter II, contains an impressive 'Declaration of Fundamental Rights'. Most of these fundamental rights are subject to limitations imposed by an Act of Parliament, leaving a wide scope for interpretation when, for example, the right to freedom of expression may be restricted by law if 'necessary in a democratic society in the interests of national security, territorial integrity or public safety'.[12]

What makes the bill of rights quite unique in the South African context, which might in theory give it some teeth, is the provision in Section 18 (para. 2): 'Except for the circumstances provided for in this Declaration, a fundamental right and freedom shall not be totally abolished or in its essence be encroached upon'. (This section apparently follows Art. 19, para. 2, of the West German Constitution.) Under Section 8, para. 1, the 'fundamental rights are binding on the legislature, the executive and the judiciary, and are directly enforceable by law'. The right of judicial review by individual application is conferred upon the Supreme Court.[13]

Unlike the Ciskei Constitution or that of the Republic of South Africa, the Bophuthatswana Cotitution therefore provides a powerful tool for the judiciary to test any Executive orders and even Acts of Parliament against the bill of rights. The quality of the judiciary and its willingness to use these powers are therefore of paramount importance.

The potential for judicial review may be illustrated by the Marwane case. Marwane, a Ciskeian, was charged under the South African Terrorism Act no. 83 of 1967, which Bophuthatswana inherited when it became independent. He contended that this Act was null and void since it was contrary to the Bophuthatswana Constitution. Heimstra, then Chief Justice of Bophuthatswana ruled that the bill of rights was applicable only prospectively and therefore did not apply to inherited legislation. At that time appeals against Bophuthatswana judicial decisions could be lodged to the Appellate Division of the South African Supreme Court in Bloemfontein. The Appellate division held that the South African Terrorism Act was inconsistent with the Bophuthatswana Constitution and therefore void in the homeland.[14]

Indeed, it is surprising to find the South African Supreme Court deciding that a South African Act was violating human rights. The Bophuthatswana Constitution was subsequently altered to clarify that the bill of rights applied to inherited legislation as well as prospective legislation. The South African Terrorism Act was thus declared unconstitutional.

Encouraging as this decision may appear, it plainly had little or no impact on government practice.

This may be illustrated by the ways the government attempts to hold down its political opponents. Mr Rocky Ishmael Peter Malebane Metsing,[15] a member of the Bophuthatswana Parliament, who fell out with the ruling party and founded the People's Progressive Party (PPP) in 1985, told us that he is barred from holding public meetings with more than twenty participants, although, he claims, his party was properly registered. However, this claim was refuted by the Deputy Minister of Justice, Mr Mothebe, who stated to us that the PPP did not fulfil the requirement of proper registration, since many of those that were on the list of registered voters allegedly were not citizens of Bophuthatswana. Under Bophuthatswana legislation only registered parties are allowed to hold meetings without prior permission by the government. Such restrictions appear clearly to be inconsistent with the Constitution guaranteeing the right to freedom of expression (Section 15) and to freedom of assembly (Section 16), and it is difficult to see how the exclusionary clause (restrictions by law are possible when 'necessary in a democratic society in the interest of national security') could be invoked in the case of a Member of Parliament who tries to achieve nothing else but a change of government by peaceful means—not even the government claims that he is a revolutionary. Even more astonishing are other restrictions he claims are imposed on his political activities:

Every meeting that I hold I have to inform the government that I am holding the meeting, and I have got to give the Minister of Law and Order a copy of my speech and tell him exactly what I am going to do there and how many people I am going to have there and give him all literature that I am going to distribute there and possibly guess what questions people might raise there and how I am going to answer them.

The leader of another opposition party not represented in Parliament, Victor Thebe Sifora, likewise claims that all his meetings have been banned since July 1986, notwithstanding numerous applications to the government. He said that the government, under various pretexts, either refused them or deferred a decision beyond the date the meetings were to take place. He raised the issue of the constitutionality of the Internal Security Act, under which the government presently operates to suppress opposition activities, with the Bophuthatswana Supreme Court. At the time of our visit the case was still pending.

Trumped-up charges are another form of harassment, as Sifora was able to relate to us from his own experience. On 27 August 1986 his office was raided by the police alleging he was suspected of hiding bombs and other explosives on his property. Some sixty-five young members of his party were arrested; he himself was detained on 30 August and subsequently taken to various prisons and police stations until he was released on 24 September and all charges against him dropped. They were (1) holding unlawful gatherings, (2) planning a *coup d'état*, (3) lining up a number of people for assassination. However, during his detention he was never formally charged. His repeated requests to see a lawyer or, at least, a member of his family were denied. Though the conditions in his cells were quite unsanitary, at least he was not tortured, thus faring better than the other detainees whose cries in neighbouring cells he was able to hear quite distinctly.

The Deputy Minister of Justice, Mr Mothebe, when we confronted him with these accounts, stressed that even under the stipulations of the Internal Security Act an arrested person would be entitled to have immediate access to his lawyer; he insisted that Sifora was duly charged, not kept incommunicado, and that his lawyer actually did have access to him.

We subsequently interviewed Mr Sifora's Johannnesburg-based attorney, who essentially confirmed Mr Sifora's version:

I cannot say that they [the police] directly refused, they tucked him away in a prison in Garankuwa, which is miles away from anywhere. We could not even locate him. They refused him access because they would not tell us where he was being kept. We tried to find out—there were a number of young children who were detained with him, and they were kept in a police station—we tried to get access to them, but the officers at the police station refused access saying that these were their instructions—which they denied when we spoke to the Attorney-General. He said that it was just the whim of the policemen in charge. . . . The Bop government particularly, when we address telexes and letters to them, they just do not reply—impossible to get any information—our problem all the time with detainees—they deliberately avoid taking calls and responding to letters.[16]

Priscilla Jana also confirmed that some of the children, arrested with Sifora, had suffered 'severe cases of assault'. She was instituting civil actions against the Bophuthatswana government in these instances.

Stewart C.J. admitted that beatings by police do happen, but he claimed not on a large scale. He also assured us that he was ready to rule against the government in cases of maltreatment of prisoners and determined to enforce the bill of rights in all cases that come to his court. Bophuthatswana has also appointed an ombudsman with wide-ranging powers to look into any complaints of government abuses. It appears, however, that most people in Bophuthatswana have little trust in these institutions and are reluctant to avail themselves of them. Legal proceedings are also costly, legal aid being practically non-existent. One of the tactics the government is said to adopt to impede the Opposition from using legal channels is to tie up Opposition members in a variety of legal cases, often on trumped-up charges, weakening them financially to the point of bankruptcy. In addition, at the magistrate's level, courts are usually known for being biased in favour of the government. Victims of such bias are in particular the unions, which are restricted to operate only if they are based in Bophuthatswana. It therefore comes as little surprise that trade unionists and other political activists prefer to be brought to courts in South Africa rather than in Bophuthatswana.

The whole fabric of justice, impressive as it may appear on paper, is considered by many residents there as a mere façade to cover up a basically unjust system of government. The Winterfeld case is one of the latest examples. In Winterfeld, a town close to the South African border, in 1986 a crowd had gathered to discuss grievances because a number of children had been detained by the Bophuthatswana police. When the police felt that the crowd became unruly, they panicked and fired into the crowd killing at least eleven people; many others were detained and brutally tortured. Eventually, a commission of inquiry was set up, chaired by one of the Supreme Court justices. Before the commission was able to carry out its work, Bophuthat-swana's President Mangope promoted two of the prime movers of the massacre, Colonel Malope and Major Mohobojane to brigadier and colonel respectively, thereby, for all practical purposes, already prejudging the commission's findings. It is this type of mockery of justice that makes the people of Bophuthatswana cynical about the government's claim of having one of the most advanced constitutions among African countries with the rule of law being cherished to the utmost extent. The Winterfeld Inquiry was never concluded and no report has been published.

The homelands' claim of 'independence' from South Africa is generally ridiculed. On the surface, all the trappings of a sovereign state are there: Parliament, government and judiciary, even military forces and diplomatic missions, though ambassadors are exchanged only with the other independent homelands and with the Republic of South Africa. However, in reality, all are totally subservient to Pretoria. This is so quite openly in the economic sphere: the homelands (but also the UN member states of Lesotho and Swaziland) form a monetary and customs union with South Africa.

Industry in the homelands is mostly owned and run by South Africans or set up by foreign investors or as subsidiaries of the giant South African business conglomerates. This is even true for the tourist industry, especially gambling casinos, which are not allowed to operate in South Africa itself and from which some of the independent homelands claim to derive a substantial portion of their budgetary income. To use cheap labour from the homelands, the South African government encourages white entrepreneurs, through financial and fiscal incentives, to set up industrial plants in areas bordering the homelands; for many inhabitants this is the only way to find employment, though lowly paid.

Dependence on South Africa is less visible in the more sensitive areas of the military and national security. However, many of the experts we interviewed confirmed that the security services of the homelands closely co-operate with their South African counterparts, and in fact are said to be controlled more or less by the latter. For example, Dean Farisani, a senior churchman detained by the Venda police from 22 November 1986 until 30 January 1987 told us that South African security policemen were present during his interrogations while in detention; he attributed his final release to the intervention of a high-ranking South African security police officer who had come from South Africa the day before. Dean Farisani's detention had received considerable international publicity and obviously threatened to become an embarrassment to South Africa, although, in theory, it was entirely an internal matter for the Venda government.

Notes

1. See, for example, the Native Land Act 1913 and the Native Trust and Land Act 1936.
2. See also J. Dugard, *The Denationalization of Black South Africans in Pursuance of Apartheid: A Question for the International Court of Human Justice*, Occasional Papers No. 8, Centre for Applied Legal Studies of the University of Witwatersrand, August 1984, pp. 5ff.
3. For further details, see the TRAC publication, *Kwandebele: The Struggle Against 'Independence'* (Johannesburg, 1986).
4. J. Yarwitch, TRAC, pt 1, p. 3 (Johannesburg, 1986).

5. J. Lelyveld, *Move Your Shadow* London, 1986) pp. 122ff; see also Leach, op. cit., pp. 82ff.
6. Lelyveld, p. 132.
7. Section 36, para. 2, of the Constitution Act, n. 20 of 1981, as amended.
8. N. Haysom, *Ruling with the Whip: A Report of the Violations of Human Rights in the Ciskei*, Occasional Papers No. 5, Centre for Applied Legal Studies, University of Witwatersrand, October 1983.
9. Haysom, p. 38.
10. Tape-recorded interview.
11. N. Haysom, *Mbangalala: The Rise of Right-Wing Vigilantes in South Africa.* See p. 87 fn. 59.
12. Section 15, para. 2.
13. Section 8, paras. 2 and 3. On the issue of the superiority of the bill of rights over ordinary legislation, see also *Cameron Smith* v. *Attorney-General* [1984] 1 SA 196 (B).
14. *S* v. *Marwane*, South African Law Reports, September 1983 (3). See also G.N. Barrie, *Marwana's Case: Echoes of* Marbury v. Madison *on the Arid Plains of Southern Africa*, André M. Thomashausen, 'Human Rights in South Africa: The Case of Bophuthatswana', *South Africa Law Journal* (1984): 469ff.
15. In February 1988, it was reported that a military coup had thrust Mr Metsing and his party into power in Bophuthatswana but 34 South African troops, 'invited' by the ruling party to assist, restored order in a few hours. See *Weekly Mail*, 12–18 February 1988.
16. Tape-recorded interview.

17 Future Developments

Time is rapidly running out for a peaceful resolution of the conflict in South Africa. Most opponents of apartheid are dissatisfied with the changes which have taken place and the government's promises of reform. Indeed, they consider these meaningless while the government refuses to contemplate the total abolition of the apartheid system. Piecemeal reforms will plainly not be accepted by the black majority.

However, Rev. Beyers Naude, until recently Secretary-General of the South African Council of Churches, assured us that there is a considerable fund of goodwill within the black community, a deep belief in human rights and acceptance of the values enshrined in the constitutions of the Western democracies. He has confidence that a black leadership in South Africa would not victimize whites and would be seeking a genuinely democratic society after the end of apartheid. His assessment was shared by most members of the non-white opposition who talked to us.

He pointed out to us, however, that the present government faces a dilemma. If President Botha were to push a reform programme too fast or too far, a substantial number of his conservative and religious supporters would switch to the right—a trend that has already been seen in the white election of May 1987. But the alternative is growing bitterness among black people, escalating violence leading to a situation of undeclared civil war—a state of affairs already existing in some parts of the country.

The dominant aspiration of the opposition, led by the ANC and the UDF, is a unitary constitutional system for South Africa based on the principle of 'one person, one vote'. However, a number of compromise proposals for power-sharing have recently been put forward in the hope of overcoming conservative resistance to that democratic outcome. In December 1986, Chief Buthelezi, Prime Minister of KwaZulu, proposed a power-sharing scheme for the whole of Natal (including KwaZulu which accounts for about 80 per cent of the population of Natal).[1]

The proposal worked out over eight months has been termed *indaba* (a Zulu word for legislative meeting). Discussions took place between groups and individuals of all races, and the proposal claims to provide a single system of provincial government in which the majority party would exercise power on the basis of universal suffrage. There would be two legislative houses. The lower would have 100 members elected by 'one person, one vote' and the upper house would have fifty members divided equally between five ethnic categories. These would be Africans, Asians, English-speakers and Afrikaners, together with a residual category for people who do not want to be identified with one of the other groups. The proposed *indaba* constitution would contain a bill of rights and other checks on the power of the majority.

The *indaba* proposal was rejected immediately following its publication both by the Botha govrnment and by the UDF and ANC. The former fears subordination of the white minority and the latter objects to its divergence from the principle of majority rule. There seems no way in which these opposing positions can be reconciled.

Another approach to reconciliation is the notion of a federal system of government for South Africa. The cantonal structure of Switzerland is offered as a parallel. This approach is adamantly rejected by the UDF and ANC, again because it conflicts with the ideal of a unitary system for the whole of South Africa. Such a solution is not ruled out by the ANC and the UDF in the longer term, but, it appears, they do not wish to pre-empt constitutional changes without a form of democratic endorsement which present conditions do not allow. It is not, however, the task of our mission to evaluate the merits and demerits of a federal constitution for South Africa, and in any event members of the mission hold different views on the subject. Furthermore, the issue may be academic because the South African government has shown no signs of making any proposals for new constitutional mechanisms based on federation.

Another topic of discussion in the area of constitutional reform is the addition of an overriding bill of rights to the South African constitution. The government had long been opposed to the idea, and many opponents of the government were also sceptical. In the first place a bill of rights would be of doubtful legitimacy unless adopted through a system of universal suffrage. Second, it is inconceivable that a meaningful bill of rights would be compatible with the apartheid system. On the other hand, some lawyers argue that the introduction of a bill of rights incorporating the standards found in the European Convention on Human Rights and the Universal Declaration of Human Rights, together with such procedural safeguards as appear in the constitutions of the United States, Italy and West Germany, would pave the way for the abolition of apartheid. It would alter the legal map of South Africa. If the fundamental rights of equal protection of the law and non-discrimination were seriously enforced, apartheid laws would be annulled. Of course, this would require the judges to interpret the bill of rights in the same spirit as the judges in the other countries which have been mentioned.

To the surprise of many lawyers, the government changed its attitude to the bill of rights issue in April 1986, when it requested the Law Commission to 'look at the function and role of the courts of South Africa as regards the protection of individual human rights and of group rights, and to advise the Government accordingly.' The reference to 'group rights' is significant. The government was evidently anxious to explore and no doubt give credibility to the notion that in a reformed constitutional system the white minority might be given some special legal protection.

The view of the Law Commission as to the meaning of 'group rights' appears to be that they are essentially cultural rights possessed by racially or culturally defined groups, for example the right to separate education in schools, as exists under the Belgian constitution.

In certain circumstances the protection of group rights may well be justified. In the South African context, however, any proposals for the protection of cultural rights will inevitably be perceived as a device for perpetuating the apartheid system. Indeed, any proposals not compatible with continued white domination are unlikely to be accepted by the present government.

If, as seems possible, the Law Commission recommends the adoption of a bill of rights, it will have to provide for the courts to have the power to annul enactments of Parliament. Such a power already exists under the Constitution in relation to the preservation of the official languages, English and Afrikaans but the other important entrenched right in the earlier Constitution, the preservation of the common roll for white and coloured voters in the Cape, was removed in 1950.[2]

The task of advising the government on a bill of rights was assigned by the Law Commission to a team of researchers led by Mr Justice Olivier. Its findings and recommendations are expected to be published during 1988.

Notes

1. *Financial Times*, 2 December 1986, p. 2.
2. Separate Representation of Voters Act 1951. For the history of that constitutional battle, see Dugard, *Human Rights and the South African Legal Order*, p. 30.

18 Conclusions

A report published by the International Commission of Jurists on the rule of law in South Africa in 1968[1] cited a document issued by the South African Government earlier that year which appeared to claim that the rule of law was sufficiently observed by giving the accused the right to defend himself in open court, and giving him the choice of counsel to represent him. This claim illustrates an attitude to the rule of law which persists in South Africa: that ritual performance of legal formalities is enough, though the substance of the law denies basic rights, or even excludes judicial intervention. An earlier congress of the International Commission of Jurists issued the following statement: 'An independent judiciary is an indispensable requisite of a free society under the Rule of Law. Such independence implies freedom from interference by the executive or legislature with the judicial function but does not mean that the judge is entitled to act in an arbitrary manner.'[2]

This, however, is not all that the Rule of Law requires of the judiciary. To quote the 1968 report: 'their devotion to the Rule of Law and the liberty of the subject should take precedence over their support for a political or social system.'[3] Evidently they must be prepared to protect the subject against the political system where individual liberty is threatened by the executive, or even by legislation which purports to abrogate basic human rights.

Nor does the maintenance of the Rule of Law depend only on the independent role of the judiciary. The government has a duty to ensure that legislation does not infringe international human rights law[4] and that the judiciary is not denied power to adjudicate in cases where human rights are at stake. Absence of such power may itself undermine judicial independence. Thus the 'Basic Principles on the Independence of the Judiciary' (the Milan Prnciples) accepted unanimously by the General Assembly of the United Nations in 1985, provide that 'the judiciary shall have jurisdiction over all issues of a judicial nature and shall have exclusive authority to decide whether an issue submitted for its decision is within its competence as defined by law.'[5]

The rule of law, in our view, is intimately linked to democracy and human rights. The rule of law is 'designed to protect certain basic democratic rights of the citizen such as freedom of the person, of expression, of movement and assembly, and of association.'[6] At the same time it follows that the rule of law must limit state power, another requirement of democracy.

The evidence received by the mission, set out in this report, demonstrates that in South Africa an undemocratic government has extended the executive power of the state (claiming to obey the imperatives of state security) so as to undermine the rule of law and destroy basic human rights. Our report reveals the processes by which this has been done. We summarise our findings as follows:

1. The Constitution

The validity of legislation passed by the Parliament is open to question (though not in terms of South African law) because the electoral process is undemocratic and unrepresentative, in that the majority of the population classified as African are denied participation. Even those classified as coloured and Indian, who may vote for candidates of their own group, do not have equal participation with the white electorate because of the separation of legislative chambers and the power of the white-dominated President's Council to override decisions of the coloured and Indian chambers.[7]

The notional supremacy of Parliament is in any event increasingly being by-passed by a largely secret system of administrative control operated by 'joint management committees' answerable to the National Security Council. This diminishes even that element of democratic participation in government which the white electorate, at least, believed itself to possess.[8]

2. Substantive Law

The security legislation[9] and the regulations issued following the declaration of a State of Emergency[10] impose or authorise numerous restrictions on personal freedom in violation of human rights.

The Internal Security Act 1982 authorises preventive detention[11], detention without trial for interrogation[12], and detention of witnesses[13].

The Internal Security Act also creates (or codifies) a series of criminal offences of a political character, such as terrorism, subversion, sabotage, and advocating any of the objects of communism. These are defined in extremely wide and often vague terms. When taken in conjunction with the procedural rules which are heavily to the disadvantage of the accused the State is provided with the means of securing the conviction of virtually any political opponent, even when that person has not exceeded the bounds of freedom of expression as protected by international human rights law.

A series of other laws authorise actions which violate fundamental rights. Examples recur throughout the report. Major examples are:

the Group Areas Act which prevents freedom of movement and residence of a person, according to supposed racial characteristics, within his or her own country;[14]

the legislation authorising forced removals;[15]

the Separate Amenities Act which allows exclusion of persons from public places and facilities on racial grounds;[16]

the legislation authorising censorship of books and other publications;[17]

legislation allowing banning or otherwise restricting meetings and processions;[18]

laws providing for discrimination in public education;[19]
The emergency regulations, made under the statutory authority of the Public Safety Act 1953, extend executive power in all these areas;[20]
Finally, under this heading, is the death penalty for offences of a political character, which for several offences is mandatory save where extenuating circumstances can be demonstrated on behalf of the accused.[21]

3. Procedure

In many respects procedural rules are contained in legislation or are expressed by the judges as common law rules which deny a fair trial to the accused, especially in political cases. Examples are:
the provisions in the Internal Security Act which create a presumption of guilt in the absence of proof of innocence by the accused;[22]
the acceptance by judges of evidence of prosecution witnesses who have been detailed under the control of the security forces before and during the trial;[23]
the refusal of bail at the direction of the prosecution;[24]
the refusal to allow detainees to give oral evidence in support of claims of unlawful detention;[25]
the inadequate provision of legal aid to provide legal representation for the accused;[26]
the practice of torture and intimidation of detainees leading to unreliable confessions which are nevertheless held admissible by some judges;[27]
rules which exclude or restrict appeals against detentions under the Internal Security Act or emergency regulations;[28]
the immunity of the security forces from liability for misconduct;[29]
the extension of the 'common purpose' rule to allow a person to be convicted of murder held to have been committed by others. (The 'Sharpeville Six' case).[30]

4. Other abuses associated with the legal process

We have found that the Government has allowed intimidation of suspects and accused persons, and interference with legal processes by the security forces (and other government agents) to take place on a large scale and in a variety of ways. We stress particularly the widespread use of torture and violence, even against children, which is habitually denied by the government and thus, though plainly illegal even under South African law, goes unpunished.[31]

We are also satisfied that detention powers, especially those under the emergency regulations, have been used in an uncontrolled and random way which could never be justified on any genuine security ground. Frequently they have been used to put out of circulation leaders of lawful organisations such as trade unions or the United Democratic Front. Although the courts have acknowledged jurisdiction to invalidate such detentions in some circumstances, there is in practice very little judicial control of these abuses.[32]

Other major abuses by the security forces are:

aiding, encouraging, or condoning violent attacks by vigilante groups on opponents of government policy (for example in the Western Cape and Natal);[33]

use of excessive force (including many killings) in crowd control operations;[34]

assaults and torture of detainees under interrogation;[35]

arrest and intimidation of lawyers representing those accused of political offences.[36]

We were also given convincing accounts of intimidation of victims of assaults to deter them from making complaints or pursuing legal remedies.[37]

We learned of many cases in which prosecutions were brought on plainly inadequate evidence, demonstrated by the acquittal of the accused or the abandonment of the proceedings at a late stage. While such proceedings are pending the defendants suffer prolonged detention or bail restrictions and considerable stress and disruption of their lives.[38] The Pietermaritzburg treason trial is an example of this form of abuse. There are also cases where decisions against the authorities, especially interdicts, have been ignored or flouted.[39]

Another increasing trend is harassment of voluntary and charitable bodies helping victims of the apartheid system, including church organisations. There has been increased use of fund raising legislation to deter the solicitation of foreign funds for purposes which the Government regards as hostile to its policies.[40]

5. Criticisms of the judiciary

A literal or 'positivist' approach to judicial responsibilities has led many judges in South Africa to forego opportunities to interpret legislation in conformity with human rights standards. But there has remained a minority of judges, especially in Natal, who have bravely resisted Government attempts to remove such rights. They have done so by using their powers to determine the meaning of legislative enactments and to declare subordinate legislation invalid on the ground of unreasonableness.[41]

The extent to which judges can mitigate the harshness of the Government's security laws and regulations has been severely reduced by recent decisions of the Appellate Division.[42] In a group of three cases heard in July 1987 they considered the exclusion by the emergency regulations of the right of a detainee to obtain access to legal advice, and the right of a detainee to be heard before the Minister ordered the extension of the detention period. Some Supreme Court judges had held that these fundamental rights could not be excluded (at least in the absence of an unequivocal intention to do so). However, the Appellate Division upheld the power of the State President to issue regulations removing any rights, however well-established in the common law. These decisions were widely regarded as sounding the death-knell for judicial intervention to mitigate the government's repressive policies.[43]

From time to time in recent years, academic lawyers have questioned whether the integrity of the judiciary is compatible with its increasing exclusion from jurisdiction over human rights issues. In 1982, Professor Raymond Wacks in an inaugural lecture at the University of Natal argued that the time had come for judges to resign in protest at the erosion of the rule of law.[44] He claimed that on the bench they had no option but to implement racist policies. Professor John Dugard disagreed.[45] He contended that the Roman-Dutch common law required the judges to advance the principles of equality, liberty, reasonableness and natural justice. In effect he asserted that the principles embodied in the international code of human rights are already part of South African law. Professor Dugard has recently acknowledged, however, that the recent Appellate Division rulings support Professor Wacks' view. 'The lack of concern shown by the court for rights judged to be fundamental by the common law, and the failure of the court to consider adequately decisions extolling the importance of these rights, suggests that it was guided, not by considerations to be found in the inherited values and principles of the common law, but by subconscious, inarticulated assumptions about the preservation of existing power structures . . .'[46] 'If the Appellate Division acts in accordance with the views of Raymond Wacks', says Professor Dugard, 'resignation may become the only decent option for the "moral judge" '[47]

Furthermore, the influence of the 'moral judge' is likely to diminish for other reasons. We have noted that Mr. Justice Milne, Judge President of the Natal Provincial Division of the Supreme Court has recently been promoted to the Apellate Division.[48] The liberal reputation of the Natal bench owes much to his leadership and his removal may well diminish it. His will be only one of eleven judges at that level. The independence and influence of the judiciary is also marred by its wholly unrepresentative character. There is no non-white Supreme Court judge and two black magistrates appointed in the Western Cape soon resigned when they were called upon to preside at political trials. The democratic lawyers' organisations, now federated in the National Association of Democratic Lawyers, to which most black lawyers belong, have opposed the acceptance of judicial office by their members, believing, like Professor Wacks, that to do so is to commit oneself to the implementation of repressive and discriminatory laws.

The criticism of partiality on the bench towards the government is also supported by a number of specific cases, including overt political statements by judges in court.[49] A matter of particular concern is that Chief Justice Rabie has remained in his post after the statutory retirement age, because, it is alleged, the Government do not wish to appoint a successor who might be less politically reliable. His failure to resign has been attacked as unconstitutional by a leading scholar.[50]

6. Is there any excuse?

When the South African Government is accused of the gross violations of human rights which have been documented in this report its response is to plead necessity or 'force majeure'. Faced with a 'total onslaught' by armed terrorists, it claims, it has no choice in defence of the State but to meet force with force, and to abandon the constraints of the rule of law. Professor Anthony Mathews examines the validity of this justification in his admirable work[51] and quotes the Canadian McDonald Commission Report on security laws in that country: 'Canada must meet both the requirements of security and the requirements of democracy: we must never forget that the fundamental purpose of the former is to secure the latter. Those who subvert Canada's democratic institutions would realise an ironic victory if Canadians were to permit their governors to violate the requisites of democracy in the course of protecting them from their opponents'.[52]

In South Africa the basic function of the security system is 'the protection of the power and privilege of the ruling minority from all forms of attack by the excluded groups'[53] Furthermore, 'the security programme is itself a massive, state-directed system of violence designed to render apartheid impregnable from attack.'[54] Since apartheid is itself a violation of human rights and has been condemned by the United Nations on many occasions as a violation of international law, measures designed for its perpetuation which also violate human rights can hardly be justified by reference to their purpose. For this reason, we reject the argument that the violations we have described are justified by the necessity of defending the security of the state.

In any event, the circumstances in which there may be derogation (exemption) from the obligations of international human rights law are strictly confined. Those obligations are a code binding on the nations of the world whether they have directly subscribed to them or not.[55]

The primary documents in the code are the Universal Declaration of Human Rights and the United Nations Charter, by which South Africa *has* agreed to be bound. The International Covenant on Civil and Political Rights, a detailed set of rules designed to implement a major part of the Charter, allows derogation in the event of war or another public emergency, but limited only 'to the extent strictly required by the exigencies of the situation.'[56] This must be determined objectively, not by the state seeking exemption. Furthermore, there can be no derogation from the obligation to respect the right to life, nor from the obligation to refrain from torture or other ill-treatment. Nor must there be discrimination on grounds of race. We conclude that the violations of human rights law identified in this report cannot be excused or justified on the basis of any supposed national state of emergency.

In the end it is the unique adherence of the South African government to a policy of legally enforced racial segregation, employed to maintain the concentration of political and economic power in a small minority of the population, largely consisting of white persons of Afrikaner descent, which lies at the root of its failure to maintain the rule of law.

The effect of recent economic and moral pressure from within South Africa and from abroad has been to force a degree of relaxation in the formal structure of apartheid but the will of the ruling minority to retain power seems undiminished. Nationalist governments in South Africa have faced a dilemma: a repressive strategy, in which human rights and the rule of law have a low priority, has become increasingly necessary to contain the huge disenfranchised majority; yet the acknowledgement of such a strategy cannot easily be reconciled with South Africa's pretensions to legitimacy within the Western liberal tradition, of which respect for human rights and the rule of law are an important element.

Our conclusion is that the dilemma has now been resolved in favour of an uncompromising assault on what is perceived as the organised extra-parliamentary opposition, regardless of liberal and humane values. Plainly the government will try as well as it can to disguise and soften its strategy under a cloak of legalism, but the disguise is wearing very thin. As this report goes to press 17 non-violent anti-apartheid organisations, including the United Democratic Front, have effectively been banned under emergency powers. As long as the apartheid system survives, the future for human rights and the rule of law in South Africa is a bleak one.

Notes

1. *Erosion of the Rule of Law in South Africa*, Geneva, 1968, p. iii.
2. *The Rule of Law and Human Rights*, Geneva, 1966, p. 30.
3. Note 1, p. iv.
4. For a concise account, see Sieghart, *The Lawful Rights of Mankind*, Oxford, 1985.
5. *International Commission of Jurists' Review*, no. 37, December 1986, p. 62.
6. Mathews, *Freedom, State Security, and the Rule of Law*, p. 269.
7. Chapter 15.
8. Chapter 14.
9. Chapters 6, 7, 8, and 10.
10. Chapter 11.
11. s. 28.
12. s. 29.
13. s. 31.
14. pp. 15–18.
15. Chapter 4.
16. Chapter 3.
17. Chapter 6.
18. Chapter 8.
19. Chapter 5.
20. Chapter 11.
21. p. 80.
22. p. 71.
23. p.75.
24. s. 30 of the Internal Security Act 1982; p. 74.
25. p. 111.
26. p. 114.
27. p. 94.
28. p. 74.
29. p. 122.

30. The Appellate Division in December 1987 upheld the convictions and death sentences imposed on 6 young participants in a protest demonstration against rent increases in the course of which a community councillor was killed. A petition for clemency to the state president was still under consideration at the time of writing. See also p. 80.
31. Chapters 11 and 12.
32. Chapter 11.
33. p. 84.
34. p. 61.
35. p. 94.
36. p. 115.
37. p. 79.
38. p. 81.
39. p. 85.
40. 3 *SAJHR* (July 1987) p. 276.
41. p. 95.
42. Omar v. Minister of Law and Order, Fani v. Minister of Law and Order, State President v. Bill 1987 (3) SA 859 (A).
43. 'Appeal Court slams the door on civil liberties', *Weekly Mail*, 10–16 July 1987, p. 5.
44. 'Wacks, Judges and Injustice', (1984) 101 *SALJ* 266.
45. 'Dugard, Should Judges Resign?—A Reply to Professor Wacks,' (1984) 101 *SALJ* 286.
46. 'Dugard, Omar: Support for Wacks' Ideas on the Judicial Process?', 3 *SAJHR* (November 1987) p. 295.
47. Ibid., p. 300.
48. p. 111.
49. 'Cameron, Nude Monarchy: The Case of South Africa's Judges', 3 *SAJHR* (November 1987) p. 338.
50. Laurence Boulle, Professor of Public Law at the University of Natal, quoted in Weekly Mail, 22–28 January 1988, p. 5.
51. Mathews, op. cit., chapter 13.
52. *Freedom and Security Under the Law*, Government Publishing Centre, Ottawa, 1981.
53. Mathews, p. 281.
54. ibid.
55. Sieghart, op. cit., p. 59.
56. Article 4; Sieghart p. 179.

19 Recent Developments

As the first edition of this report went to press in February 1988 seventeen non-violent anti-apartheid organizations, including the United Democratic Front, were prohibited under the Emergency Regulations from carrying out any of their ordinary activities. This drastic new curb by the Government on the expression of dissent was not unexpected; indeed it was entirely consistent with the broad conclusion of our inquiry, namely that the maintenance of white minority rule under the system of apartheid was incompatible with the rule of law and internationally accepted human rights principles. Since February 1988 there has evidently been no substantial change in the white supremacist policies of the regime. Detentions without trial have continued, complaints of torture and violence towards those opposing the apartheid system are still frequent, more political executions have taken place, and there has been no amelioration in the pattern of censorship and suppression of free speech which we described. We have little reason to alter our pessimistic forecast of a bleak future for human rights in South Africa while apartheid survives.

Indeed, as the following account of recent developments shows, violations of human rights and the rule of law have in some respects become even more serious. The success of the Conservative Party in the election of May 1988, which made it the official parliamentary opposition in place of the Progressive Federal Party, put pressure on the National Party Government to present a more 'right-wing' stance. Most disturbing, for lawyers, is the spectacle of a judiciary which has relinquished even more completely than before its role as guardian of human rights against the excesses of the executive arm of government (see p. 164).

(see p. 164)

Following the sequence of chapters in the original report we comment on events which have taken place in the period from the end of February 1988 until the end of March 1989.

The Legal structures of apartheid

The process of dismantling the apartheid legislation which enabled P.W. Botha to claim that a process of reform was under way in South Africa has largely ceased. Indeed, in some respects there has been a regression by the introduction of more stringent apartheid laws. An amendment to the Group Areas Act sought to impose harsher penalties on those who infringed it. At the time of writing it has not been passed but it is far from clear that it has been abandoned.

Following the achievement of power by the Conservative Party in some localities in the elections of October 1988, the power to exclude black people from certain public places under the Separate Amenities Act was reasserted, e.g. in Boksburg, Transvaal. This was a regression to the 'petty apartheid' which the Government had claimed was on the way out. The Government is responsible for allowing the restoration of segregation by the retention on the statute book of the Separate Amenities Act, which allows local authorities discretion to practise apartheid in public facilities. If it is genuinely opposed to such apartheid, it should seek to repeal the Act.

Freedom of movement: forced removals

The practice of forced removal of black families resident in areas reserved for or destined to be assigned to white occupation has continued. The township of Oukasie, near the white town of Brits, was declared an 'emergency camp' under the Prevention of Illegal Squatting Act (see pp. 19 and 30), a curfew was imposed and the area sealed off to all but residents, health workers, state and court officials and soldiers.[1] This step paves the way for the forced eviction of the residents with the minimum of publicity, as has happened in other areas (see p. 31).

At the end of 1988 the Government introduced a Prevention of Illegal Squatting Amendment Bill to extend the already sweeping powers of local authorities and to limit further the discretion of the courts to restrain landowners from carrying out evictions and demolition of homes. For example, the Bill classifies the dependants of farmworkers and retired farmworkers as squatters who may be evicted without the right to seek protection from the courts.

Rights of summary eviction and demolition have been slightly curbed by court decisions limiting the scope of the clause in the Act which ousts its jurisdiction, but the new Bill will prohibit any application for judicial relief without proof of bad faith.

The number of squatters in the Eastern and Western Cape, the Transvaal, and Natal at the end of December 1987 was estimated to be 935,798, of whom 914,101 were said to be in the Pretoria/Witwatersrand/Vaal region, and none was on any official housing waiting list:[2] 230,000 squatters are estimated to live in Soweto alone.

In addition to the action taken against squatters, there have been many other evictions and threatened evictions in pursuance of the Government's homeland policies.

Education

From March to May 1988 there were extensive school boycotts, especially in the Western Cape and the Cape Peninsula. A reason was the exclusion of pupils refusing to undertake not to take part in activities outside the school curriculum. But many thousands of pupils also stayed away to protest against the harassment and detention of teachers by the security forces. For example, in Tembisa at the end of April, 10,782 secondary school pupils boycotted schools for four days over the detention of a teacher detained under Emergency Regulations.[3] In Soweto there was a two-month school boycott to protest against the detention of some 200 fellow students. This ended on 13 July following a meeting with teachers, parents and clergy.[4]

Government pressure on universities to restrict political activities by students was alleviated by a court decision declaring that the Government's new conditions for giving subsidies were void for vagueness and grossly unreasonable.[5]

However, early in 1989 new regulations were issued by the Department of Education and Training empowering the director-general (see p. 99) to refuse school admission to any applicant 'if he is of the opinion that such a person's presence at the school will be prejudicial to the interests of the school or the provision of education'. This wide power was claimed by the Government to be necessary to 'normalize' education by barring 'troublemakers'. However, the new restrictions led to incidents of violence in Soweto when pupils were refused admission. The African Teachers Association said there was severe overcrowding in schools—due to failure of the Government to provide resources for black children. Teachers in Soweto withdrew their labour and said that the new regulations were 'a deliberate attempt by the Department to disrupt education in our schools and to further its political aims'.[6]

Freedom of speech and expression

The Government has continued to exert tight control over the media, under the powers which it has given itself under the Emergency Regulations (see pp. 91–4). Before the end of 1987 warnings had been sent to a number of newspapers (among them *New Nation*, *South*, *Work in Progress* and *Weekly Mail*).

In January 1988 amendments to the media regulations were proclaimed to relax the Minister's obligation to warn that he is considering using his powers to close down or censor a paper. The *New Nation*, which is published by the Catholic Church, unsuccessfully challenged the new regulations. Its publication was prohibited by the Minister from 22 March to 10 June 1988.

Other papers have been subjected to periodic bans and seizures. *South* was banned for one month from 10 May 1988, and later in the year the *Weekly Mail* was banned for one month. These and other papers have also complained of constant police harassment, including raids and detentions of staff members. The editor of *New Nation*, Zwelakhe Sisulu, was detained without charge or trial for over two years until his release in August 1988. Since then, he is subjected to restrictions which prohibit resumption of his work as a journalist.[7]

Many other kinds of publications were confiscated in 1988, including an educational publication which contained Nelson Mandela's speech from the dock in 1956. The publishers challenged the seizure of 14,300 copies but their application was dismissed by the court.[8]

Censorship also extends to films. All film and video material has to be submitted to the censor before it can be shown to any audience, public or private. After 'Cry Freedom' had been approved for public viewing by the Publications Appeal Board, and it was already being screened, all copies were seized by the police from distributors and cinemas under the Emergency Regulations.

Considerable pressure has also been brought to bear by the Government on the presence of foreign journalists in South Africa. Several of them in 1988 were deported or had applications for renewal of work permits rejected. It is widely believed that these decisions are linked to the process of censorship, and are made to punish or neutralize those journalists who give unwelcome publicity to human rights violations by the regime.

The Government attempted to impose additional control on the media by requiring registration of 'news agencies' with the Director-General of Home Affairs.

Under considerable pressure this regulation was first suspended and then, on 9 September 1988, repealed. Journalists led a campaign against these registration requirements and it seemed likely that there would be a mass refusal to register.[9]

The editor of the *Weekly Mail* has complained that the censorship in South Africa has become such a complex web of statute and regulation that it is no longer possible to know in advance how one can avoid infringing the law. He gives as an illustration the National Key Points Act of 1980, which forbids the depiction of any 'key point'. However, no one can be told what are the 'key points'. Accordingly, one can know what is unlawful only after breaking the law.[10]

Freedom of association

Under an amendment by the State President of the Emergency Regulations extending the power to restrict activities of organizations and individuals, the Minister of Law and Order banned the United Democratic Front and another seventeen organizations opposed to the apartheid system on 24 February 1988. Since then, yet more organizations have also been banned, including the Committee for the Defence of Democracy—a new organization launched in the aftermath of the February bannings and immediately banned in its turn—and the End Conscription Campaign. Fifty organizations have been banned since 1948, but the number of bannings in 1988 far exceeds those in any other year.

The bannings in 1988 were carried out by issuing orders under the Emergency Regulations prohibiting the organizations from 'carrying on or performing any activities or acts whatsoever.[11]

In the case of COSATU, the Congress of South African Trade Unions, the ban was limited to non-trade-union activities—but its officials have claimed that in reality many campaigning activities directly linked to its trade union functions will be affected.

To some extent those who were active in the banned organizations have been able to continue their opposition in other ways, either by joining or founding new organizations or by acting individually, but the Government's actions have plainly inhibited seriously the opportunities for the expression of political opinion and for peaceful political action.

The restrictions on the UDF may well have contributed to the continuance of the bloody conflict between supporters of Inkatha and others in the Pietermaritzburg area. At the time of the banning of the organization, UDF leaders were actively seeking to negotiate a peace settlement between the warring groups. Their application to the Minister of Justice for the restrictions to be modified to enable them to continue this important task was turned down.

Such constructive initiatives have also continued to be severely curtailed by action against individuals. Arrest and detention powers under the Emergency Regulations and the Internal Security Act have obviously been used primarily against political activists holding leadership positions in anti-apartheid organizations, especially those organizations which have been banned. International pressure (and, recently, well-coordinated hunger strikes by detainees) have evidently induced the Government to release a number of detainees, but it has kept them under strict control after release by imposing extremely onerous conditions on their behaviour. As in the case of Zwelakhe Sisulu, mentioned above, many ex-detainees are prevented even from resuming their ordinary work, let alone attending meetings and engaging in political activity. Another example is the case of Raymond Suttner, a law lecturer who is not allowed to enter any educational institution.[12]

Another recent development threatening to have a severe effect on anti-apartheid organizations is the Government's attack on foreign funding. The euphemistically named Promotion of Orderly Internal Politics Bill proposed that the Minister of Justice be given power to 'restrict' an organization which in his opinion was using foreign funds for political aims. Funds held by such an organization could be seized by the Government and those receiving such funds sentenced to fines and a prison sentence of up to ten years.

After widespread criticism the Government abandoned its Bill, but in February 1989 it introduced a Disclosure of Foreign Funding Bill which seems likely to be enacted. It makes no specific reference to curbing political activity but provides sweeping powers for the Government to gain access to information about the source of funding of any organization. There is already legislation—the Affected Organizations Act and the Fund Raising Act— which will allow the Minister to dispose of funds received from foreign sources once he has been able to identify them. Since it is widely believed that many opposition groups rely heavily on financial assistance from abroad this new legislation may be a further significant restraint on their activities.

Freedom of assembly

The Minister of Justice renewed on 31 March 1988 under s.46 of the Internal Security Act a comprehensive ban on all outdoor gatherings except for funerals and sports occasions, save where special permission is obtained from the local magistrate or the Minister of Justice himself. He also banned indoor meetings promoting educational boycotts and illegal strikes.[13] Under the Emergency Regulations it has become common practice to restrict funerals where the death has arisen in any political context. This practice continued in 1988 and orders were frequently made under the State of Emergency even where the comprehensive ban applied.

The wish of many people to celebrate the 70th birthday of Nelson Mandela obviously caused the Government considerable anxiety and they did their utmost to frustrate the public events which were planned. Where permission to hold gatherings was applied for it was refused. A ban on a concert at the University of the Western Cape was set aside by the court but it was too late because the police had already dispersed the audience.[14]

In September 1988 the Commissioner of Police banned a conference called by COSATU and other groups to discuss the new Labour Relations Amendment Act (see below) and other issues. At least twenty-four people involved in the organization of the conference were detained for several days beforehand. The Government claimed that the conference was aiming to disrupt the forthcoming municipal elections.

Trade unions

The Labour Relations Amendment Act came into effect on 1 September 1988 after its introduction had been delayed by protests from both employers and trade unions. The protests had included a well-supported national stay-away from work on 6, 7 and 8 June 1988. The *South African Journal on Human Rights* comments that 'the trade unions are now faced with the most challenging and concerted efforts yet by the Government to subdue them'.[15]

The elements in the new law which have caused most concern are the following:

(1) Sympathetic or secondary work stoppages by those not directly involved in an industrial dispute become unfair labour practices, hence unlawful. Strikes are unlawful even by those directly involved in a dispute if there has previously been a strike about a similar issue within the previous twelve months.

(2) The former immunity of trade unions against liability for damages for interference with a contractual relationship occurring as a result of a trade dispute is removed, unless the union can show that the interference occurred without its authority. The immunity is also removed where damage arises from an illegal strike or from criminal acts.

(3) The opportunity for lawful strike action after the breakdown of conciliation procedures is greatly reduced by the introduction of much more complex and bureaucratic disputes procedures which must be exhausted before a lawful strike can be undertaken. This seriously weakens the negotiating power of the trade unions.

The new law has already given rise to actions for damages brought by employers, including a 1.7 million rand action against the Food and Allied Workers Unions.

Beyond the sphere of labour relations law, repression of trade unions under emergency powers and by extra-legal violence has continued. COSATU has recently reported a series of police raids on its offices and the homes of its officials.[16] The General Secretary of COSATU was unable to address the conference of Commonwealth Foreign Ministers in Harare in February 1989 because the Government refused him a passport.

In the main body of our report (p. 63) we pointed out that trade-union law was an area in which there had been some progress towards equality, at least within the collective bargaining process. The new legislation, coupled with continued harassment of the predominantly black trade unions by the agents of the Government, reflects an apparent determination to reverse this trend. It is not surprising that a government still seeking to maintain minority rule recognizes that the collective power of the trade unions is a major obstacle to its strategy.

The right to personal freedom

In the year that has passed since our report was completed there has been no relaxation in the complex network of laws and strategies which restrict the freedom of those who oppose apartheid. The Internal Security Act 1982 remains in full force. The State of Emergency (see also p. 162) was renewed for a further year on 10 June 1988 and seems certain to be further renewed in 1989. Under these laws a large number of people, including children, remained imprisoned without trial and in very many cases without having been charged with any offence or even informed of the reason for their detention. A spate of political trials took place, many resulting in conviction and imprisonment. Death penalties were imposed and in several cases carried out for essentially political offences. Personal freedom was also restricted increasingly, especially in parts of Natal, by the extra-legal violence of vigilantes and others unknown, in circumstances justifying the suspicion of Government approval, if not active support.

It does appear, however, that the total number of detainees without charge is now substantially less than before and that the Government is operating a policy of more selective detention of those whom it regards as leaders of opposition groups. However, it is often overlooked when considering the figures sometimes produced by the Government itself that, in addition to those detained under the Emergency Regulations or under the provisions of the Internal Security Act allowing detention without charge (sections 28, 29 and 31), there are many who are detained after being charged who are awaiting trial and there are many more serving sentences of imprisonment after convictions which would not have been imposed in a system observing international human rights standards.

Thus the Human Rights Commission (Fact Paper FP1) estimates that there were 178 detentions under security legislation in the first half of 1988 and that the figure for those detained under emergency regulations during the State of Emergency of 1988/9 is likely to be no more than 2,000, by comparison with an estimated figure of 25,000 emergency detainees in 1986/7. The Government has, however, claimed that in the week 9–15 February 1989, 316 people were held under s.29. This is assumed to be the total held, not the number newly detained in that week. At the same time the Government claims only 884 emergency detainees in custody who have been held for more than thirty days, among whom fifty-two are children under 18.[17]

Government figures have always been found to be seriously understated, but their own figures are still sufficient to justify a sense of outrage. The European Court of Human Rights has recently condemned the British Government for permitting detention without charge for up to seven days under the Prevention of Terrorism Act. Detention without charge of several hundred people for over thirty days and of some of these for more than two years is an affront to the civilized values which the South African Government still sometimes claims to uphold and a gross abuse of Human Rights.

Space does not permit examination in detail of the political trials which have taken place since publication of our report but some of them, referred to in the report but now further advanced or concluded, must be mentioned.

(a) The Transvaal UDF treason trial

This case (now usually known as the Delmas trial, after the town where most of it took place) was still in progress when our report was completed (p. 75). There were originally twenty-two defendants, among whom were leading officials of the United Democratic Front. Of the nineteen remaining defendants at the end of the trial in September 1988, four were convicted of treason and seven of terrorism. The sentences of the former ranged between twelve and six years' imprisonment; of the latter one was sentenced to five years in prison and the remainder received suspended sentences but are prohibited from political activity for five years. The charges were that the accused participated in a conspiracy between the ANC, UDF, and the South African Communist Party to overthrow the state by violence. There was no evidence of violence by any of the accused and the whole case was based on inferences which the judge drew from remarks made in a large number of taped telephone conversations, video recordings of meetings, and evidence of informers and alleged accomplices many of whom had been detained by the police for many months. The three who were given the longest prison sentences also happened to be the three of the defendants who held the most senior positions in the UDF. They had been refused bail during the three and a half years while the trial was in preparation and in progress. The defence case was that there was no conspiracy and the aim of the UDF was merely to put pressure on the Government to bring about a process of peaceful change. The judge concluded that treason and terrorism could be committed without actual or intended violence, where violence was an inevitable consequence of the actions of the accused. As many observers have commented, the judge's findings blur the distinction between lawful political dissent and criminal activity. Not only has the UDF been banned under the State of Emergency; it has in effect been found to be an unlawful organization under the common law.

In another trial not yet completed, Moses Mayekiso, general secretary of the National Union of Metal-workers, and others are accused of treason in forming and organizing community associations aimed at ameliorating the appalling living and social conditions in the township of Alexandra. The Government alleges that the true purpose of their activities is to usurp the role of the Government itself. Yet the Government itself denies the accused participation in any democratic process. The trial has been in progress for more than a year and if it results in a conviction will narrow the boundaries of dissent even further than the Delmas judgement.

(b) The Sharpeville Six case and capital punishment

The Sharpeville Six, who had been convicted of the murder of a community councillor during protests at rent increases in the townships of the Vaal Triangle in 1984, were on death row when our report was published and an international campaign for clemency was being mobilized. However, in March 1988 clemency was refused by the State President and their execution was imminent. A last-minute application to the trial judge led to its postponement while the court considered whether the claim of a prosecution witness that he had testified falsely under duress was capable of vitiating the convictions. An even stronger ground for upsetting the convictions, and yet more for commuting the death sentences, was that the accused had not been found by the court to have been directly involved in the killing at all. The finding—a tenuous one at best—was merely that they had shared a 'common purpose' with the actual killer or killes to carry out the murder. This ground had, however, already been rejected by the Appellate Division and could not be re-argued.

The international campaign attracted support from many governments, including those of the United States, Britain and West Germany. After a series of further legal manœuvres, all unsuccessful, the State President relented and the Six were reprieved, but long prison sentences were substituted.

The campaign for the reprieve of the Sharpeville Six did not, however, save the lives of a number of others sentenced to death following trials arising out of political 'unrest' or other political causes. In November 1988 it was estimated that a total of over 300 people were on death row having been sentenced to death for a range of offences (see p. 80). Of these it was estimated that eighty-three had been convicted of unrest-related activities.[18] During the height of the Sharpeville Six campaign, no political executions took place, but two men, Kholisile Dyakala and Zwelindumile Mjekula were executed on 24 November. A last-minute stay was granted to Paul Setlaba, and in February 1989 his sentence was commuted to imprisonment. At the same time it was reported that sixteen others on death row had been granted clemency. At least sixty political prisoners are believed still to be awaiting execution.

(c) Political trials in progress

Throughout South Africa, political trials are in progress, many of them for offences which can attract the death penalty. On 9 February 1989 the newspaper *South*, published in Cape Town, commented as follows:

The South African Government has in recent years increasingly resorted to the courts to counter its political opponents. The number of political trials currently handled by courts throughout the country are too numerous to mention. The abundance of these trials often leads to important trials going unnoticed. Last month two important trials in the Western Cape were concluded with little publicity.

The paper then proceeds to list eighteen major trials currently in progress including trials for treason and terrorism. In Upington, a remote town in the Northern Cape, twenty-five people were convicted in 1988 of murder, applying the same 'common purpose' doctrine as in the Sharpeville Six case, none of them having been found to have been directly involved in the single killing alleged to have taken place. Argument is still proceeding as to whether there were 'extenuating circumstances' justifying waiver of the death penalty.

Since all those accused in the courts could be detained indefinitely under the Internal Security Act or the Emergency Regulations, it must be supposed that the proliferation of trials is itself directed by the Government's political strategy. Because of the wide and uncertain scope of the security offences and the prosecution's procedural advantages (summarized on pp. 145 and 146) conviction is probable and acquittals can be nullified by new charges or emergency detention. An advantage to the regime of pursuing cases through the courts is that the detention of political opponents while awaiting or undergoing a trial is more easily justifiable to the international community than detention without trial. For example, the British Government still expresses reluctance to protest at the suppression of political opposition in South Africa where legal processes are being pursued. Furthermore, in the absence of any effective legal aid, the opposition is put to considerable expense and difficulty in arranging legal representation.

During 1988, vigilante and other violence towards opponents of the apartheid system has increased and there have continued to be frequent claims that the security forces have actively assisted the vigilantes or have themselves initiated violent attacks on members of the opposition or their premises. At the same time there has evidently been a marked failure by the authorities to trace and bring to book those who have been guilty of crimes against political opponents of the government. For example, during 1987 and 1988, the headquarters of COSATU in Johannesburg was destroyed by fire-bombs, Khotso House, headquarters of the South African Council of Churches and office of several anti-apartheid organizations was severely damaged, and the headquarters of the Catholic Bishops Conference in Pretoria was also set ablaze. No arrests have been made for any of these crimes.

In our report we commented on the failure to prosecute policemen apparently guilty of shootings and killings. At that time no action had been taken against the policemen responsible for killing three young people in the 'Trojan Horse' incident (pp. 82, 83, 119–20). In March 1988, when the inquest finally took place, a magistrate held the police officers 'negligent'. However, in November 1988, the Attorney-General of the Cape declined to prosecute them. (Until then he had failed to reach a decision.) The families of the deceased have now launched a private prosecution against thirteen policemen and soldiers.[19] But this means that they carry the financial burden of fighting the case.

In addition there have now been some prosecutions of policemen for killing civilians. However, in one case in February 1988, a policeman sentenced to death for murder had his sentence commuted by the State President to eight years' imprisonment. Two other policemen were reprieved at the same time as the Sharpeville Six. No policeman has been executed for murder in an 'unrest' situation, though many hundreds of people have been killed by security forces (see, for example, the Uitenhage case, p. 61).

In 1988, violence escalated in the Pietermaritzburg area of Natal and many people believed to be supporters of the UDF have been killed. A much smaller number of people believed to be members of Inkatha have been killed and the events have been characterized by the Government as 'black on black' violence. However, there is considerable evidence that the authorities have favoured Inkatha and that the Government has given at least tacit support to Inkatha as a means of suppressing the UDF in the region (see p. 158).

An agreement was reached between COSATU, many of whose members were also attacked, and Inkatha for the peaceful adjudication of disputes by a Complaints Adjudication Board whose convenor is Mr Justice Leon, a retired judge of the Supreme Court. In its first report the Board found evidence that two leading Inkatha members (sometimes referred to as 'warlords') had used 'acts of intimidation, violence and threats of extreme violence, directed against residents of the area on the grounds of their membership of organisations whose policies differed from those of Inkatha'. The two Inkatha members then withdrew from the hearing and it appears that the agreement is in jeopardy. It would indeed be tragic if this attempt to prevent loss of life in Natal were to fail.

The State of Emergency

The State of Emergency was renewed for a further year on 10 June 1988 and the regulations issued under it have followed the same form as the previous regulations, but some of the provisions have been strengthened in order to repair limitations revealed by adverse court decisions or to reflect changes in policy.

For example, all restrictions imposed during the prior emergency are automatically continued—previously they lapsed at the end of the emergency period. Major changes were made in the regulations affecting the media and censorship, which were considerably tightened, for example by extending the definition of 'subversive statement'. One extension clearly intended to inhibit opposition to the forthcoming municipal elections was to make it a subversive statement to incite or encourage the public to boycott such an election. (In fact there was a substantial boycott: only a very small number of black people voted in the elections in October 1988.)

Undoubtedly the emergency regulations have continued to have a major effect on the media and on the expression of dissent, as has been seen. But the number of emergency detentions has been reduced (see pp. 158–9).

As to the treatment of detainees, reports of torture persist. The Human Rights Commission was formed in September 1988 by church leaders and other eminent South Africans to investigate and monitor violations of human rights in South Africa. In its first report on detentions (Fact Paper 1) it says

Over the years and right up to the present time, there has been a continuous stream of allegations of torture and assault in detention. Court proceedings abound with such allegations, and these can only be considered the tip of the iceberg. . . . The whole subject is far too extensive to receive more than passing mention in this Fact Paper, but will form the subject of a separate Paper in future.

Plainly the continuance of such reports of torture demands urgent action by the Government, which has claimed to be ready to discipline anybody guilty of it.

Children

The particular plight of children in South Africa, who were estimated to account for some 40 per cent of those detained under the State of Emergency of 12 June 1986 (see p. 101), has been highlighted by an international campaign beginning with the conference convened by Archbishop Trevor Huddleston in Harare in September 1987.

At that conference several children testified about the brutal treatment they had received at the hands of the South African police, including torture by electric shocks, suffocation and violent beatings. Their testimony was supported by doctors, psychologists, and other health workers who in several cases had travelled from South Africa to the conference at considerable personal risk. The evidence given at the conference has been summarized in *Children of Resistance* by Victoria Brittain and Abdul Minty.[20] Since then the reduction in the total number of detainees has included a proportionate reduction in the number of child detainees, but doubt has been cast on Government claims that no children below the age of 15 are detained. At the time of the Harare conference the Minister of Law and Order made this claim but evidence of the detention of at least one 14-year-old was immediately provided by the newspaper *South*, with a photograph of the child's birth certificate.

In July 1988, the Minister again claimed that there were no children under 16 left in South African prisons. Dr Max Coleman of the banned Detainees'

Parents Support Committee gave the names of several children whom he said were then in prison.

In October 1988, it was reported that a 13-year-old boy had been brought to court as a state witness in a political trial after having been held in custody for six months. The boy said he did not know why he was in court, nor did he know the eleven accused. The judge, Mr Justice Didcott, ordered the immediate release of the boy.[21]

In February 1989, the Minister, Mr Vlok, announced in Parliament that there were fifty-two children under 18 currently in detention.

Administration of justice

In our report we drew attention to the way in which the Appellate Division had reversed a number of decisions by lower court judges which invalidated certain emergency regulations and actions of the Government in pursuance of them. As a result of the Omar decision in July 1987 (see p. 96), many lawyers believed that the door had been closed to any effective challenges to the emergency regulations.

Unfortunately, subsequent decisions have reinforced that view and the comment has been made that, in the light of those subsequent decisions, 'Omar cannot be regarded as the low water mark in judicial conservatism'.[22]

The Public Safety Act 1953, under which the State of Emergency was declared, and from which the power to proclaim emergency regulations derives, contains an 'ouster' clause, purporting to remove the jurisdiction of the courts to pronounce on the validity of a regulation. Hitherto, the courts had avoided the effect of this clause by holding that it could not displace their power to determine whether a regulation was or was not *ultra vires* its statutory source.

In State President v. UDF and State President v. Release Mandela Campaign,[23] the Appellate Division appeared to abandon this power and to accept that in matters of state security it had been deprived of any ability to safeguard the citizen from abuse. The view of leading academic lawyers is that the courts have now recognized that general principles of administrative law applicable in all other cases do not apply to security matters. Chief Justice Rabie, who has presided over this process of with-drawal by the courts from their traditional role as champion of individual liberty, has now retired. However, Haysom and Plasket say 'it is difficult to imagine how even a reconstituted Appellate Division could rescue our system of administrative law from the treatment it has received at the hands of the Rabie court . . .'[22]

Mr Justice Friedman, in a subsequent case where the same issue arose,[24] spoke out strongly against the decisions of the Appellate Division but was forced to hold himself bound by them. Shortly afterwards he resigned from the bench.

Another judge, Mr Justice Didcott, has publicly criticized the Government and the Appellate Division in a lecture which has now been published.[25] He said:

In our country . . . we witness power exercised under the authority of duly enacted legislation, but in many directions beyond the reach of the law and, in that sense lawlessly. This is what we mean by saying that, though we are ruled by laws, we lack in those areas the rule of law. And what Nazi Germany shows us is that, once such areas include the various fields of personal liberty, as they certainly do in our case, the lawlessness of which I talk may pave the way to tyranny.

These sentences express in a very concise form the conclusion we reached in our report. Mr Justice Didcott goes on in his lecture to place some hope, as other liberal judges have done[26] in the prospect of a Bill of Rights.

We referred in our report to the examination of this topic by the South African Law Commission, which the Minister of Justice requested it to undertake in April 1986 (pp. 142–3). No report has yet been published but in an interview published in the *South African Journal on Human Rights*,[27] Mr Justice Olivier, who is conducting the investigation, acknowledged that

Racial discrimination is not reconcilable with a normal bill of rights. The introduction of a credible bill of rights must therefore of necessity be accompanied by the scrapping of apartheid from the statute books. The first step should be the protection of the individual against the power of the state. This would have to be followed, however, by measures to protect the civil rights of citizens and to eliminate discrimination at all levels.

To implement such a programme would require the end of white minority domination and the total replacement of the present system under a democratic constitution. It is hard to imagine the present regime surrendering in the way Mr Justice Olivier seems to envisage. Nevertheless, if it lives up to his comment, his report should prove to be a powerful criticism of the present policies of the South African Government.

Notes

1. 4 *SAJHR* p. 263.
2. Ibid.
3. 4 *SAJHR* p. 262.
4. 4 *SAJHR* p. 419.
5. *University of Cape Town* v. *Minister of Education and Culture*: see 4 *SAJHR* p. 262.
6. *Weekly Mail*, 20–26 January 1989.
7. Human Rights Commission, *Focus on Human Rights*, 10 December 1988.
8. 4 *SAJHR* p. 411.
9. 4 *SAJHR* p. 410.
10. *Focus on Human Rights*, op. cit., p. 14.
11. *Focus on Human Rights*, p. 5.
12. *Human Rights Update*, vol. 1, no. 4, p. 13.
13. 4 *SAJHR* pp. 255 and 406.

14. 4 *SAJHR* p. 406.
15. 4 *SAJHR* p. 401.
16. *Weekly Mail*, 10–16 February 1989.
16A On 22 March 1989, COSATU'S lawyer Mr. Nicholas Haysom presented a dossier containing evidence of 29 incidents of active co-operation between policemen and Inkatha 'warlords' in the detention, interrogation, shooting and harassment of residents of Imbali Township; *Weekly Mail*, 23–30 March 1989.
17. *Weekly Mail*, 24 February–2 March 1989, p. 35.
18. IDAFSA Briefing Paper, Ottawa, Canada.
19. Johannesburg *Sunday Star*, 12 February 1989.
20. V. Brittain and A. Minty, *Children in Resistance* (Kliptown Books, 1988).
21. Johannesburg *Star*, 21 October 1988.
22. Haysom and Plasket, 'The War against Law: Judicial Activism and the Appellate Division', 4 *SAJHR* p. 303.
23. 1988 4 SA 830 (A) and 903 (A).
24. *Natal Indian Congress* v. *State President*, 16 September 1988.
25. 'Salvaging the Law', the Second Ernie Wentzel Memorial Lecture, 4 October 1988. An extract is published at 4 *SAJHR* p. 355.
26. e.g. Mr Justice Leon, when Chancellor of the University of Natal in 1985: see 2 *SAJHR* p. 60.
27. 4 *SAJHR* p. 99.

Index